Godfrey Sturgeon

Lightweight Cycle Catalogues
Volume II

The John Pinkerton Memorial Publishing Fund

Following the untimely death of John Pinkerton in 2002, a proposal was made to set up a fund in his memory.

The objective of the Fund is to continue the publishing activities initiated by John Pinkerton, that is to publish historical material on the development of the bicycle of all types and related activities. This will include reprints of significant cycling journal articles, manufacturers' technical information including catalogues, parts lists, drawings and other technical information.

Published by the John Pinkerton Memorial Publishing Fund, 2007

ISBN 978-0-9552115-8-4
Printed by Quorum Print Services Ltd. Cheltenham.

The John Pinkerton Memorial Publishing Fund Publication List:-

Lightweight Cycle Catalogue Volume 1
An Encyclopaedia of Cycle Manufacturers - compiled by Ray Miller
Frederick H Pratt and Sons - Complete Cycle Engineers - Alvin J E Smith
The Electric-Powered Bicycle Lamp 1888-1948 - Peter W Card
The Pedersen Hub Gear - Cyril J Hancock
It wasn't that Easy. The Tommy Godwin Story - Tommy Godwin
The End to End & 1000 Miles Records - Willie Welsh
The Origins of Bicycle Racing in England: Technology, Entertainment, Sponsorship and Publicity - Andrew Ritchie

All publications are available through the Veteran-Cycle Club Sale Officer.

CONTENTS

Introduction . . . 5

Overview . . . 7

W & R Baines . . . 9

Carpenter Cycles . . . 25

Granby Cycles . . . 37

R O Harrison . . . 47

Higgins Cycles . . . 55

Macleans Featherweight Cycles . . . 63

Mercian Cycles Ltd . . . 73

Paragon Cycles . . . 81

Mal Rees Cycles . . . 89

The Saxon Cycle Engineering Co Ltd . . . 99

E Stephens . . . 117

Viking Cycles Ltd . . . 135

INTRODUCTION

The Lightweight Cycle Catalogues, Volume I, the first John Pinkerton Memorial Publishing Fund's publication was well received by V-CC members and other cyclists with an interest in the subject. Six other books have been published since then and in the meantime the V-CC Club Sales Officer has been questioned many times about the possibility of publishing a second volume of Lightweight Cycles Catalogues.

So here we present an interesting mix of marques with no clearly defined manufacturing period. The twelve manufacturers are a selection of those offering lightweight cycles in the pre- and post-World War II (WWII) eras and includes one still offering cycles at the present time. One ceased manufacture before WWII, two stopped in the 1950s and the rest ceased during the 1960s.

One marque, Granby, started manufacture before the first World War (WWI), seven set up after WWI in the 1920s, two started in the 1930s and two began operations after WWII.

I would like to thank the twelve marque enthusiasts and other V-CC members mentioned in the texts, who provided the material that has been assembled in this book. Also those persons mentioned who provided much knowledge of their activities with the various marques, as mentioned in the texts, are gratefully acknowledged. The preparation of the edited texts by my wife and the layout and design by Brian Hayward are also much appreciated.

Cyril Hancock

Chairman

John Pinkerton Memorial Publishing Fund Committee

OVERVIEW

This second volume contains a very interesting selection of lightweight frame builders. It includes Granby who might well deserve the title 'Father of British lightweight bicycles'. For it was almost certainly Granby that was the first builder to copy the Bastide bicycle made in France and became the first British maker of the definitive lightweight cycle design that is still used today in Britain and all around the world.

To understand the importance of Granby and Bastide a short explanation is necessary. Bastide frames were built in Paris from c1910 with mainly English Reynolds tubing with lugs and fittings provided by BSA. They featured some quite radical ideas for the time: 26in wheels, calliper brakes operated by cable on the side of the rim; this offered quick wheel removal, 10.5in high bottom bracket, horizontal top tube and tapered straight seat and chainstays brazed into place. The Constrictor Tyre Company imported the first Bastides and they were the sensation of the 1913 Olympia show. The traditional English racing bike for road or track sometimes used 26in wheels but the bottom bracket height was normally near 12in necessitating a dismount when stopping, the top tubes sloped down to the head and cranked seatstays were bolted to the seat lug and rear dropout with also cranked, often two part chainstays. And the frame was much larger – it was ridden with the saddle almost as low as it would go. Bastide's frames were smaller and ridden with about 3–4in of seat pin showing. The net result was a machine with far sleeker and less cluttered appearance. Granby clearly copied the Bastide design; they claimed in later advertising that they were building this design of frame from 1913, they were certainly advertising it by 1915. So why is this so important? It was this new design that was used by all British framebuilders in building serious fast bicycles from the 1920s onwards É and many of the design features were also later incorporated into utility bicycles too. We cannot simply credit Granby with this change for there was much talk in the cycling press about the advantages of lower, simpler and more efficient bicycles and *Cycling* in particular pushed the advantages of the new design but Granby were almost certainly the first to show the way forward.

This volume includes two of the first lightweight builders to follow Granby with the new design – Saxon and Maclean. Don Maclean together with Harry Bailey it is thought opened a small shop at 39 Landseer Road, North Holloway in 1918 or 1919. Many years ago I interviewed an old employee of Saxons, Don Salmon, who had first worked for Don Maclean at the beginning and he had lots to tell on both companies. By about 1920 Maclean began to build lightweight racing frames in the new style. Saxon was not quite the typical small lightweight frame builder. Founded in 1919 in east London it was a company on similar lines to Sun making a full range of bikes including roadsters – a very early Saxon frame is known which incorporated features (straight seatstays, bolted rather than brazed into place) of both the new lightweight design and the older design. This frame was claimed to be from around 1922 which I think entirely plausible. By 1923 however Saxon's frames were wholly of the new design.

The rest of the builders here in this volume represent many different aspects of the smaller British framebuilders, several are very small; Stephens, Paragon and Carpenter with less than 100 frames a year being produced on average. These were for the most part one-man builders and two frames a week is a good average when repairs and other jobs are involved also. They were producing mainly for riders in their own locality and did not market their frames through other shops unlike most of the makers described in volume 1.

Baines stands out on account of it being the only one featured here to make a business of building 'funny' frames – their Flying Gate design was built in reasonable numbers both post and pre-war and then taken up again in the late 1970s by Trevor Jarvis. It is one of the most typical of the funny frames being designed before the notorious ban by the Road Time Trials Council in 1938 on clearly visible builders names. The RTTC ban was an attempt on the part of the body regulating time trials to uphold the total amateur status of the sport – they were anxious that manufacturers would not benefit from riders' successes by pictures appearing in the cycling press with clearly visible maker's names. This attempt at a ban continued certainly until the early post-war years but was never successful. However the emergence of 'funny' design frames has often been attributed to it. The evidence for this effect is not at all compelling; most of the 'funny' frame designs had appeared well before the ban. But as we find with most of the makers building 'funny' frames the vast majority of the frames they built were the 'funny' design, the Flying Gate.

Higgins on the other hand was a different type of specialist builder; he made a name for himself with some of the most splendid tricycles ever made in the UK. The only builder of tricycles to rival Higgins must be George Longstaff in the 1980s and 90s. He also built some quite splendid solos and especially tandems which were one of the first in the UK to have modern tandem geometry. Perhaps his interest in trikes gave him an insight into tandem geometry.

By contrast Viking was more similar to Saxon though their period was post WWII rather than between the wars despite being founded at a similar time to Saxon. They were not a true small builder and built a large variety of machines including some quite innovative children's machines. The Viking All-Size was a very clever design that grew with the child for a year or two extra than a standard design. I have a very fond spot for the All-Size as this was the bike I learnt to ride on. Their success in post-war years was due in large part to publicity gained by racing and the energy and influence of a few enthuisastic members of staff. It certainly proves the point that racing is an excellent form of publicity – Viking's bikes moved upmarket and included some really rather nice top-end race models as well as a good base of sports models built with more modest components and tubing.

Mal Rees is a great example of another type of builder – he did not in fact build his own frames; they were not even built on the premises. He commissioned freelance framebuilders to build frames specifically for his shop and were badged as Mal Rees. These were certainly not inferior to those built by a small one man builder – it certainly could be argued that these freelance builders were a great deal more experienced and could turn out a truly superb frame. One of the builders used by Mal Rees, Bill Hurlow, I consider to be probably the top builder of his era. The Hurlow frames I have encountered are the most accurate and beautifully built frames I have seen. He was more famous for the frames he built for Condor and later under his own name but the Rameles model produced for Mal Rees was the equal of any work he did for Condor. Wally Green was another freelance builder for Mal Rees – he was a real specialist in this type of frame in the 1950s and early 1960s and built frames for many shops across north London as well as a few under his own name.

Mercian stands out by being one of the few in the UK to still be building steel frames. Almost all of the other makers featured in this volume and in Volume 1 do not have a continuous lineage of building steel frames. They have, particularly since the 1960s, made a very good business of exporting their frames especially to the USA. Curiously they still use a very old fashioned method of building their frames; the frames are still to a large extent brazed in an open hearth. This method is claimed to reduce the chances of overheating the tubes though I would consider this claim highly questionable.

Last and certainly not least, R O Harrison was a highly respected framebuilder in the 1930s and through to the 1950s – in post-war years he obviously must have employed other builders but the quality of the frames still surviving certainly suggests he kept a close control on the standard of workmanship in his workshop. He built a 'funny' frame design, the Shortwin but this could not be described as a success – about three are known to survive. His standard frames, many of which have finely crafted lugs survive in good numbers.

There are many top builders who have yet to be featured so the hope is that there will be more volumes in this series. These volumes have opened up a lot more information on British lightweight builders. I hope that the readers enjoy the discovery process as much as I have done over the last twenty-five years.

Hilary Stone

W & R BAINES

Willie and Reg Baines' father had a cycle shop that was trading before 1900. There is a photograph of his shop taken in 1904 on display in the National Cycle Collection at Llandrindod Wells, together with many photographs of the W & R Baines workshop and showroom premises taken around 1937.

Reg Baines joined his father in the shop in 1919 at the age of 14, but even before that he had to assist in the workshop each evening after school from 5 to 7pm and again on Saturday mornings. At that young age he learned to braze and stove enamel with the best of them. Willie Baines joined the company on leaving school in 1921. At this time there was insufficient work for the three of them so Reg left and joined the Jowett car company in Bradford and became a draughtsman. After a few years Reg rejoined the company and the brothers formed the W & R Baines Company around 1928.

The company had been building standard frames, but in 1934 Reg designed and built the first vertical tube frame in order to achieve a shorter distance between the wheels and to be more responsive. The name given to the frame was VS37, due to its 37" wheelbase. Full-scale manufacture did not commence until 1936 when the new factory was built in Idle Road.

With Reg's engineering background, the works were well laid out and the frames well made, with machine cut mitres, good quality brazing and face plate correctness. The lugs were neatly filed, but not ornate. The paint spraying was kept in-house and again great care was taken to ensure that a good finish was achieved. The stove enamelling was undertaken in a thermostatically controlled gas heated oven which held five frames. Later they produced the longer wheel base International TT, which again proved very popular. In the search for information, Dave Murgatroyd has been very helpful as he knew Willie Baines. He was told the frame number book was thrown out by a female employee when they moved from the Eccleshill premises, so our knowledge is rather hit-and-miss, though we have over thirty names on the owners' list. Four types of traditional and three 'gate' type frames were produced covering the requirements of practically all classes of cyclist.

At this time Reg also designed the sloping top tube frame with a small front wheel, as seen on the aerodynamic time trial bikes of recent years. This was tested out at various meetings in the North of England with some good results being achieved, but the design itself was ridiculed and never took off. It proved to be ahead of its time but with the successes that people were having on the 'Gate', it presumably would not have seemed worthwhile continuing with its development.

During the war years, Baines' did war work although a number of frames came out of the back door. The supply of top lug and bottom bracket lugs dried up and as frames were fillet brazed in these areas, pre-war frames are rather sought after as they are lugged and workmanship is very good, though the lugwork is not ornate.

The company closed in 1958 but the frame building stopped in 1952. Some frames were then built by John Mapplebeck to complete the outstanding orders. A copy of a letter from Willie Baines to Nick Tithecott states they supplied a number of cycles to the New York Cycling Club; these had the lamp brackets on the left fork blade.

The frame numbers and dates are difficult to determine correctly due to the loss of the records. An attempt to put together a list of old frame numbers in relation to their age did not produce a true sequence. The following frame numbers and dates have been agreed to give a reasonable history.

Frame number	Probable date of manufacture	Frame number	Probable date of manufacture
43	??	906	1939
182	1936	943	1939
343	mid 30's	1248	1947
424	1938	1383	1949
441	1938	1478	1950
786	1938	1829	1950's
830	1938	(last known number)	

Frame numbers were stamped on the fork stems and on the rear left hand drop out. It is known that the frames produced during the 1939 – 1945 war were lugless, but no definite numbers have been recorded.

There is now a very nice cast model available of the "Flying Gate" which has been reproduced from frame number 43, a complete bike with all the period equipment. This belonged to George Baines and is currently on display at the National Cycle Collection. The cast model can be obtained from Trevor Jarvis, Tel.01584 811451. E-mail: jarvistandp@aol.com

Trevor Jarvis and Derek Kitchener

Catalogue lent by David Murgatroyd which he believes is a copy of the 1937 publication.

Baines
SUPER RESPONSIVE
CYCLES.

TERMS OF BUSINESS

A DEPOSIT OF 20/- IS REQUIRED WHEN ORDERING, AND THE BALANCE OF CASH IS DUE WHEN ACCOUNT IS PRESENTED BEFORE DISPATCH.

CARRIAGE

All cycles and frames are despatched carriage paid to nearest railway station in Great Britain and Northern Ireland, and crate and packing free of charge, and on receipt should be signed for "Unexamined," and any damage notified to the Railway Company and ourselves.

W & R BAINES

BUILDERS OF SUPER RESPONSIVE CYCLES

GUARANTEE

W. and R. Baines GUARANTEE that all precautions have been taken to obtain excellence of workmanship and materials, and should any defect occur within five years of purchase, and in original owner's possession, the defective part will be replaced free of charge, which does not include cost of postage, and must be sent carriage paid.

This GUARANTEE is limited to the supply of a New Part, and we do not hold ourselves responsible for any consequential damage or expense due to defective parts.

Tyres, Rims, Saddles, Chains, Gears and other component parts are usually Guaranteed by the various Makers, and our name should be mentioned in any correspondence to them. This Guarantee does not apply to defects caused by wear and tear, misuse or neglect.

WORKSHOPS & BUILDING DEPARTMENTS:

WEST ST., ECCLESHILL, BRADFORD, YORKS

Where all communications should be addressed

TELE PHONE / GRAMS BRADFORD 4679

SHOWROOMS & SALES DEPOTS:

IDLE ROAD, ECCLESHILL, BRADFORD

4, PICCADILLY, KIRKGATE, BRADFORD

6, COMMERCIAL STREET, SHIPLEY

FOR YOUR INTEREST

The V38 and VS37 ultra short wheelbase designed frames were an instant success from introduction, and the demand for them exceeded all our expectations. The riders out to improve their times have realised the certain advantages these frames can give them, and the success in this direction has been proved by unsolicited letters of appreciation that we are receiving daily, which inform us of successes in Mass Start, Hill Climbs, Road and Track Events.

These frames are of registered design, and the registration numbers are as follows: V38, No. 816135; and VS37 No. 816136.

In undertaking to build and supply to your particular requirements, we are prepared to build to any angle, or design. Our long experience and the varied specifications we have built to have given us complete mastery over the individually built frame.

We make a point of having in stock lug sets to build to all anticipated angles, and by this foresight we avoid any necessity to force a lug to a particular angle. The rough and ready method of forcing only means leaving the lugs and tubes in a tensioned condition, which eventually develops into a distorted tube or a total fracture.

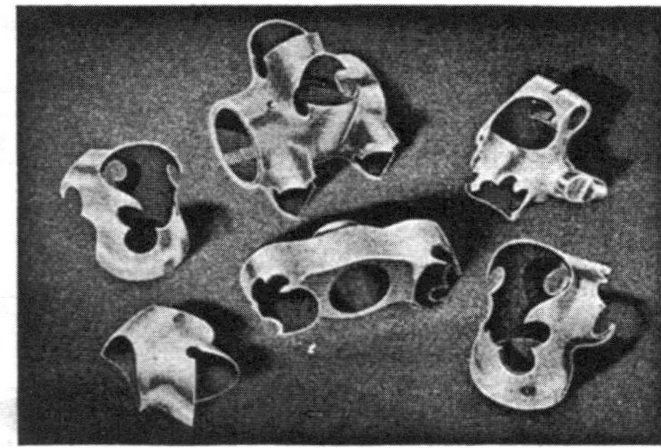

Particular attention is given to the tubing. All tubes are carefully mitred to reach and occupy the full length of the lug, an important factor when using hand-filed and lightened lugs. the ordinary method of brazing a frame and then lining it up afterwards, wrenching a tube here and there in order to obtain a correct angle did not find favour with us, and went to great expense to design a special plate erecting jig for the assembly of the main frame triangle. Every frame is erected and pegged ready for brazing on this jig, and after brazing the frame is again placed on the jig and passed out only after careful checking.

We are one of the very few Lightweight Cycle Manufacturers who have their own enamelling plant, and have recently introduced a new process for anti-rusting frames before enamelling.

Enamelling is by up-to-date high pressure spraying, and we offer a wide range of colours and contrasting shades. All chrome plating is on a special nickel and copper base, the extra copper deposit helping considerably in the prevention of any moisture reaching the tubing and eventual peeling of the chrome.

W.R.B. WESTFIELD

Cash Price £9 12 6

All Chrome Plated Head, 5/- extra

WESTFIELD VARIABLE

With choice of Simplex Professional du Monde or Cyclo Oppy 3-Speed Gear, two Brakes. Other specification exactly as Single Speed Model.

Cash Price £10 17 6

SPECIFICATION

FRAME. Reynolds 531 Tubing, Upright Frame, 73° Head, 73° Seat. Baines Special. Lightened and Hand Filed Lugs of attractive design. Any Frame size to order. Bracket height 11 in. Special Short Rear Triangle incorporating our own design Chain Stays allowing full tyre clearance. Wheelbase 41 in. Brazed on fittings.

FORKS. Special Gauge Blade of Reynolds 531 Tubing, ⅞ in. Chater round or D to O Section. No. 2 Rake or to order. Brazed on adjustable lamp bracket.

CHAIN WHEEL SET. Williams C1000 Lightweight Racing, 46t or to order.

CHAIN. Coventry Roller.

PEDALS. Light Steel Continental Racing.

WHEELS. 26 in. x 1¼ in. built with Dunlop Light Gauge Rims. B.W. Light Racing Hubs. Double Butted Spokes. Two fixed Cogs on Single-Speed Model. Variable Model has special Rear Hub to take Boss Type Freewheel. Dunlop High Pressure Wheels and Tyres 5/- extra.

TYRES. Dunlop Sprite, Silver Sprite, or Speed.

BRAKES. Front or Rear LAM Light Steel Continental.

SADDLE. Brooks B17 Range or Flyer.

BARS AND STEM. Chrome Highgates, Bailey, Binda, Tour de France, or to order. Lightweight 2 in. or 3 in. Adjustable Extension.

GUARDS. Bluemels White Noweight.

FINISH. Baines Stoved Synthetic Enamel or Chromatic Lustre in any colour. Chevron on Seat Tube. Special anti-rust process before enamelling. Chrome Front and Rear Tips. All Chrome Fork optional.

EQUIPMENT. Tecalemit oiling throughout, gun supplied. B.S.A. Pattern Box Spanner, Bluemels Inflator.

WESTFIELD FRAME

With Front Forks, Chainwheel Set and Seat Pillar.

Cash Price £4 19 6

Praise from
LONG ISLAND, NEW YORK
U.S.A.

. . . When I unpacked the Special American Model VS37 you have kindly built for me it caused quite a sensation amongst the New York Clubmen; on trying it out all agreed it is all you say—SUPER RESPONSIVE. L. A. H.

W.R.B.

"International T.T." Road Model

The CHOICE of the Massed Start and Road Racing Experts

Designed in conjunction with one of the most successful massed start experts of the day, who says: "A revelation to ride; responsive to every effort; perfect steering and control."

Cash Price £12 12 0

International T.T. Massed Start Model

Exactly to above specification, but fitted with Sprint Wheels built with Sportal Dural, Tabucchi, or Constrictor First Choice Wood Rims, Wolber Tour de France, or Dunlop Cotton Tubulars. Spearpoint Extension in place of Guards.

Cash Price £12 19 6

SPECIFICATION

FRAME. Reynolds 531 Butted Tubes. Frame sizes 21 in., 22 in., 23 in., or to order. 73° Upright Head, 72° Seat. Wheelbase 39½ in. or to order. Bracket Height 11 in. with 26 in. wheels. Special Registered Design Frame incorporating Vertical Tube giving three-point suspension to top tube. Additional Light Struts to rear drop outs and seat tube giving scientific rigidity to Chain Stays and Rear Triangle.
FORKS. Special Gauge Blades of Reynolds 531 Butted Tubing. No. 2 Rake Fork ⅞ in. Round Section. Fork Crown designed to match frame lugs. Brazed on Chater Adjustable Lamp Bracket.
CHAINWHEEL SET. Williams C1000 or C1200 Lightweight Racing.
CHAIN. Renolds best Roller.
WHEELS. Dunlop High Pressure 26 in. or 27 in., Chrome Rim, Solite Hubs, Continental Double Butted Spokes.
TYRES. 26 in. x 1¼ in. Dunlop High Pressure Rib and File Tread.
BRAKES. Front and Rear "LAM" or Gloria Tour de France Continental Light Steel.
SADDLE. Brooks B17 Range or Flyer.
HANDLE BARS. Chrome Highgate, Bailey, Binda, Tour de France, or any popular Continental Type on KROMO 2 in. or 3 in. Adjustable Raised or Level Extension.
GUARDS. Bluemels White Noweight or Ultralite. Dural optional.
FINISH. BAINES STOVED SYNTHETIC ENAMEL or CHROMATIC LUSTRE IN ANY COLOUR. Special anti-rust process before enamelling. Contrasting coloured Chevron on Seat Tube. Chrome Plated Head and Head Lugs. Chrome Front and Rear Tips. All Chrome Front Fork optional.
EQUIPMENT. Tecalemit oiling throughout, gun supplied. B.S.A. Pattern Box Spanner; Bluemels Inflator. Feeding Bottles Extra.
GEAR. Simplex 3-Speed Champion du Monde Professional or Cyclo Oppy.

This design has proved its superiority time after time in a most convincing manner.

Extras on Both Models

CHATER CHAIN WHEEL SET and HEAD FITTINGS, 17/6.
A.V.A. DURA BARS and STEM with HIDUMINIUM SEAT PILLAR, 6/6 extra.
AIRLITE CONTINENTAL HUBS, 13/- extra.
INTERNATIONAL T.T. FRAME, £6.

Praise from
LIVERPOOL

. . . I have just had a long weekend on my "INTERNATIONAL T.T." and covered about 200 miles; I find its performance marvellous, and must thank you for the finest bicycle and workmanship I have yet seen. M. N.

W.R.B. V.38 Road Model

The Really Rapid Hill Climber

Incorporating the now famous Short . . Wheel Base Frame of Registered Design

Cash Price **£9 12 6**

V.38 **SRINT MODEL**

Exactly as above specification but fitted with Sprint Wheels built with Tabucchi Best Flat Wood Rims, Dunlop Cotton Tubulars. Spokes tied and soldered. Less Guards, but with Spearpoint Extension.

Cash Price £10 10 0

SPECIFICATION

FRAME. Built of Reynolds 531 Butted Tubes. 73° Head, 73° Seat. Upright Frame. Baines Special Lightened and Hand Filed Lugs of attractive design. Frame of special design incorporating vertical tube giving three-point suspension to top tube, and at the same time allowing an ultra-short Wheel Base of only 37¾ in. Any Frame size to order. Bracket height 11 in. Usual brazed on fittings.

FORKS. Special Gauge Blades of Reynolds 531 Tubing No. 1 Rake or any Rake to order, ⅞ in. round or D to O optional. Machined Crown designed to match Frame Lugs. Brazed on Chater Adjustable Lamp Bracket.

CHAINWHEEL SET. Williams C1000 Lightweight Racing 46t or to order.

CHAIN. Coventry Roller.

PEDALS. Light Steel Continental Racing.

WHEELS. 26 in. x 1¼ in. built with Dunlop Light Gauge Endrick Rims. B.W. Light Racing Hubs. Double Butted Spokes. Cog sizes to order. DUNLOP HIGH PRESSURE WHEELS AND TYRES, 5/- extra.

TYRES. Dunlop Sprite, Silver Sprite, or Speed.

BRAKE. Front or Rear "LAM" Light Steel Continental.

SADDLE. Brooks B17 Range or Flyer.

HANDLEBARS. Chrome Highgate, Bailey, Binda, Tour de France, Pelissier, or any popular bend to order. Lightweight 2 in. or 3 in. Adjustable Extension.

GUARDS. Bluemels White Noweight.

FINISH. Baines Stoved Synthetic Enamel or Chromatic Lustre in any colour. Special anti-rust process before enamelling. Contrasting Chevron on Upright Tube. Front and Rear Ends Chrome Plated. All Chrome Front Fork optional. Chrome Head and Head Lugs 5/- extra.

EQUIPMENT. Tecalemit oiling throughout, gun supplied. B.S.A. Pattern Box Spanner; Bluemels Inflator.

V38 FRAME with Front Forks, Chain Wheel Set, and Seat Pillar, Front and Rear Chrome Ends. **£5 5 0.**

The Ideal Ladies' Model, light in weight and very tractable.

Praise from
ESSEX

. . . The workmanship and finish is all that can be desired, and the frame to ride is a revelation. H. W.

W.R.B. Continental CHAMPIONSHIP MODEL

as used by the Continental ACES in the World's Championship Road Events

Cash Price £14 5 0

Continental Road Model

Exactly as above specification, but with Dunlop High Pressure Wheels with Rib and File Tyres or Jenatzy Oversize Continental, Bluemels Noweight Guards or Super Dural.

Cash Price £13 12 6

Airlite Continental Hubs 13/- extra on each model.

FRAME only with Durax four fluted Cranks, Front Fork, and Seat Pillar, £6 7s. 6d.

SPECIFICATION

FRAME. Built of Reynolds 531 Steel Tubes and Stays throughout. Genuine Continental Light Cast Lugs finely cut away to Continental design. Head Angle 73°, Seat Angle 71°. Other Frame measurements compare with true Continental design as favoured by the International Road Race entrants. 11 in. Bracket height with 26 in. wheels. Wheel Base 42½ in. Inserted Fork Races taking large size Balls. Continental design Seat and Chain Stays of light taper gauge allowing full tyre clearance so essential for long distance events. Continental Drop Out Ends (Osgear Type to order). Usual brazed on fittings. Any Frame size to order.

FORKS. Special 2½ in. Rake Continental Oval to Round Blades of Reynolds 531 Butted Tubing giving light easy steering. Wide Continental Light Cast Crown designed to match Frame Lugs. Brazed on Lamp Bracket and Mudguard Eyes.

CHAINWHEEL SET. DURAX Nickel Chrome Steel. Three Arm Fixing Cranks with four finely cut flutes, 46t or 48t Chain Ring.

CHAIN. Renolds best Roller.

GEAR. Simplex 3-Speed Champion du Monde Professional or Cyclo Oppy.

PEDALS. Pierre Lyotard Duralumin, 4 in. wide.

WHEELS. Continental Sportal Dural or Tabucchi Flat Wood Sprint Rims, Solite Hubs, rear hub suitable for Simplex Cogs, Continental Double Butted Spokes tied and soldered.

TUBULARS. Wolber Tour de France or Dunlop Cotton.

BRAKES. Front and Rear "LAM" Dural, or Gloria Dural Tour de France, Silver Cables.

SADDLE. Brooks B17 Range or Flyer, on Hiduminium Seat Pillar.

HANDLEBARS. A.V.A. Dura Bars and Stem, expander fitting. Choice of Magne, Pelissier, Aerts, or Leducq, on 3 in. or 4 in. Extension.

GUARDS. Spearpoint Extension.

FINISH. Super Continental Metallic Light Blue, Bronze, Grey, or any colour to order. Special anti-rust process before enamelling. Two colour lining on all tubes. Continental Seat Tube Chevrons and Bands; Chrome Plated Front and Rear Stay Ends. All Chrome Head 5/- extra.

EQUIPMENT. Tecalemit oiling throughout, gun supplied. B.S.A. Pattern Spanner; Bluemels Inflator.

Praise from *CO. ANTRIM* *Nr. Ireland*

. . . I received my Baines cycle to-day and I am more than pleased with the appearance and workmanship. I certainly have a cycle that I am proud of. D. C.

W.R.B.

PATH-TRACK MODEL

Cash Price £14 5 0

SPECIFICATION

FRAME. Built of Reynolds 531 Butted Tubing, 22 in. or to order. 75° Head, 73° Seat. Rear track ends. Special short rear triangle. Bracket height 11½ in. with 27 in. wheels, wheel base 39½ in. or to order. Brazed on fittings to order.

FORKS. Special gauge blades of Reynolds 531 Butted Tubing. No. 1 rake. D to round or ⅞ in. round.

CHAINWHEEL SET. Chater Lea or B.S.A. 1 in. x ⅛ in. pitch. Size to order.

CHAIN. Coventry Elite Block. 1 in. x ⅛ in.

WHEELS. Best Tabucchi or Constrictor sprint rims and tubulars to choice. Airlite Continental equal flange hubs, spokes tied and soldered, 14 x 16 gauge.

SADDLE. Brooks B17 Champion Range on straight seat pillar.

HANDLEBARS. Sibbit, Continental or to order, on Toni Merkens special adjustable extension.

PEDALS. Webb or Brampton, solid centre.

LUBRICATION. Tecalemit nipples to wheels, bracket, top and bottom fork races.

FINISH. Front and Rear Tips Chrome Plated. All Chrome Fork optional, any colour enamel or BAINES Durable Chromatic Lustre finish in blue, green, or red only. Chrome Head and Lugs 5/- extra.

EQUIPMENT. Tecalemit Oil Gun and B.S.A. Pattern Four-Way Box Spanner.

TRACK FRAME

With Front Forks, Chainwheel Set, and Seat Pillar.

£6 15 0

Praise from

WALLASEY

. . . I received my frame in good order and must congratulate you on a most beautiful job of work.

W. R.

W.R.B. VALKENBURG CONTINENTAL

Cash Price £11 7 6

Airlite Continental Hubs 13/- extra

CONTINENTAL FRAME only with front fork and Durax Chain Wheel set £5 10 0. Front and Rear Chrome Ends 10/- extra.

SPECIFICATION

FRAME. Built of Genuine Continental Featherweight Lugs, finely cut away to Continental design, Frame of true Continental measurements as approved by well known English and Continental riders. All Tubes and Stays are of Reynolds 531. Head Angle 73°, seat angle 71°. 11 in. Bracket Height with 26 in. Wheels. 42¼ in. Wheel Base.

FORKS. Special 2½ in. Rake Continental Oval to Round Blades of Reynolds 531, giving light easy steering. Inserted bearing races. Wide Continental light crown, designed to match frame lugs, brazed on lamp bracket and guard eyes. Continental Design Seat and Chain Stays of special light taper gauge, allowing for full tyre clearance so essential for long distance competition work. Special Continental Drop Out Ends. (Osgear type to order). Usual Brazed on fittings. Any Frame size to order.

CHAINWHEEL SET. DURAX Continental Light Nickel Steel. 3 pin fixing. Grooved Cranks. 46t or 48t with 6½ in. cranks.

CHAIN. Reynolds best Roller.

PEDALS. Pierre Lyotard Light Steel Continental Tour de France.

WHEELS. Dunlop High Pressure 26 in. or 27 in. All Chrome Rims. Solite Hubs, rear Hub to take Simplex Cogs. Genuine Continental Double Butted Black Spokes Tied and Soldered.

TYRES. Dunlop High Pressure Rib and File, or Jenatzy Simplex Oversize Continental.

BRAKES. Two "LAM" Light Steel Continental. Silver Cables.

SADDLE. Brooks B17 Range or Flyer.

HANDLE BARS. Binda, Tour de France, or any Popular Bend on Continental Extension. Expander Bolt Fitting.

GUARDS. Bluemels White Noweight or Light Dural.

GEAR. Simplex 3 Speed Champion Du Monde Professional or Cyclo Oppy.

EQUIPMENT. Tecalemit Oiling throughout, gun supplied. B.S.A. pattern box spanner, Bluemels inflator.

FINISH. Continental Metallic Light Blue, Bronze, Grey, or to order. Special anti rust process before Enamelling. Shaded Silver Front and Rear Tips. Seat Tube Chevrons and Continental Bands. All Frame tubes super-lined in contrasting colours. Chrome Plated Front and Rear Ends 10/- extra.

Praise from
CAMBRIDGE

. . . I feel I must congratulate you on turning out such a fine finished cycle.
P. A. D.

W.R.B. ECCOLITE

Cash Price £10 10 0

With Chater Fittings, 20/- extra.

A.V.A. Dura Bars, Stem and Hiduminium Seat Pillar, 6/6 extra.

All Chrome Finish on Special Copper Base, 25/- extra.

Airlite Continental Hubs, 13/- extra.

ECCOLITE FRAME with Front Forks, Chain Wheel Set, and Seat Pillar, Front and Rear Chrome Ends, All Chrome Head.

Cash Price £5 5 0

SPECIFICATION

FRAME. Built of Reynolds 531 Butted Tubes. Frame size to order. 74° Head, 72° Seat or any degree optional. Baines Special Lightened and Hand Filed Lugs of attractive design. Chain Stays of special design, allowing for full tyre clearance. Forward Drop Outs. Track Ends to order. Bracket height, 11 in. with 26 in. wheels. Wheelbase 39½ in. to 41 in. as desired. Usual brazed on fittings.

FORKS. ⅞ in. round of Reynolds 531 Butted Tubing. Solid Fork Crown designed to match Frame Lugs. No. 1 Rake or to order. Brazed on adjustable Lamp Bracket.

CHAINWHEEL SET. Williams C1000 Lightweight Racing, size to order.

CHAIN. Renolds Elite Roller.

PEDALS. Webb Solid Centre or Pierre Lyotard Continental.

WHEELS. 26 in. x 1¼ in. Dunlop High Pressure, Chrome Rims, Featherweight Hubs or Solite, Double Butted Spokes. Cog sizes to order, 27 in. wheel optional.

TYRES. 26 in. x 1¼ in. Dunlop High Pressure, Rib and File Tread.

BRAKE. Lam or Gloria Tour de France Light Steel Continental. Front or Rear.

SADDLE. Brooks B17 Champion Range or Flyer, on straight Kromo Seat Pillar.

HANDLEBARS. Chrome Shallow Highgate, Bailey, Binda, or any popular Continental type. Kromo Adjustable Stem, 2 in. or 3 in. Extension.

GUARDS. Bluemels White Noweight or Ultralite.

FINISH. Any colour Stoved Synthetic or Baines Durable Chromatic Lustre in any colour. Special anti-rust process before enamelling. Front and Rear Chrome Ends. All Chrome Head and Head Lugs. All Chrome Fork if desired.

EQUIPMENT. Tecalemit oiling throughout, gun supplied. B.S.A. Pattern Box Spanner, Bluemels Inflator.

Praise from

NORTHAMPTON

. . . I am now the proud owner of what I consider the nearest approach to a perfect cycle that sets a new standard in the cycle world. C. P. F.

W.R.B. V.S. 37 ROAD MODEL

Registered Design No. 816136

ULTRA-SHORT WHEELBASE. The most popular Frame design of the year. Enjoy easier cycling by riding the most responsive Frame yet built.

Cash Price £11 5 0

V.S. SPRINT MODEL

Specification as Road Model but with the following alterations:—

RIMS. Fonteyn Sportal Dural or Tabucchi Flat Wood. Spokes tied and soldered.

Tubulars. Dunlop or Tour de France.

Less Guards but with spearpoint extension.

Cash Price £12 5 6

On all Models Airlite Continental Hubs ... ... 13/- extra.
Chater Chain Wheel and Head Fittings ... ... 17/6 extra.

FRAME. Built of Reynolds 531 Butted Tubes. Frame size to order. 74° Head, 72° Seat, or any degree optional. Baines Special Lightened and Hand Filed Lugs of attractive design. Frame of special design, incorporating Vertical Tube, giving three-point suspension to Top Tube. Additional Struts to Rear Drop Outs and Seat Tube, giving scientific rigidity to Chain Stays and Rear Triangle. Bracket height 11 in. using 26 in. wheels. Usual brazed on fittings. Wheelbase 37¾ in., with 26 in. Wheels or any Wheelbase to order.

FORKS. Special Gauge Blades of Reynolds 531 Tubing. No. 1 Rake Fork or any Rake to order, ⅞ in. round or D to O optional. Machined Crown designed to match Frame Lugs. Brazed on Adjustable Lamp Bracket.

CHAINWHEEL SET. Williams C1000 Lightweight Racing.

CHAIN. Reynolds Elite Roller.

PEDALS. Webb Solid Centre or Pierre Lyotard.

WHEELS. Dunlop High Pressure 26 in. x 1¼ in. Chrome Rims, BW Featherweight Hubs, or Solite. Continental Double Butted spokes. Cog sizes to order, 27 in. optional.

TYRES. 26 in. x 1¼ in. Dunlop High Pressure.

BRAKE. Front or Rear Lam, or Gloria Tour de France.

SADDLE. Brooks B17 Champion Range or Flyer.

HANDLE BARS. Chrome Highgate, Bailey, Binda, Tour de France, or any popular Continental type, on Lightweight 2 in. or 3 in. adjustable extension.

GUARDS. Bluemels white Noweight, Ultralite, or Dural.

FINISH. Baines Stoved Synthetic Enamel or Chromatic Lustre in any colour. Special anti-rust process before enamelling. Front and Rear Chrome ends, all Chrome fork optional. Chrome Head and Head Lugs, 5/- extra. All Chrome Plated on Special Copper Base, 25/- extra.

EQUIPMENT. Tecalemit oiling throughout, gun supplied, B.S.A. pattern box spanner, Bluemels inflator.

CONTINENTAL V.S. 37 MODEL

Exactly as Road Model but with the following Continental fittings:—

BRAKE. Lam or Gloria Super Dural Front or Rear.

CHAINWHEEL SET. Continental Durax, grooved cranks.

PEDALS. LYOTARD DURAL 4 in. RACING.

BARS AND STEM. A.V.A. Super Dura, Magne, Pelissier, or Aerts, Bends on Super Dura Extension, 3 in. or 4 in. with Expander.

HUBS. SOLITE. Light Steel.

Cash Price £11 19 6

Praise from

SURREY

. . . I am more than pleased with the finish and performance of my VS37 cycle, and must thank you for this excellent job. C. J. A.

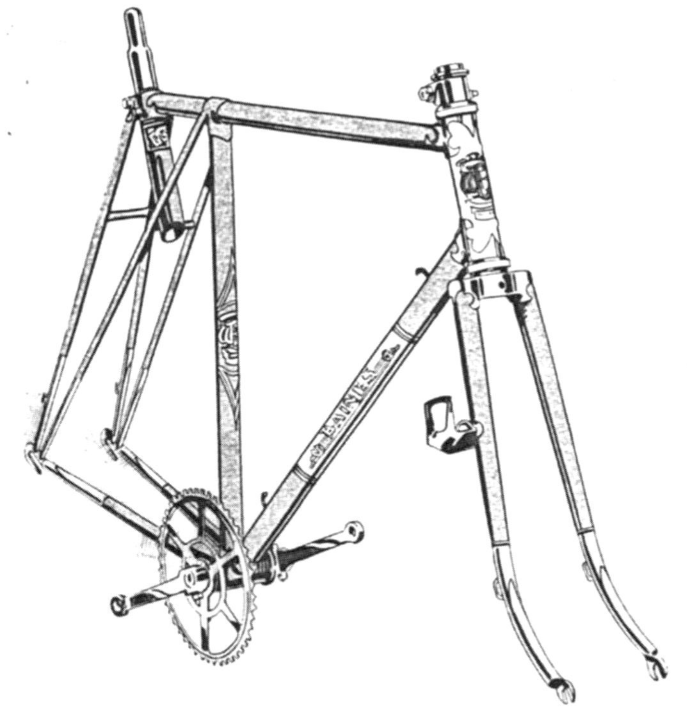

The BAINES V.S. 37

HANDBUILT SHORT-WHEELBASE FRAME

The New Design Frame with distinct advantages.

SPECIFICATION

FRAME. Reynolds 531 tubing. Frame size to order. 74° head and 72° seat, or optional. Baines special lightened and handfiled lugs of attractive design. Forward drop–outs. Track ends to order. Special design frame incorporating a vertical tube giving three point suspension to top tube. Additional light struts to rear drop-outs and seat tube giving scientific rigidity to chain stays and rear triangle. Bracket height 11 in. using 26 in. wheels.

FORK. No. 1 rake of special design. 531 tubing. ·⅞ in. round or D to round optional. Solid fork crown designed to match frame lugs.

WHEELBASE. 37¾ in. using 26 in. wheels.

FITTINGS. Williams C.1000 Lightweight Racing chainwheel set. Brazed-on mudguard eyes, pump pegs and Chater adjustable lamp bracket. Tecalemit oil nipples to bottom bracket, fork head clip and bottom frame race.

FINISH. Special Anti–rust process before enamelling. Baines' stoved Synthetic enamel or durable chromatic lustre in any colour. Attractive Chevron design on vertical tube. Front and rear chrome ends. All chrome front fork optional. All chrome heads 5/– extra. All chrome finish on copper base, 25/– extra.

With Baines Fittings - - **£5 15s.**

Extra for Chater Chainwheel Set and Head Fittings ... ... 17s. 6d.

Since the BAINES Short wheel-base design was first introduced we have been copied by many, but at what cost?

In attempting to attain the same short base as the BAINES, you are offered short top tube, bent or distorted tubes and seat tubes at an alarming angle, etc., which either cramp or throw the riders weight out of balance and offer no alternative riding position.

The advantages of the BAINES Frame Design

- Any top tube length.
- Any angle seat tube as you you would order on an orthodox frame.
- Short chain stays givlng rigidity to drive.
- Vertical tube strengthening front triangle.
- Additional light struts to rear triangle.
- Full clearance for mudguards and toe clips
- An ideal design for Road or Track.

Praise from

BROOKLYN, NEW YORK
U.S.A.

. . . After using my American Model VS37 for several months I wish to state that it is the most lively and responsive cycle that I have ridden. My riding partner, who also is a proud Baines owner, asks me to thank you for the marvellous job you made of his VS37model. F. S.

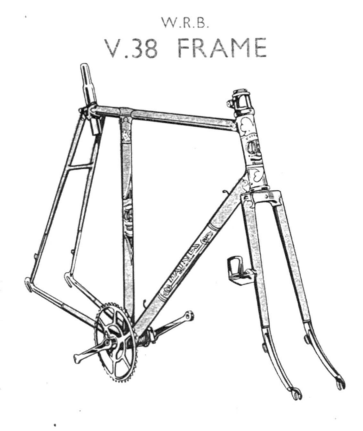

W.R.B.

V.38 FRAME

SPECIFICATION

FRAME. Built of Reynolds 531 Butted Tubes. 73° Head. 73° Seat. Upright Frame. Baines Special Lightened and Hand Filed Lugs of attractive design. Frame incorporating Vertical Tube giving three-point suspension to Top Tube, and at the same time allowing an ultra-short Wheelbase of only 37¼ in. Any Frame size to order. Bracket height 11 in. Usual brazed on fittings.

FORKS. Special Gauge Blades of Reynolds 531 Tubing. No. 1 Rake or any Rake to order, ⅞ in. round or D to O optional. Machined Crown designed to match Frame Lugs. Brazed on Chater Adjustable Lamp Bracket.

WHEELBASE 37¼ in., using 26 in. wheels.

FITTINGS. Williams C1000 Lightweight Racing Chain-wheel Set. Brazed on Mudguard Eyes, Pump Pegs, and Chater Adjustable Lamp Bracket. Tecalemit oil nipples to Bottom Bracket, Fork Head Clip, and Bottom Frame Race.

FINISH. Special anti-rust process before enamelling. Baines Stoved Synthetic Enamel or Durable Chromatic Lustre in any colour. Attractive Chevron design on Vertical Tube. Front and Rear Chrome Ends. All Chrome Front Fork optional. All Chrome Head 5/- extra. All Chrome Finish on Copper Base 20/- extra.

With Baines Fittings **£5 5 0**

Extra for Chater Chainwheel Set and Head Fittings, 17/6.

WHEN ORDERING YOUR BAINES FRAME

IT IS IMPORTANT when ordering your VS37 or V38 Frame to state clearly the size of wheels that will be used. Should you be using 26 in. with full equipment for road work and 27 in. for weekend events, our standard build covers your requirements.

But owing to the modern trend of larger frames, many riders have found it an advantage to use 27 in. wheels generally, that is with guards and brakes, and in these cases we have to make allowances for this when building, so it is important you mark your order clearly as to build required.

Praise from

DOUGLAS I.O.M

. . . You have certainly made a marvellous job of my V38 frame. It has exceeded all my expectations.

S. J. H.

We shall be pleased to quote for any repairs, wheelbuilding, gear repairs, frame and fork repairs, re-tracking and alterations, also re-enamelling and re-chroming to any make of cycle or tandem.

ANY ALTERNATIVE SPECIFICATION QUOTED FOR ON APPLICATION.

CARPENTER CYCLES

Carpenter cycles are acknowledged by connoisseurs to be one of the best lightweight cycles. They always made orthodox frames of the highest quality and their elegant proportions, superb finish and fine workmanship established a reputation for quality and performance that many thought was not surpassed by any other frame builder.

Established in the early 1920s, the earliest catalogue available to the author, dated 1927, gives their address as H Carpenter & Son, Head Office and Works, 43 Penton Street, London, N1. Certainly they had been trading for several years previous to this date – in 1925 they had introduced a range of imported Sprint wheels. They were located near 'The Angel' of Islington, a locality that was becoming well known to lightweight cycle enthusiasts. Several of the famous 'names' in frame building had their shops in this area of London. Even at this early period the range of Carpenter frames included two sporting tandems, a 'Special Record Tricycle', two path frames and both gents and ladies sports models. Clearly they had already become involved in sporting events with some success. They claimed that they were also innovators of some note, having introduced the hollow spindle and forward quick release rear ends which were then adopted by other manufacturers. This claim is not upheld however by other evidence.

In 1929 they introduced a Duralinium hub. In the early 1930s reference is made in the catalogues to 'Reynolds high-manganese butted tubing' and in 1935 this is referred to as 'Reynolds HM or 531 tubing'.

During WWII, bomb damage to the Islington area caused them to move from Penton Street and at some time towards the end of the war, they relocated to Kingston-on-Thames. The address became F H Carpenter, 52 Surbiton Road, Kingston-on-Thames, Surrey. They continued their business at this location throughout the 50s and 60s and had considerable success in competition events with riders such as Mike Gambrill, Robin Buchan and Jack Manning. In the 1960s, F H Carpenter fell ill and had to retire from the business. For a short period, Carpenter frames were manufactured under licence by Swindon Cycles, 90 Commercial Road, Swindon. Colin Cape frames were also made there. It is thought that this business closed in the early 1970s.

During the time they were based in Kingston, the Carpenter shop became the centre of sporting cyclists in the area. Frank Carpenter was a leading figure in the Festival Road Club and the shop became its unofficial second clubroom. Frank was President of the Club for many years. The shop was well known for its friendly atmosphere and Mrs Carpenter ran the shop's administrative side and kept detailed records in her precise handwriting. She ran a 'book' for the younger riders which enabled them to buy equipment by spreading repayments over a period of time. Known by club members as 'Mrs C', she was liked and respected by all who dealt with the shop. Frank was regarded with some awe and respected for his fanatical attention to detail. He offered advice and guidance to young riders and had ridden competitively in his younger days. However, he could be a little feisty if materials delivered to him or any sub-contracted work were not up to his high standards.

Keith Mitchell remembers Frank Carpenter during the early 1960s when, like most other artisan frame builders, he worked on his frame building in a tiny workshop at the back of his shop in Surbiton Park Terrace, while his wife minded the shop! He was a total perfectionist and at that time he filed his own lugs, mainly using Nervex Professional, which were not good enough for him so he spent hours filing each set until they were absolutely smooth and sharp. Frank was conservative and not overkeen on adopting the heavier seat stays and ultra-close clearances which came into fashion, preferring slim and elegant seat and chain stays. His perfectionist tendencies led him to examine each pair of Reynolds forks minutely, usually complaining how they were now made by machines and that the blades no longer came in matching pairs!

Frank was also an ace wheel builder, which also set him apart from others, at the time of 7-ounce wood insert sprint rims. We time triallists wanted them with 24 or 28 spokes and 5-ounce tyres, which we then rode over potholed roads! Any defective wheel with a shake of more than about 5mm was declared 'trueable, but needs a new rim really!'

Frank evidently supplied wheels to leading competition cyclists of the time, including Reg Harris.

A number of successes were achieved by notable riders who used Carpenter frames. Some examples are:

Bill Inder, who rode frame number 5279, had with two other founder members, brought cycling to Woking in 1922 and by 1928 had formed the West Surrey D A. A rider of no mean ability, he told tales of daily mileages of more than 100 miles in the early years, carrying camping kit on dreadnought cycles with 28 x $1^1/_2$" wheels and tyres. He became the President of the West Surrey D A in 1955, continuing in office until his death in 1992.

Jack Manning, who rode frame numbers 4146 and 4215, was notorious for racing anything anywhere. Jack was a superb rider whose racing career was severely curtailed by the outbreak of WWII. He was the last man to win a cycle race at Brooklands on the Campbell circuit. He worked as a toolmaker with an aircraft company. After the war he took part in many top-class events using his Carpenter frames. He was invited to join the first Milk Race team, but declined due to his wife's concern about him attending the race.

CARPENTER CYCLES

Mike Gambrill, was a well-known rider of the 1950s and a member of the Clarence Wheelers. One of Mike's best races was the 'Epic Dresden Madison' of 1959 in which he was paired with Norman Sheil. Fresh from their success of a few days earlier in Leipzig, the pair faced stiff opposition from riders from Berlin and the local Dresden Matadors' team. Mike's younger brother Robin was paired with Ken Craven. At half distance a new 20km track record time of 25min 31sec was set. The British pair took first place with 21 points and a track record of 40km in 51min. 41.2sec. (29.5mph). Mike rode a 26-inch Carpenter track frame in this event.

John Froud of the Festival Road Club, rode in the Tour of Britain, the Milk Race and the Peace Race (Berlin – Warsaw – Prague).

Jim Wheeler rode for the Festival Road Club and won the Bath Road 100 in 1961 with a time of 4hr 2min 27sec. In the same year Jim, together with the twin brothers John and Brian Froud, won the National Championship 100 team award.

Robin Buchan who rode frame number 4756, was a member of the Norwood Paragon C C. The 1960 Olympics saw Robin travel to Rome as reserve for the team pursuit and road team. He set a record for the 24hr Senior Men's class in 1971, covering 483.84 miles.

Notable personalities who worked with Carpenters were:

Harry Grey who worked with H Carpenter at the Penton Street address as a frame builder and was reputed to have slept in the shop cellar for a period when digs were not available.

Freddie Smeeth was a wheel builder-cum-mechanic at the Carpenter shop

Johnny Vaughan, who from 1959-63 worked as a frame builder with Carpenters, was also a keen competition cyclist and rode Time Trials during this period.

Carpenter's adopted a simple sequential numbering system for their frames. The numbers are stamped on the underside of the bottom bracket and on the front fork tube. Examples, which have been verified by copy of original receipt, are:

Frame	Date
3511	1st May 1938
4176	10th October 1947
4532	8th August 1950
5378	24th February 1962
5473	4th April 1964

The earliest frame number on the register is 3050 and the latest is 5752. It is reasonable to draw from the verified dates that Carpenters produced around 100 frames per year and this makes dating frames a relatively easy job.

The marque enthusiast maintains a register of frames and their details and is happy to assist in dating frames for owners. He would like to acknowledge the assistance of many people who helped provide the background information on the Carpenter cycle business and in particular Valerie Walker and Keith Mitchell.

John Gill

Catalogue kindly supplied by John Gill is for the 'Season 1932'

Catalogue for Season 1932

H. CARPENTER & SON

Specialists in Modern "Lightweight Cycle and Tandem Construction.

H. Carpenter & Son

**43 PENTON STREET,
LONDON, N.1.**

(NEAR "THE ANGEL," ISLINGTON)

Telephone ... ... NORTH 0176

Business Hours 8.30 a.m. till 8 p.m.
Thursdays 8.30 a.m. till 1 p.m. Saturdays 8.30 a.m. till 6 p.m.

AGENT

INTRODUCTION

Ever since our establishment, we have specially devoted all our energy and knowledge, together with our very wide experience, to the manufacture and improvement of the Lightweight bicycle. We were the Pioneers and Original Inventors of the Hollow Spindle, and the Forward Release rear fork end, now universally adopted by the leading makers all over the world.

The question of weight reduction is of the utmost importance to the Lightweight builder. Cutting down weight can only be carried out to certain limits, and it is only by selecting the very best materials and cutting out all superfluous parts of the lugs, and using only "A" quality tubing, and perfectly mitreing the joints before brazing, that this object is achieved. We do not believe in fanatical weight-saving ideas.

We employ no piecework labour, and can therefore guarantee the utmost attention and efficiency in the smallest detail to every machine. We do not profess to make the fastest cycle on earth, but we do profess to build a racing cycle equal to any maker in the trade, possessing the essential qualities of Lightness, Strength and Rigidity. Our cycles have been very successful both on path and road and we have hundreds of testimonials from satisfied owners.

You will undoubtedly wonder why we are able to sell our cycles cheaper than other Lightweight builders. This is only made possible by the reason that we have no heavy advertising bills to pay for, and we do not keep a lot of racing men, and advertise their wins week after week. These heavy expenses are thus avoided, and the saving is passed on direct to our customers; we have found from past experience that our cycles are "Silent Salesmen."

Our deferred payment system is financed entirely by ourselves, and all the prices are plainly marked under the various illustrations in this catalogue. There is no publicity or irritating enquiries made, as long as we have a substantial male guarantor who is a householder. Our system is considered the fairest yet placed before the rider.

All our cycles and frames are dispatched carriage free, except to Ireland and the extreme northern parts of Scotland, and the Continent.

2

OUR GUARANTEE.

We guarantee all our cycles, tandems and frames, for a period of Five Years. If any defect takes place during this time, same not having been caused by misuse, accident or neglect, we will make good such damage Free of Charge. Any defective part must be sent to us carriage paid, giving full details of complaint, date when purchased, and from whom. This guarantee Does Not apply to machines bought secondhand, or if anybody has had repair of same except ourselves.

Specialities of other manufacturers, such as Tyres, Saddles, Rims, Speed Gears, etc., are Not covered by our guarantee, but should be sent direct to the makers. Every fitting on a Carpenter cycle is guaranteed.

HIRE PURCHASE TERMS AND CONDITIONS.

After the agreed deposit, the balance is to be paid in eleven monthly instalments; the first instalment becomes due one month from date of delivery, and the remaining instalments on the same day in each succeeding month, until the whole is paid.

If any instalment is not paid within twenty-one days from date due, the balance of the whole of the remaining instalments shall become immediately due and payable, any indulgence allowed by us not prejudicing our rights.

Any default in payments relieves us of liability under our guarantee.

SPECIAL FEATURES.

Brazed on Pump Pegs, Reflector Boss, and Mudguard Eyes, on all models except Path Machines. Also lamp bracket if desired.

QUICK RELEASE, to both wheels, and special self-centring device to rear wheels, giving Automatic Chain Adjustment.

MUDGUARDS. All our guards are quick release. Spring Clips instead of straps are used, and the stays are fitted to brazed-on eyes. This enables them to be detached in 5 seconds.

All complete machines are fitted with Bluemel's 15″ pump and Bluemel's reflector.

All machines are also fitted with Tecalemit oil gun nipples. Tecalemit gun supplied Free.

CHROMIUM PLATING.

Properly executed, Chromium Plating is undoubtedly the finest finish procurable, for service and appearance, but it is a very expensive process, and the cost can only be reduced by omitting an essential part of the treatment. On certain models where we specify Chromium plating, we guarantee it to be the finest procurable.

3

Special Path. Model A.

Weight 17 lbs.

A perfectly rigid, light and lively machine, designed to respond to every ounce of energy expended, very close built for 27″ wheels. When ordering, it should be stated whether this model is required for cement tracks only, or for combined use for cement and grass.

FRAME	Built with Reynolds High Manganese Butted Tubes, any Size to Order, all Lugs Specially Cut Out and Lightened, Pull Back Type Rear Fork-ends, all Round Front Forks, Wheelbase 42″ or to Special Order, Bracket Height with 27″ Wheels, 10¾ for Cement, 11¼ for Grass.
WHEELS	Constrictor Best, 27″ Wide Flange Special Light Path Hubs, Spokes Tied and Soldered.
TYRES	Constrictor Silk Championship, for Cement, or Silk Grass Track, the Best Obtainable.
SADDLE	Brooks' Sprinter, or Ormond Sprinter.
HANDLEBARS ...	Any shape to Order, Special Light Gauge.
CHAIN	Renold's 1″ block, ⅛ or 3/16.
PEDALS	B.S.A. or Chater Lea, B.O.A. on Brampton Model.
FINISH	Any Desired Colour, Front Fork Plated all over.

Brampton Fittings £9 10 0

Easy payments, £3 deposit and 11 payments of 13/6.

Chater Lea or B.S.A. £10 15 0

Easy payments, £3 deposit and 11 payments of 16/-

Many National Championships have been won on machines of our make during the past few years, also hundreds of pounds in prizes.

4

Ladies' Sports. Model B.

Weight 26lbs.

The Ideal mount for the sports girl. The seat tube is butted 12" up from the bracket. This ensures perfect rigidity, easy running and elegant. A marvel on hills; makes cycling a real pleasure.

FRAME	Built with Reynolds A Quality Tubes, Top Tube Straight or Splayed to choice. Specially Lightened Lugs, Tapered Stays, Forward Release Rear Ends, D to O Forks, 2" Rake, Solid Ends. 10¼" Bracket height, 41½" Wheelbase, Any Size Frame to Order.
WHEELS	Endrick, or Narrow Section Steels. Double Cogged Hub, Fixed and Free Wheel, any Size to order. Butted Spokes.
TYRES	John Bull Speed, Dunlop Road Racing.
HANDLEBARS ...	We recommend North Road, but you may have any Bar to Order, Plated or Celluloid Covered, adjustable.
CHAIN	Brampton, Coventry, or Renold's.
SADDLE	Gough or Leatheries, Terry Pattern.
BRAKE	Pelissier or Resilion. Front or Rear.
PEDALS	Lady's Rat-trap or Rubber.
MUDGUARDS ...	Bluemel's Noweight, Spring Clip Fitting.
FINISH	Best Black or colour to choice. Plated Crown and Front Fork Ends. Usual Parts Super Plated.

Brampton Fittings £7 10 0

Easy Payments: 20/- deposit, and eleven payments of 13/3.

B.S.A. or Chater Lea Fittings ... £10 0 0

Easy Payments: 30/- deposit, and eleven payments of 17/6.

5

"The Clubman." Model C.

Weight 26 lbs.

A fast touring mount, very rigid and light, perfectly tracked, easy steering, and a revelation on hills.

FRAME	Built with Reynolds A Quality Tubing. Parallel Top Tube. Specially Lightened Lugs, perfectly mitred and brazed. Forward Release Rear Ends, Forks D to O, 2" Rake, Solid Ends. Built Any Size to Order. Bracket Height 10¼", Wheelbase 41¼".
WHEELS	Endrick or Narrow Section Steels, Plated or Black. Double-geared Hubs, Butted Spokes, two fixed, or one fixed and one Free Wheel. Any Gears to Order.
TYRES	John Bull Speed, Dunlop Racing.
HANDLEBARS ...	Any shape Bend and Clip to Order, Plated or Celluloid Covered.
CHAIN	Coventry, Brampton or Renold's.
SADDLE	Brooks, C32, Challenge, Racing.
BRAKE	Front or Rear Pelissier, or Resilion.
PEDALS	Brampton Race.
MUDGUARDS ...	Bluemel's Noweight, Spring Clip Fitting.
FINISH	Best Black, or colour to choice. Plated Crown and Front Ends. Usual Parts, Super Quality Plating.

Brampton Fittings £7 10 0

Easy Payments: 20/- deposit, and eleven payments of 13/3.

B.S.A. or Chater Lea Fittings ... £10 0 0

Easy Payments: 30/- deposit, and eleven payments of 17/6.

6

"Super" Clubman. Model D.

Weight 24¼ lbs.

This model really is "Super" Light, Rigid, Fast and Responsive. If you wish to improve your times this season, this is "IT." Just look at the graceful lines; a real thoroughbred, and every component used in its construction is the finest obtainable.

FRAME	Built with Reynolds High Manganese Butted Tubes, Lugs, specially cut out and lightened, perfectly mitred and brazed, forward release rear ends.
FRONT FORKS ...	Our new design as illustrated, very resilient, absorb all road shocks, 2, 3, or 4" rake at ends, or standard pattern if required.
WHEELS	Endrick Lightweight Rims, Plated or Black, Bayliss Wiley "Featherweight" Hubs. Black Butted Spokes. Two Fixed Cogs, any Gears to order.
TYRES	Dunlop Speed, or Englebert Amber, or to choice.
HANDLEBARS ..	Any pattern, bend to order, celluloid covered, on adjustable stem.
CHAINWHEEL AND CRANKS	Williams Special "Lightweight" Set.
CHAIN	Renold's roller, or Coventry Elite.
SADDLE	Brooks, B.17, or Mansfield "Ormond," or to choice.
BRAKE	Resilion Cantilever, front or rear.
PEDALS	Solid Centre Race, or Boa.
MUDGUARDS ...	Bluemel's New Noweight, Spring Clip Fitting.
FINISH	Any Desired Colour, Plated Crown and Front, and Rear Fork Ends, Usual Parts Chromium Plated.

Brampton Fittings £8 15 0
Easy Payments: 30/- deposit, and eleven payments of 14/6.

B.S.A. or Chater Lea Fittings ... £11 0 0
Easy Payments, £3 deposit, and eleven payments of 16/6.

7

Special Record Tandem. Model E.

Weight 43 lbs.

Designed for racing or touring, this model still holds several records. Brampton Models can have single or lateral stay frame to order. Chater Lea Models can be built of 12a or the new No. 14 design, with Cross-Over Drive, with stays brazed direct to rear bracket, giving a little shorter wheelbase.

FRAME	Reynolds A Quality Tubes, all Lugs Specially Lightened, Wheelbase 65". Bracket Height 10¾". Any Size Frame to Order.
WHEELS	Endrick or Westwood, 13 x 15 G Butted Spokes, Double Cog Rear Hub, Perfectly Rigid and True.
TYRES	Dunlop Tandem or John Bull Service.
HANDLEBARS ...	Any Shape, Celluloid Covered, in Adjustable Clips, Rear Bar on T Clip, or to Order.
CHAINS	Coventry, Brampton or Renold's.
PEDALS	Brampton Racing.
SADDLES	Brooks C 32, Challenge Racing.
BRAKE	Pelissier or Resilion, Front or Rear.
MUDGUARDS ...	Blumel's New Noweight, Spring Clip Fitting.
FINISH	Best Black or colour to choice. Plated Crown and Front Fork Ends. Usual Parts Super Quality Plated.

Brampton Fittings £14 0 0
Easy Payments: £4 deposit, and eleven payments of £1/0/9.

Chater Lea Fittings £16 10 0
Easy Payments: £4/10/0 deposit, and eleven payments of £1/4/6

Lady Back Model, 7/6 Extra.

8

Special 3 Speed Touring Tandem. Model F.

Weight 50 lbs.

An ideal touring tandem, fitted with "Cyclo" 3-speed gear and two special Cyklbrake Hubs, Derailleur Bracket and Brake Arm Lugs, brazed to stays; quickly detachable wheels and brake cables.

FRAME	Built with Reynolds A Quality Tubes, Brampton Lugs and Fittings. All lugs cut out, forward release rear ends, solid front ends, wheelbase 65", bracket height 10¾", any size frame to order.
WHEELS	Endrick or Westwood 26 x 1⅜, 13 x 15 G, Butted Spokes, on Cyklbrake hubs, any combination of gears to order.
TYRES	Dunlop Tandem, or John Bull Service.
HANDLEBARS ...	Any Shape Celluloid Covered, in Adjustable Clips, rear bar on T clip, giving choice of four positions.
CHAINS	Coventry, Brampton, or Renold's.
PEDALS	Brampton Racing, rubber rear if desired.
SADDLES	Brooks, C.32, Challenge.
MUDGUARDS ...	Bluemel's New Noweight, spring clip fitting.
FINISH	Best Black, or colour to choice, plated crown and front fork ends, usual parts, super quality plated.

Brampton Fittings £17 0 0

Easy Payments: £5 deposit, and eleven payments of £1/3/6.

Lady Back Model, 7/6 Extra.

9

3-Speed Super Touring. Model G.

Weight 30 lbs.

An ideal Touring or Business Machine, with "Cyclo" 3-speed and Two Hub Brakes. Any combination of three gears desired. Hills do not matter to the riders of this model. The low gears make climbing easy, and the two powerful hub brakes are adequate for any descents.

FRAME	Built with Reynolds A Quality Tubes, all Lugs cut out and Lightened. Bracket Height 10¾", Wheelbase 43". Forward Release Rear Ends, Cyclo Bracket Brazed to Stay.
FORKS	D to O Section, Heavy Butted Blades and Column, the Blades have a 3" Rake, giving Wonderful Comfort and Steering.
WHEELS	Endrick or Westwood Rims, with either two Perry or two Solo Hub Brakes, Fitted with Cyclo 3-Speed Chain Gear, Black Butted Spokes.
TYRES	Fort Dunlop or John Bull Service, or to Order.
HANDLEBARS ..	Any Shape Bend in Adjustable Clip, Celluloid Covered.
CHAIN	Coventry, Brampton or Renold's.
SADDLE	Brook's B66, or Terry's C.T.C., or to Order.
PEDALS	Racing or Roadster Rat Trap or Rubber.
MUDGUARDS ...	Bluemel's New Noweight, Spring Clip Fitting.
FINISH	Best Black or Colour to Choice. Usual Parts Super Quality Plated.

Alternative same price specification with this model include the new Sturmey-Archer 3-speed and Perry Hub Brake combined, or the new Cyclo Tank 3-speed and Two Resilion Brakes.

Brampton Fittings £9 15 0

Easy Payments: 30/- deposit, and eleven payments of 17/-.

B.S.A. or Chater Lea Fittings ... £11 10 0

Easy Payments: £3 deposit, and eleven payments of 17/6.

10

Special Record Tandem Frame.

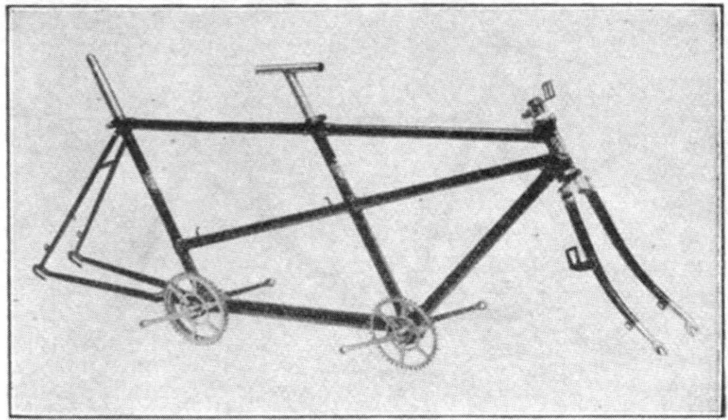

Weight 22 lbs.

It is no idle boast when we state Record model. Our tandems have broken several Place to Place records. You cannot buy a faster machine. Built on practical lines, Rigid, Responsive, and dead True. Built with Brampton Superb or Chater Lea Fittings.

Built any size to order. Wheelbase 65". Bracket Height 10¾". Brampton model 1⅞" Chain Line, No. 14 Chater Lea 1½" Chain Line, Reynolds A Quality Tubes. All lugs specially lightened and fish-tailed. Straight round tapered seat and chain stays. Brazed-on Mudguard Eyes, Pump Pegs, Reflector Boss, Lamp Bracket if desired. Complete with all interior fittings, Seat Pins, and Chain Wheels and Cranks.

Forward Release or Draw Back Rear Ends, Solid Recessed Front Ends.

FINISH. Best Black, or colour to choice. Plated Crown and Front Ends.

Brampton Fittings £9 0 0

Easy Payments: £3 deposit, and eleven payments of 12/6.

Chater Lea Fittings £10 10 0

Easy Payments: £3 deposit, and eleven payments of 15/6.

11

Special Taper Tube Model.

Weight 10¼ lbs.

This model is the very essence of rigidity, and its construction eliminates the possibility of distortion occurring at the bracket. Furthermore, there is no increase in weight over our standard model.

Patent No. 259026.

Built throughout with straight tapered tubing of the highest quality, forward release rear ends, solid front ends. Brazed-on Mudguard Eyes, Pump Pegs, also Lamp Bracket if desired.

Complete with all interior fittings, Seat Pin, Chain Wheel and cranks.

FINISH. Best Black, or Colour to choice. Plated crown and front ends. Usual parts super quality plating.

Brampton Fittings £3 10 0

B.S.A. or Chater Lea Fittings ... £4 10 0

Frames only, not supplied on hire purchase terms.

SPECIAL RECORD TRICYCLE.

FRAME	Reynolds A Tubes, Specially Lightened Lugs. Size to Order. Wheelbase 38", Bracket Height 9½".
WHEELS	26 or 27" Constrictor Best Sprint Rims.
TYRES	Constrictor No. 3, or to Order.
AXLE	Abingdon, 30", 28" Axle 10/- extra.
SADDLE	Brook's B.17, or Ormond.
CHAIN	Coventry Elite, or Reynold's roller.
BRAKE	Front Pelissier.
FINISH	Any Colour, Fronk Fork Plated all over.

Brampton Fittings £17 10 0

B.S.A. or Chater Lea Fittings ... £19 0 0

You cannot buy a faster Trike. Dead true, very rigid.

12

The Clubman Frame.

Weight 10¼ lbs.

Built any size, with best quality Reynolds A quality tubing. Parallel top tube, all lugs perfectly mitred and brazed. Forward release rear ends, solid front ends, Bracket height 10¼", Brazed-on Pump Pegs, Mudguard Eyes, and Reflector Boss, Lamp Bracket also, if required. Complete with all interior fittings, chain wheel and cranks.

FINISH. Best Black, or colour to choice, plated crown and front fork ends. All usual parts super quality plating.

Brampton Fittings	**£3**	**0**	**0**
Chater Lea Fittings	**£4**	**0**	**0**
B.S.A. Fittings	**£4**	**5**	**0**

OUR SPECIAL "SUPERLITE" FRAME.

Built with Reynolds High Manganese Butted Tubes, special light gauge, all lugs cut away and lightened as far as is practicable with safety. We do not believe in fanatical weight-saving. Forward release rear ends, solid front ends, D to O front forks 2" rake, 10¾" bracket height. Built any size to order. You may have our new resilient front forks if desired, complete with Conloy Seat Pin and Pelissier "Lauter-weight" Chainwheel and Cranks. Guaranteed weight 8 lbs.

FINISH. Any desired colour. Plated crown, and front and rear fork ends.

Special Superlite Fittings ... **£5 0 0**

Frames only, not supplied on hire purchase terms.

13

Carpenter's Famous Leather Bags.

For years we have been noted for our Leather Bags, and we now offer better value than ever before. Several improvements have been incorporated for this season. All sizes are now fitted with a steel bar across the back, which not only retains the shape of the bag, but also allows the straps to pass round, and so obviates the necessity for sewing or riveting; also they now all have a pair of cape straps fitted at top of bag. You cannot obtain a better bag, irrespective of price.

Made from specially selected hides, bound edges, entirely waterproof. Special sizes made to order in two days.

Large Size, fitted with Two Side Pockets, for camera or maps. Size, 13" x 9" x 5". **8/6** each.

Same Size Bag as above, without the side pockets, 13" x 9" x 5". **6/6** each.

Small Size, 11½" x 6" x 4" **4/6**. Very neat and compact. We also stock Brooks, Gough and Midland Bags.

14

CARPENTER'S FAMOUS OILSKIN CAPES. WITH "COOLER" SHOULDER VENTS.

The only Cape for the real Clubman, made with the hem 126 inches wide. This allows the Cape to Cover the Bag at Rear, and come well forward also. These Capes are proofed again after they are sewn, and are therefore entirely Waterproof at the Seams, the "Cooler" Ventilated Shoulders obviate the "Ballooning" when riding in a strong wind, and also keep the wearer much cooler, than the ordinary Cape does.

Made in one size only, 42" x 126".

BLACK, **11/-**,

KHAKI, **12/-** each. Post Free.

ZIP Fastening to Cape or Leggings, **3/-** extra.

Sou'Westers to match, Black or Khaki, **2/6** each.

Oilskin Leggings to match, Black or Khaki, **7/6** pair.

Also Paget and Brook's Capes and Leggings in stock, current Prices. Post Free per return.

15

CARPENTER'S HAND-MADE CYCLING SHOES.

These Shoes are made specially for us by a well known London Clubman, his skill in Shoecraft, combined with our Knowledge of what the Clubman requires, results in the Finest Shoes possible to obtain for Appearance, Comfort and Durability. Our new Range of Styles appeal to every class of Rider.

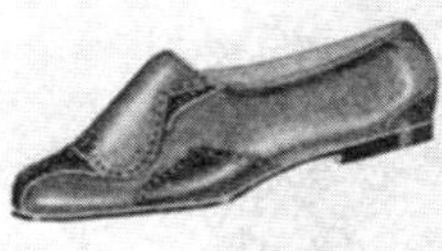

LIGHTWEIGHT Racing Shoe, with Flap-over Tongue, Low Cut, Snug Fitting Heel, Supple Chrome Calf Uppers, Flexible Sole, Black with Tan Trimmings, White Eyelet Holes. **15/-**

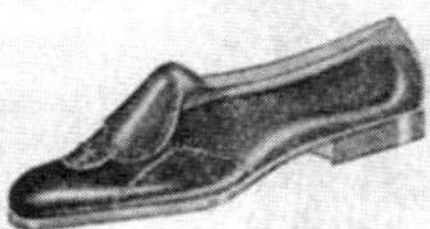

The "CLUBSHOE" with Flap-over Tongue, Supple Chrome Calf Uppers, Medium Heel, Stiffened Back, Neat Pedal Patch, Correct Cut and fit.
Black, **14/6** Brown, **15/6**

The "TOURIST," a very SmartAll-Weather Shoe, Best Willow Calf One Piece Upper, Broad Elastic Strap under Flap, Very Snug and Comfortable. A Really High-grade Shoe.
Black, **15/6** Brown, **16/6**

The "RYDEWALK," a New Introduction, Ideal for Cycling or Walking. Box-hide Uppers, Stout Sole and Heel. Will Keep Out the Heaviest Rain, and Stand up to the Hardest Wear, with Full Freedom.
Black, **16/6** Brown, **17/6**

All above Shoes stocked in sizes from 5 to 11. Special sizes made to order, **2/6** extra.

GABY Pattern Shoes, British make, Box Calf uppers, a very popular Cycling Shoe, small leather strap fastening. Black only, **10/6**.

Special line of French cycling shoes, at clearance price, **7/6**. Unrepeatable when stock is exhausted. Sizes 5 to 8 only.

16

HANDLEBAR STEMS, SEAT PINS AND BENDS.

Highest Quality Plating. British Manufacture.

No. 1.	No. 2.	No. 3.
Plated 3/-.	Plated 3/6.	Plated 3/6.
Chromium 4/-.	Chromium 4/6.	Chromium 4/6.

Curved Stems: Plated 3/-, Chromium 4/-. Expander Bolts 6d. extra.

Chater Lea 1¾ Extension 6/3, Chromium 7/6.

Major Taylor Extension 7/6, Chromium 9/-.

Tandem T Seat Pin, Square Back with Rear Bar Clip, 8/- each.

Tandem Rear Bar and Seat Pillar Clip, 2/8 each, for T or Straight Seat Pins.

SEAT PILLARS.

L. Pattern, 8", 1/3; 12", 2/-; Best Plating.

L. Pattern, 8", 2/-; 12", 2/9; Chromium Plated.

Straight Pattern, 10", 1/-; 12", 1/3; Best Plating.

Straight Pattern, 10", 1/9; 12", 2/-; Chromium Plated.

Curved Pattern, 9", 1/6; 12", 2/-; Best Plated.

Curved Pattern, 9", 2/3; 12", 3/-; Chromium Plated.

Constrictor Conloy, 3/6 each.

"High Manganese" Seat Pins., 1oz. heavier than Conloy, 2/9 each. Chromium Plated 3/3. All sizes.

HANDLEBAR BENDS.

Largest Stocks in London. Every known bend in stock. All level grip and fitted with brazed-on ferrules. The celluloid-covered bends are ⅞ diameter over all. To avoid straining, open your handlebar clip when fitting.

	Marsh.	Southall	Lauterwasser.	Highgate.
Rough	2/-	2/-	2/-	2/6
Plated	3/6	4/-	4/-	5/-
Celluloid Covered ...	4/6	5/-	5/-	5/6
Chromium Plated ...	5/-	6/-	6/-	6/6

17

WHEELS.

All Carpenter Built Wheels are Correctly Trued and Tensioned.
Any Combination of Rim and Hubs Dispatched same day as Ordered.

ENDRICK OR WESTWOOD RIMS.

Brampton "Superbe" D.C. Hubs, Locked Cones, Butted Spokes	15/- 12/6
Bayliss-Wiley "Featherweight" Hubs	25/- 22/6
B.S.A. or Chater Lea D.C. Hubs	26/-
Cyklbrake "Solo" or Perry Hub Brake, Front Wheel only ...	20/-
Cyklbrake "Solo" or Perry Hub Brake, Rear Wheel only ...	22/-
Sturmy Archer 3-Speed, Rear Wheel only	30/-
Sturmy-Perry, Combined 3-Speed and Hub Brake, Rear Wheel ...	40/-

EXTRA STRONG TANDEM WHEELS.

Endrick or Westwood Rims, Brampton D. C, Tandem Hubs, 13-15G, Spokes	20/- 17/6
With Constrictor Light Steel Large Flange Hubs	40/-
Cyklbrake or Perry Hub Brake, Front Wheel only	23/-
Cyklbrake or Perry Hub Brake, Rear Wheel only	26/-

SPRINT WHEELS.

Brampton "Superbe" Hubs, any Pattern "Boa" Rim, 15 x 17G Spokes	25/-
Ditto with Constrictor Best Rims, 26 or 27"	32/-
Ditto with Tabucchi Flat or Crescent Rims	30/-
Bayliss Wiley "Featherweight" Hubs, in any of above, extra	10/-
B.S.A. or Chater Lea Hubs, in any of above, extra	11/-
Conloy Tubular Rims and Brampton Hubs	46/-

Extra for Tie and Soldering Spokes, 1/6 per pair.

Let us quote you for your Wheels, we are recognised as the quickest and cheapest Wheel Builders in the Trade. Estimates dispatched per return post, Wheels dispatched same day as ordered.

REPAIRS AND ENAMELLING.

One New Frame Tube, 7/-, Two New Tubes 12/6.

Cutting down Frame and Fork, 15/-.

New Fork Stem 4/-, New Fork Blade 4/-, Two Blades 6/-.

New Tapered Chain or Seat Stays, 10/-.

New Set of Tapered Chain and Seat Stays, 17/6.

Brazing-on Fork Lamp Bracket, Pump Pegs, Reflector and Mudguard Eyes, 5/-.

Enamelling Frame and Fork, Black 7/-, Colour 8/-.

Enamelling Tandem Frame and Fork, Black 14/-, Colour 16/-.

Plating Fork Crown and Ends 3/-, Tandem 3/9.

Plating Rear Ends 3/6, Tandem 5/-.

We specialise in repairs to any make of cycle or tandem. Send us details of work required. We will quote you per return post.

18

EXTRA, AND ALTERNATIVE EQUIPMENT, ETC.

CHROMIUM PLATING.

Of the highest quality only. Includes Fork Crown and Front Forkends on Frames, and all usual bright parts, also Rims and Brake on Cycles.

	Frame.	Cycle.	Tandem Frame.	Tandem.
BRAMPTON	6/-	10/-	8/-	15/-
CHATER LEA ...	10/-	20/-	14/-	25/-
B.S.A.	8/-	15/-		

EXTRA PLATING.

Plating Rear Forkends, Nickel 4/-, Chromium 6/-.
Plating Fork all over, Nickel 5/-, Chromium 7/6.
Plating Frame and Fork all over, Nickel 20/-, Chromium £2/5/0.

FLAMBOYANT FINISHES.

For this Special Finish Frames are Dull Plated all over. Prices include both Front and Rear Forkends plated. Any colour obtainable.

With Nickel-Plated Forkends .... Cycle 12/6, Tandem 20/-.
With Chromium-Plated Forkends ... Cycle 17/6, Tandem 25/-.

TAPERED FRAME TUBES.

(Patent No. 259026.)

Can be had on any of our models, 7/6 extra. Eliminates bracket distortion, and ensures an extra rigid frame.

SADDLES.

On models where Challenge C32 are specified: Brooks B.17 6/- extra. Terrys 7/6, Lycett Aero 4/- extra.

TYRES.

On models where Dunlop Racing or John Bull Speed are specified:
Fort Dunlop or John Bull Gristly, 6/- per pair extra.
Englebert Amber or Constrictor No. 3, 7/6 per pair extra.

HANDLEGRIPS.

Constrictor Long Sponge 1/3 extra; Long Anti-Shock 2/6, Short 2/-.
John Bull Air Cell Eccentric Grips 1/6, Shockstop 1/6 extra.

CHAINWHEELS AND CRANKS.

Pélissier "Lauterweight" Chainwheel and Cranks fitted to any Brampton Cycle or Frame, 10/6 extra. Chromium Plated 13/6.

SUNDRIES.

Veeder Cyclometer 7/9, Trip Model 18/6.
Fork Blade Clip for same, 1/3.
Bag Supports 1/- and 1/6.
Lucas Challis Bell 2/9, Chromium Plated 3/3.

ALL EXTRAS REQUIRED ARE TO BE PAID FOR WITH DEPOSIT ON ORDER.

19.

GEAR TABLE

Chain-wheel No. of Teeth	Cog. No. of Teeth	Diam. of Wheel. 26 in.	27 in.	28 in.	Chain-wheel No. of Teeth	Cog. No. of Teeth	Diam. of Wheel. 26 in.	27 in	28 in.
	12	91.0	94.1	98.1		12	99.6	103.5	107.3
	13	84.0	87.4	90.5		13	92.0	95.5	99.0
	14	78.0	[illegible]	84.0		14	85.4	88.7	92.0
	15	72.8	[illegible]	78.4		15	79.7	82.1	85.8
	16	68.2	70.8	73.5		16	74.7	77.6	80.5
42	17	64.3	[illegible]	69.2	46	17	70.3	73.0	75.7
	18	60.6	63.0	65.2		18	66.4	69.0	71.6
	19	57.5	59.6	60.9		19	63.0	65.4	67.8
	20	54.6	56.7	58.8		20	59.8	62.0	64.4
	12	95.3	99.0	102.2		12	104.0	108.0	112.6
	13	88.0	91.3	94.8		13	96.0	99.7	103.4
	14	[illegible]	84.8	88.0		14	89.1	93.5	96.0
	15	76.2	79.2	82.1		15	83.2	86.4	89.5
44	16	71.5	74.2	77.1	48	16	78.0	81.0	84.1
	17	[illegible]	69.	72.[illegible]		17	73.4	76.2	79.0
	18	63.5	66.0	68.4		18	69.3	72.0	74.6
	19	60.2	[illegible]	64.8		19	65.7	68.2	70.7
	20	[illegible]	59.4	61.6		20	62.4	64.8	67.2

CYCLING HOSE.

Best Black or Fancy Designs, 3/6, 4/6. Super Quality, 6/6 and 8/6 per pair.

TIGHTS.

Best Black, Double Seated, Specially Cut to Ensure a Perfect Fit 5/6, 7/6.
Super Quality, All Wool, 10/6 and 12/6 pair.

ALPACA JACKETS.

Well Cut and Tailored, 6/6, 8/6, 10/6 each.

BLACK RACING JERSEYS.

Button at Shoulder, 3/6 and 4/6. Super Quality, 8/6 and 10/-.

KHAKI SHIRTS.

4/6, 6/6. Shorts to Match, 4/6 and 6/6.

Let us know your requirements, we have it in stock. Remember all Orders Dispatched same day. Post Free.

ALL MAKES OF TUBULAR TYRES IN STOCK.
POST FREE. PER RETURN.

The Walthamstow Press, Ltd., 183, High Street, E.17.

GRANBY

Bill Ewing, or Ewings, established the marque Granby before WW1. In the 1914 Kelly Directory for Lewisham, he is listed as 'Cycle Manufacturer at 324 New Cross Road'. Being next door to a well-known south London landmark, The Marquis of Granby public house, the marque acquired an easy-to-remember name at an easy-to-find location.

During 1915, a Catford Cycling Club Gazette carried the following advertisement.

Speedmen
When requiring a new racing cycle call at The Granby Cycle Works, 324, New Cross Road, S.E., and inspect our new Path and Road Racing Cycles. No bolted joints, perfect rigidity with lightness, straight back stays tapering to the fork end with which the wheel can be removed and replaced in 15 seconds. Prices from £6 15s. Other racing cycles from £5
All classes of repair undertaken.

With this provenance, and there being strong indications that trading started in 1912, the marque can make a reasonable claim to be the first of the British lightweight frame builders.

Advertising ceased during 1916 whilst Ewing(s) served King and Country. Post-war he was joined by another recently demobbed Catford rider, Percy Dean, with whom he had ridden a tandem on 50-mile and 12-hour Catford events prior to the war.

Under the proprietorship of Ewing(s) and Dean, the marque flourished in the immediate post-war period. Contemporary advertisements based on competition results show most of the leading national and commonwealth riders were riding machines built at The Granby Cycle Works. Advertising claimed that Granby cycles were the only British-built cycles placed in the finals of both the 1920 and 1924 Olympic Games.

From their earliest advertisements, it is clear that Granby were in the forefront of technical innovation, the quick release fork end (reg. design no. 670117) and 'Double D' tube construction (reg. design no. 670116) being the earliest.

The innovation for which the marque is synonymous is that of taper tube frame construction. A patent application for this type of construction was made in 1925 by W E Ewings, P J Dean and H B Harris. This was accepted in October 1926 as patent specification 259026. Early in 1926 Granby Cycle Works advertisements appeared for this type of frame. More or less at the same time Selbach, another leading South London frame builder, advertised taper tube frames. It is believed that he had shared the undoubtedly high cost of the initial batch of taper tubing and lugs. Taper tube frames were built in search of the Holy Grail sought by most frame builders, that of a 'stiff' frame. These frames were of two types, those having the three main triangle tubes tapered and those with the seat and down tube tapered, but a parallel top tube. The latter was known as the 'Taperlite' model.

Production flourished during the 1902's and 30s, the marque being highly regarded by club riders and racing men locally and throughout the UK and overseas. Judging by the regular, often half a page, advertisements in Cycling, much business was conducted by mail order. A range of specialist singles, tandems and tricycles were catalogued.

Both Ewings and Dean retained close contact with the Catford CC, as can be affirmed by reference to Southcott and Reynold histories of the club. During the late 1930s, changes occurred affecting the marque. In 1935 a move was made a few doors along the New Cross Road to larger premises at 338, then Bill Ewing died, and by 1938 Percy Dean became the sole proprietor.

The catalogue shown, although undated, is believed to be 1937/8. It is clear that production was aimed very much towards the serious clubman who wanted a high-class machine for use on club runs with the hard riders, for long distance touring, time trials or track work. All of the components and options offered in the catalogue are of a high quality, hence expensive, this being during a period of relatively low wages. Both the Taperlite and Aldek models were favourably reviewed in Cycling during the late 1930s. According to Cyclo advertising material, the record breaker Evelyn Hamilton was, at about that time, riding a Granby.

Soon after the start of WWII, South London became a prime target in the blitz. The late Reg Reynolds, who at that time had a machine on hire purchase from the shop, indicated that the shop closed immediately at the outbreak of war never to re-open as a cycle shop.

The post-war austerity period saw the re-emergence of the marque, but under a different management structure. Ron Argent, another respected Catford CC racing man, who during the war ran an engineering business in Erith, acquired the name. Percy Dean remained for a few years connected with the frame building side of the business. Argent, an entrepreneur with various interests, owned a number of cycle shops in northwest Kent. Production of lightweights continued, often using oddments remaining from pre-war stock. In 1954 a catalogue was produced showing the tradition Granby range of machines. However, the marque never regained its inter-war pre-eminence producing lightweight frames, although Peter Beardsmore of Medway Wheelers did ride a Taperlite Granby when he won the BBAR in 1948. During this period, technical innovation continued, one notable example being a stem/handlebar extension with fixing arrangements nearly identical to current practice, including the use of socket head screws. This was reviewed and marketed in 1948. Other innovations at about this time were a headset with a novel locking arrangement and an oversized bottom bracket that accommodated an eccentric carrier for the bottom bracket axle, thus allowing easy adjustment of the chain without releasing the rear wheel.

A member of the Dean family has informed me that no records or documentation associated with the marque are known to exist. The frame numbering system would need the expertise of Bletchley park to made any sense of the numbers, totalling about fifty frames, which are currently recorded. Identification and dating of Granby frames is difficult, but some of the following features may be used as a guide. Pre-1940, the frame number was stamped under the fork crown on the bottom of the steerer tube, in addition to the bottom bracket. No Taper Tube models were produced before 1925. Known frame numbers for Taper Tube models with indented chain stays are 2841, with copy of original order dated 14/11/28, 2835 and 733 believed to be 1929. Square section chain stays were introduced in 1930, and known machines are 3351 ordered before 1932, 869 and 1579, a ladies machine dated 1934. All these were Taper Tube models. Frame numbers for four others are TT2272 ordered 29/12/36, 2440 ordered in 1937, 2120 with 338 New Cross Road transfer, 1936-1939 and 2497 ordered in 1938. Machines produced under Ron Argent's ownership of the marque are, 2573 ordered June 1947, GS 253 built to owner's specifications 1946/47 and 401 2923 purchased from the 1951 Earls Courts Show stand.

Few pre-war head badges and even fewer examples of transfers survive today. From the examination of frames, head badges were uncommon, three types are known to exist. One pre-1930 example is known to exist on a Taper Tube frame. The other pre-1930 Taper Tube frame appears never to have carried a metal badge. The 'fan' style badge with the 338 New Cross Road marking was, in all probability, used on a few early post-war Argent built frames.

The number of machines recorded by the V-CC Marque Enthusiast are as follows:

Granby		**Argent**	
Frame	No	Frame	No
Early Double D	1	Regent	2
Pre-1930 Taper Tube	2	Consort	1
Ladies Taper Tube	1	Skylon	1
Pre-1940 Taper Tube	14	Taperlite	2
Pre-1940 Taperlite	11	Unidentified	8
Taper Tube Tricycle	1		
Tandem	3		

By the late 1960s, the Granby marque, together with many other respected lightweight frame builders had slowly faded into obscurity; a sad ending to a pioneering, innovative and one-time leading marque.

David Hinds

Catalogue and leaflet kindly loaned by Mike Madgett . Mike' 'guestimate' for the date is 1938/9

A. E. MADGETT,
Cycle Agent,
DISS.

"GRANBY" CYCLES

LMA

THE WORLD'S BEST
BICYCLE

MANUFACTURED BY
GRANBY CYCLES
338, NEW CROSS ROAD,
LONDON, S.E.

By courtesy of "The Bicycle"

LIGHTWEIGHT & RACING LIST

GRANBY CYCLES

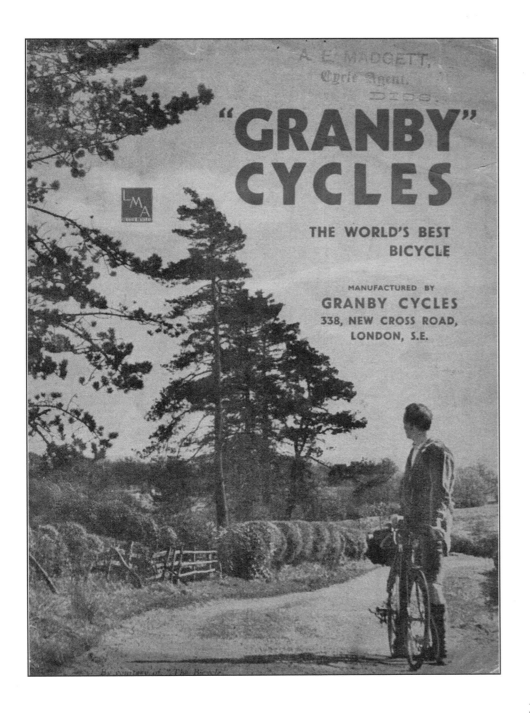

Our Speciality is the building of Cycles of Highest Quality to meet customers' own special requirements. Twenty-five years ago we set out to improve the lightweight cycle. We originated the design of the present and now universal lightweight, also the Taper Tube frame. During that period we have continually effected improvements and perfected design. The "Granby" is the last word in modern design and is recognised as THE WORLD'S BEST BICYCLE. Send Your Specification and we will quote without obligation. Our experience is at your service. We can unfailingly give you the best advice on any point.

338
NEW CROSS RD.
LONDON
S.E.14

PHONE
TIDEWAY 3398

TERMS, Etc.

A nominal bona fide deposit of £1 is required with all orders. Balance upon completion. Customer is notified when machine is ready for despatch. All machines or frames are very carefully packed and sent carriage paid per passenger train, at our risk, to address. Please state when ordering whether you desire to take advantage of our Easy Payment system, or whether you desire to purchase for cash.

ORDERS.

An Order Form is enclosed for customers' convenience, and also a Quotation Form for enquiries for price. An ordinary written specification will do as well. Upon receipt of an order, we send a complete Copy of Specification in detail for checking over and reference, to avoid any possible error. Any discrepancies should be notified at once.

FORKS.

The "Granby" Resilient Fork Blade (Ref. letter G) is the blade we recommend for touring and for road racing. This blade is finely proportioned from tapering gauge metal and so curved to distribute the stresses along the whole length of the blade. D to O section. It is a particularly safe blade and very resilient. This blade is very costly to produce, but is fitted as standard unless otherwise ordered.

THE WORLD'S BEST BICYCLE

GRANBY "Lightweight" Club Model

UPRIGHT OR STANDARD ANGLES

This machine can be built to any angles and equipped to your own specification.
Quotation by return.

SPECIFICATION

Frame—Chrome-Molybdenum or Reynold's H.M. Steel, D to O Fork Blades, Tapered Seat and Chain Stays, Granby rear Release. Standard Wheelbase 41ins., Bracket height 10¼ins. (or dimensions to order), "Upright" or standard angle design, (For further particulars see frames, page 10).

Wheels. 26in × 1¼in. Light Steel Endrick. D.B. Spokes. Constrictor light steel hubs.

Brakes. Two Resilion.

Chain. Coventy Elite.

Saddle. B 17, "Flyer" or Terrys.

Handlebars. Any shape.

Pedals. BOA or Brampton Race.

Guards. Blumfield "No-Weight,"

Brazed-on-Attachments—Mudguard Eyes, Pump Pegs, Reflector Eye, Chater Fork L Bracket if desired—either side. (Hub brakes can be substituted for either or both rim brakes at same price).

Finish. Best black enamel after rust proof preparation. Usual plated parts chromium.

The above Specification can be altered in any item to meet customer's requirements at difference in price of interchanged parts.

Model built with
Standard Frame Tubes £9 5 0

Easy Payments **17/9** deposit, and
11 monthly payments of **17/9**

Model built with
Taper Tubes £9 10 0

Easy Payments, **£1 2 9** deposit, and
11 monthly payments of **17/9**

B.S.A. or Chater-Lea fittings **£2** extra.

The Machine is built with a view to use as a club machine, and also, when stripped and fitted with Sprints, Road Racing. The frame is built with that purpose in view, and the whole construction makes for the utmost efficiency in that direction.

GRANBY "Aldek"

ANGLES 73° HEAD
71° SEAT
OR TO ORDER.

SPECIFICATION

Frame. Size to order of Chrome-Molybdenum tubing.

Wheels. 26in. × 1¼in. Endrick Chrome on "Sivada" Hubs.

Chain. Renold.

Saddle. Brooks

Handlebars. Any Shape.

Brakes. 2 "Grip-it" De Luxe.

Guards. Featherweight.

CASH ONLY £8 : 10 : 0

3

GRANBY "Road Racing" Model

BUILT TO ANY ANGLES.

SPECIFICATION

Frame. Chrome-Molybdenum or H.M. steel. Frame angles suitable for road racing, or to special order.

Wheels. 26in. or 27in. Constrictor. First choice flat rims "Solite" light steel hubs. Constrictor ADDER Tubulars. Spokes D.B. tied and soldered at crossings.

Chain. Coventry Elite.

Handlebars. Racing.

Brake. Front Bowden. CONLOY or Pelissier.

Saddle. B 17 Ch. Narrow. (Specification varied to suit customer's requirements at difference in costs).

Finish. Black, usual plated parts chromium.

CHAMPIONSHIPS have been won all over the World on "Granby" racing machines. These machines are designed essentially for speed and are the result of a long experience of building for Champions.

Standard Frame Tubes - £10 : 10 : 0
Easy Payments, **£1 1 6** deposit, and
11 monthly payments of **£1**

Taper Tube model - £10 : 15 : 0
Easy Payments, **£1 6 6** deposit, and
11 monthly payments of **£1**

B.S.A. or Chater-Lea fittings **£2** extra.

GRANBY "Path Racing" Model

SPECIFICATION

Frame. Chrome-Molybdenum or H.M. steel, Path Angles.

Wheels. 27in. × 1in. Constrictor flat rims, No. 1 Silk Path tyres. Tied spokes.

Saddle. B17 Sprinter.

Handlebars. Sibbit, Triumph, or to order.

Chain. Renold's 1 in. × ⅛in. Block.

Pedals. Brampton Race or BOA.

Finish. Black, usual plated parts chromium.

Standard Frame Tubes - £10 : 15 : 0
Easy Payments, **£1 7 0** deposit, and
11 monthly payments of **£1**

Taper Tube model - £11 : 0 : 0
Easy Payments, **£1 12 0** deposit, and
11 monthly payments of **£1**

B.S.A. or Chater-Lea fittings **£2** extra.

4

The GRANBY "Taperlite"

THE LIGHTEST, STRONGEST & MOST RESPONSIVE LIGHTWEIGHT CYCLE IN EXISTENCE

This Super Light machine is designed to meet the requirements of the Lightweight Enthusiast.

For a machine of this type to give entire satisfaction, no strength can be sacrificed. The ENORMOUS STRENGTH of TAPER TUBES combined with that of Chrome-molybdenum or H.M. Steel, allows of considerable weight reduction without loss of strength and rigidity.

Every part, even the most inconsiderable, where weight can be reduced without sacrificing strength, has had careful attention. New Lugs have been designed. Also a New Type of Resilient Fork Blades is fitted.

Special Light Rims and Spokes reduce weight where most effective as regards Life and Speed.

A very careful selection has been made in the use of Components where ounces or parts of ounces could be saved. A policy of saving weight by the use of inferior parts has been rejected.

Alloy Parts are only used where they can be safely and after long tests. The metal used is the Highest Quality Light Alloy known suitable for the purpose, i.e., DURALUMIN. This metal has the extraordinary high tensile strength of 26 tons per square inch.

The Complete machine equipped with D.C. hub, Bluemel guards and brake weighs only

22¾ lbs. Guaranteed Weight.

The machine has a wonderful feeling of Life such as is possessed by no other cycle, and when handled feels like a feather.

NOTE that the Chainwheel and Cranks are of light steel, not alloy, as we do not consider that a successful crank in alloy has yet been produced.

The Granby Cycle Works have brought twenty years of experience in lightweight construction to bear on the designing of this machine. We have delayed the production of a machine of this ultra-light type because we preferred not to put such a machine on the market under our name until we could fully satisfy ourselves that it could be done in such a manner that would be a further testimony to the quality of our productions and give entire satisfaction. The machine has undergone test after test, and it is a superfine article.

We make this machine to order, and are prepared to fit any equipment or components, and in such a case the standard specification is to serve as a guide as to what the ultimate weight will be, after making allowance for the difference in weight of the interchanged or added parts.

SPECIFICATION

Frame. Built with special light "Granby" lugs. Light gauge Taper Tubes of tapering gauge in Chrome-molybdenum, H.M. or "531" Steel. Taper seat and chain stays—chain stays are squared at bracket end to give a good clearance for the tyres. D to O fork blades of resilient type of taper gauge. B.S.A. front fork ends of solid drop-out type. "Granby" Rigid Seat Lug. All lugs are fish-tailed and tapered to a fine finish.

Chainwheel and Cranks. These are very light and of high quality steel. Williams' new pattern flush fitting cotters 5/- extra.

Wheels. Solite or Featherweight Steel hubs. Double-butted spokes, light Endrick or high-pressure rims.

Tyres. Constrictor "Viper" wired-on Road tyres with special Constrictor inner tubes to prevent blistering, or Dunlop high-pressure.

Chain. Coventry " Elite " roller.

Handlebars. Polished " Hiduminium " on " Kromo " clip. Constrictor Grips.

Saddle. Mansfield Duralumin saddle.

Seat Pin. Polished Duralumin straight "12"

Pedals. Quil pattern rat-trap—alloy.

Brake. Front Bowden Dural.

Guards. Bluemel " No-weight " clip on.

Finish. Any Colour finish with Chromium plated front and rear fork ends (except Chromium plating all over, which would be an extra). Flamboyant Fnishes 7/- extra.

PRICE : As Specification **£11 : 5 : 0** With Sprint Wheels and Constrictor Tubulars **£12 : 15 : 0**

Guaranteed Weight with steels as specification 22¾ lbs.

FRAME ONLY. Complete with chainwheel and cranks and forks and seat pin £5 : 5 : 0

Guaranteed Weight 8 lbs. 6 ozs.

5

GRANBY "Continental"

2 Dural Bowden. Dural Bars. Any Colours. Panelled and Lined. Continental Chain-wheel and Cranks or C 1200. H.P. Wheels and Tyres. **£12 : 10 : 0**

2 Bowden (Steel). Brooks Saddle B.17. H.P. Wheels. C 1000 Chain-wheel and Cranks. Black Enamel - - - - - - - **£10 : 10 : 0**

Any 2 Colours 7/6 extra

As above with Osgear **£13 : 12 : 0**

With Simplex **£14 : 0 : 0**

As above with Osgear **£11 : 12 : 6**

With Simplex **£12 : 0 : 0**

6

GRANBY "Continental"

In H.M. - "531" or CHROME-MOLY. STEEL

IN ANY TWO COLOUR ENAMELS
with Plated Crown

This frame is built by us from the best Continental Lugs which are cut out and tapered to a fine finish. Front forks are Oval to Round section with forged steel crown, tapered seat stays and chain stays. Continental Angles or to special requirements. Solid steel fork ends.

Continental Chainwheel and Cranks in Nickel Chrome steel, four fluted or C 1200	£6 : 2 : 6
In B.S.A. or Chater-Lea fittings - - - - - - -	£6 : 10 : 0
In Black Enamel Granby fittings - - Williams C 1000 Chainwheel set	£5 : 2 : 6
In two colour enamel	£5 : 10 : 0

EXTRAS
Chrome Plated front and rear ends 7/6
Taper Tubes 5/-

7

GRANBY "Club" Tourist

UPRIGHT OR STANDARD ANGLES

An Ideal Light Touring Mount equally suitable for Club Riding.

SPECIFICATION

Frame. Chrome-Molybdenum or Reynold's H. M. Steel. Upright design or standard angles or any special angles (for further particulars see frames page 10).

Wheels and Brakes — (Alternatives). **Rear Wheel**—Sturmey Archer Three-speed Hub Brake.

Tyres. Dunlop Speed or Sprite, 26in. × 1¼in. or ⅜in.

Chain. Coventry Elite.

Handlebars. Any shape, Light Kromo stem.

Saddle. B 17 "Flyer" or "Terry"

Pedals. BOA or Brampton Race.

Guards. Bluemel "No Weight."

Brazed-on Attachments. Mudguard eyes, pump pegs. reflector eye, lugs for brake arms, Derailleur bracket. Others to order.

Finish. Best black enamel after rust proof preparation. Usual plated parts chromium.

The Granby Club Tourist can be built to your own specification, and particulars can be varied in any direction at difference in cost.

Quotation by return.

Particular attention is given by our experts to the fitting of speed gears to these models, especially the the Derailleur type, which calls for expert knowledge and experience. Every gear is in perfect working order before it leaves our Works.

Model built with Standard Tubes £10 17 6

Easy Payments. **£1 0 10** deposit, and 11 monthly payments of **£1 0 10**

Model built with Taper Tubes £11 2 6

Easy Payments. **£1 5 10** deposit, and 11 monthly payments of **£1 0 10**

B.S.A. or Chater-Lea fittings **£2** extra.

GRANBY WHEELS

Spokes used in our wheels are specially treated

HUBS RECOMMENDED BY US

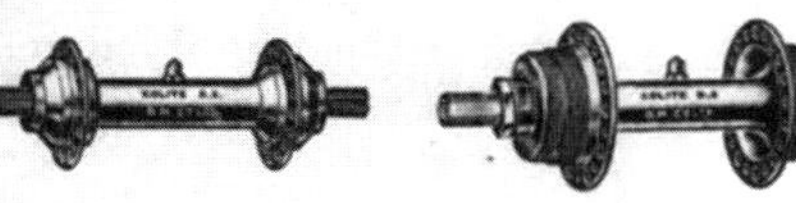

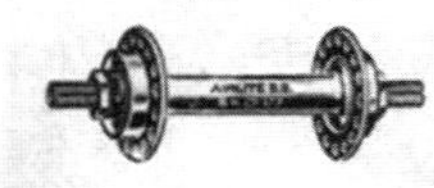

RIMS	HUBS: SIVADA	SOLITE	AIRLITE	AIRLITE CONTINENTAL
CHROME ENDRICK	15/-	25/-	31/6	37/6
DUNLOP HIGH PRESSURE	19/6	27/-	33/.	39/9
CONLEY ASP	44/6	52/9	58/-	66/-
CONLEY SPRINT	42/-	51/-	56/-	64/-
CONSTRICTOR 1st CHOICE SPRINT	34/6	41/6	47/6	54/-
BOA or VIPER SPRINT	26/9	35/-	41/-	48/-

Tied and Soldered 2/- per pair extra. Other wheels quoted by return.

The GRANBY "Club Tandem"

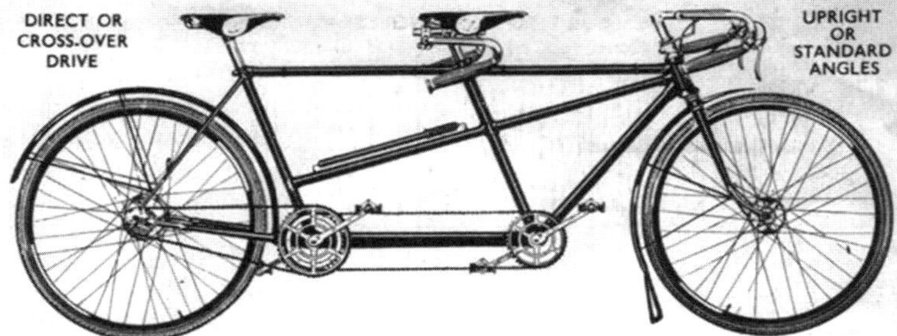

SPECIFICATION

Frame. Chrome-Molybdenum Steel or Reynold's tubing. D to O fork blades, tapered chain and seat stays, forward opening or "Granby" Release rear fork ends. Standard wheelbase 65½in., bracket height 10¾in. (or dimensions to order). All lugs finely cut-out and tapered down. Further particulars see "Tandem Frames."

Wheels. 26in. × 1⅜in. Endrick Tandem Rims. 12 × 14 g. single butted Spokes. Sturmey Archer Tandem Hub Brakes.

Tyres. Dunlop Tandem or to order.

Saddles. Brooks' "Champion" series S25R or Terry's C.T.C.

Chains. Coventry Elite roller.

Pedals. Brampton Race or B.O.A.

Handlebars. Any shape to order, fitted with adjustable clips front and rear, celluloid covered or plated.

Brakes. Resilion or Constrictor brakes may be substituted for hub brakes—double cogged rear tandem hub—no extra.

Mudguards. Bluemel "No-weight."

Brazed-on Attachments. Mudguard eyes, pump pegs, reflector eye and lug for brake arm. Others to order.

Finish. Best Black Enamel after rust-proof preparation Usual plated parts Chromium.

Special Finishes. See under "Tandem Frames."

In "Granby" Fittings	Williams' Best Chainwheel and Crank Set	£15 : 3 : 0
In Brampton Fittings		
In Chater-Lea Fittings	- - - - -	£17 : 8 : 0

The "Granby" Tandem can be built to your own specification and particulars can be varied in any direction at difference in cost. Quotation by return. Any model can be supplied on Hire Purchase Terms.

SPECIFICATION

Design as illustrated, or to any of the designs on page 11 (Ref. letters "C"-"O" or "L"): In Reynold's High Manganese or Chrome-Molybdenum Steel; All Lugs cut out and tapered down to a fine finish; **Direct Drive**—Williams' Best Chainwheels and Cranks. Sizes to order. Standard frame dimensions—Wheelbase 65½in., Bracket height 10¾in.; Usual Brazed-on Attchments—Mudguard eyes and pump pegs; Plain forward opening rear release or "Granby" rear release. No extra for special frame dimensions, including wheelbase and bracket height.

In Black Enamel (usual plated parts chromium) **£9 : 15 : 0** **In Chater-Lea Fittings** (usual plated parts chromium) **£12 : 0 : 0**

EXTRAS. Any Colour Enamel 5/-; Flamboyant finishes (Ruby, Amber, Green or Blue) 25/-; Chromium plated front and rear ends 13/-; Nickel plated frame and fork 35/-; Fork only 8/-; Chromium plated frame and fork £3 : 5 : 0; Fork only 10/6.

OTHER FRAME DESIGNS. Any special frame can be built to order including The Brampton Lateral Stay Model. The frames under Ref. Letters "C" and "O" can be built with a gradually rising top tube to allow of a short rear seat tube and yet obtain an adequate length of head.

9

GRANBY FRAMES

"UPRIGHT" OR "STANDARD" ANGLES

IN CHROME MOLYBDENUM, "H.M. or "531" STEEL

GRANBY SPECIAL FRAME

The Granby frame is built on jigs to ensure accuracy. All lugs fishtailed and chamfered to a fine finish. Any type of rear fork ends. Square tapered chain stays and taper back stays. Granby resilient fork blades with solid ends. Head clip fitting. Williams C 1000 Chainwheel set. Standard Wheelbase 42 × 10½in. bracket height. All necessary brazed-on attachments. Plated parts chromium.

GRANBY TAPER TUBE FRAME

The Granby Taper Tube Frame is the very essence of Rigidity and its construction which is based on sound scientific principles completely excludes any possibility of Whip or distortion. It shows no increase in weight. It is light, exceptionally strong and lively.

Details—Top tube 1in. dia., parallel. Seat tube, 1⅛in. to 1⅛in. at seat. Bottom tube taper 1⅜in. to 1⅛in. at head. Usual plated parts chromium

PARALLEL FRAME TUBES

COLOUR	Price			6 monthly payments of
Black - - -	£3	19	0	15/10
Any colour - - -	£4	2	0	16/4
Flamboyant colours -	£4	6	6	17/4
Nickel plated all over -	£4	15	0	19/-
Chromium plated all over	£5	9	0	21/10

TAPER TUBE FRAMES

COLOUR	Price			6 monthly payments of
Black - - -	£4	4	0	16/10
Any colour - - -	£4	7	0	17/5
Flamboyant colours -	£4	11	6	18/4
Nickel plated all over -	£5	0	0	20/-
Chromium plated all over	£6	14	0	22/10

B S.A. or Chater-Lea fittings **£1** extra, to be paid with deposit.
These frames can be built to any special angle or measurements (see chart below).
When ordering frames please be careful to state the type of **rear fork ends** and also the **brazed-on attachments** required.

GUIDE TO FRAME DIMENSIONS WHEN ORDERING SPECIAL SIZES

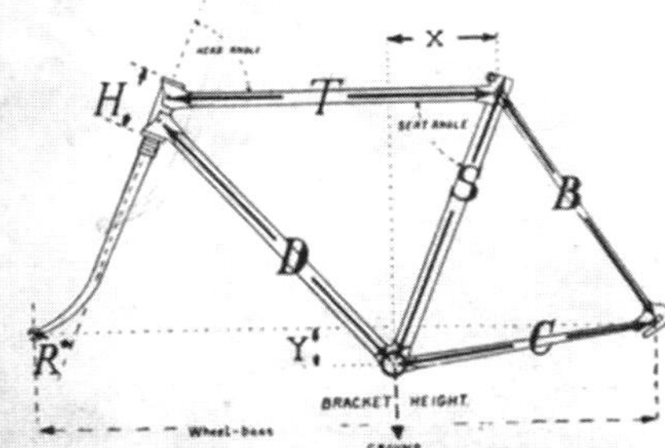

The diagram will assist when ordering **frames of special dimensions and angles** (no extra charge is made for this). It is not always necessary to give every dimension, the important ones will do. If not convenient to give angles, the measurements "X" will serve as well.

The diagram shows blades and other ends, etc., under reference letters. We are, however, prepared to fit any type of fork or ends at no extra charge.

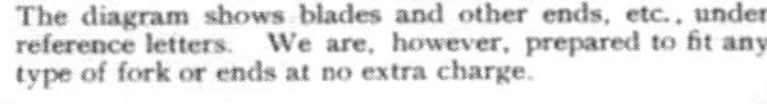

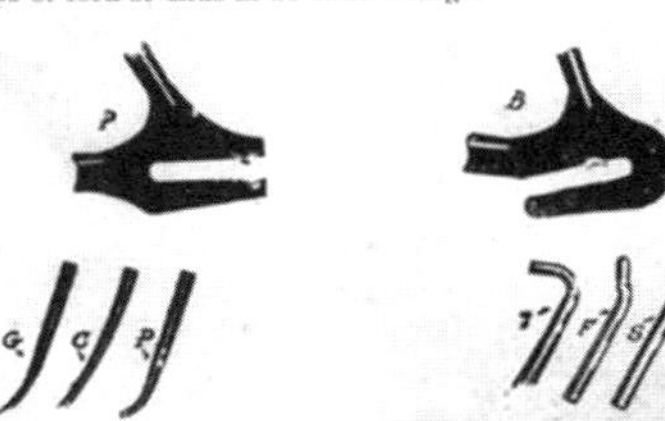

COST TO YOUR OWN SPECIFICATION

Send the enclosed Blue Quotation Form filled in in accordance with your own requirements, and we will quote you by return, and at the same time advise you to your advantage.

EXTRAS. Plating Nickel plated frame and fork all over **16/-**; Fork only **5/-**; Chromium plated frame and fork all over, **30/-**; Fork only, **7/6**; Chromium plated front and rear ends, **8/6. Enamel**—Any colour (Coloured Bands on seat tube no extra), **3/-**; Flamboyant Ruby, Amber, Green or Blue, **7/6**; C 1200 Chainwheel Set **7/6**.

10

The GRANBY "Touring Tandem"

DIRECT OR CROSS-OVER DRIVE

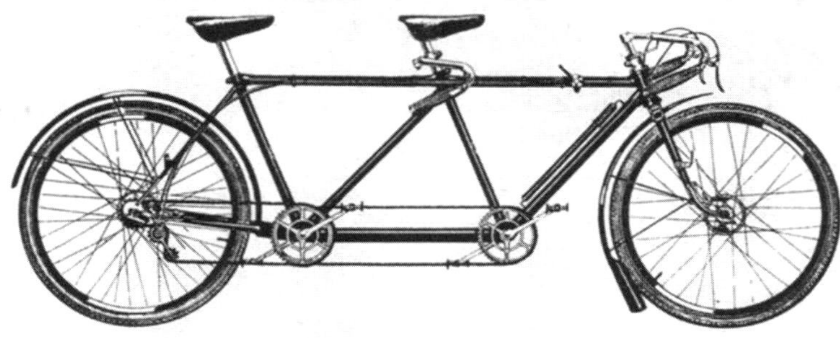

In "Granby" Fittings In Brampton Fittings	Williams' Best Chainwheel and Crank Set	£17 : 5 : 0
In Chater-Lea Fittings	- - - - -	£19 : 10 : 0

This Tandem can be built and equipped to your own specification. Quotation by return.

SPECIFICATION

Frame. Chrome-Molybdenum Steel or Reynold's Tubing. Details as "Club" Tandem. Further particulars see "Tandem Frames"

Wheels & Brakes (Alternatives). **Rear Wheel.**—Sturmey Archer Three-speed Hub Brake, "Solite" and "Cyclo" Three-speed Gear with Resilion Brake.

Front Wheel. Sturmey Archer Hub Brake or Tandem Hub with Resilion or Constrictor Brake. Endrick Tandem Rims 26" × 1⅜". 12 × 14 g. single butted Spokes.

Tyres. Dunlop Tandem.

Saddles. Brooks' S 25 R or Terry's C.T.C.

Chains. Coventry Elite roller.

Pedals. Brampton Race.

Handlebars. Any shape to order, adjustable clips, celluloid covered.

Mudguards. Bluemel "No-weight."

Brazed-on Attachmentr. For guards, pump, reflector, derailleur and brake arm. Others to order.

Finish. Best Black Enamel after rust-proof preparation. Usual plated parts Chromium.

Special Finishes. See under "Tandem Frames."

FRAME DESIGN C

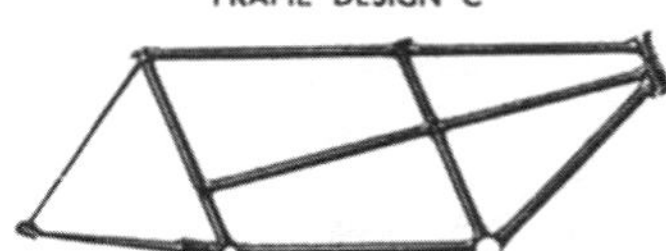

FRAME DESIGN O

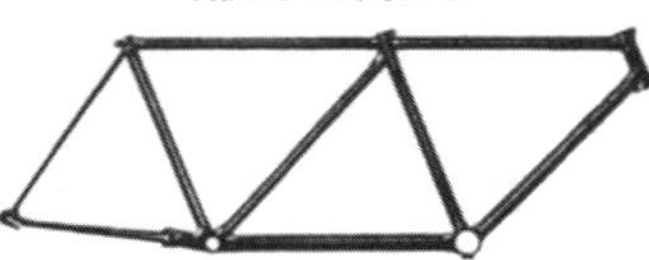

FRAME DESIGN L

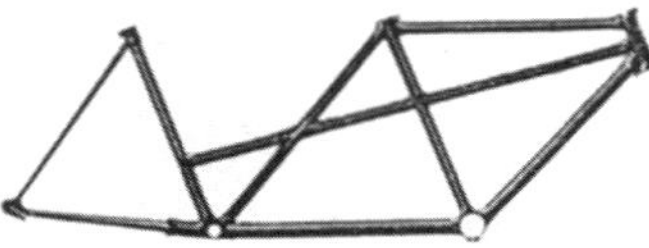

Track and Alignment are most important in a tandem. If these are not correct, the machine will never give entire satisfaction. Great care and attention is given to this feature by our experts during building. The frames are again tested before enamelling and the complete machine after assemble. We can therefore Guarantee that all "Granby" Tandems are sent out Correctly in Track.

TAPER TUBES

A TAPER TUBE FRAME BUILT FROM A & P CHROME-MOLYBDENUM STEEL IS

THE BEST CYCLE FRAME NOW OBTAINABLE

No other Frame has the same STRENGTH, RIGIDITY AND LIFE

The Rider of a T. T. Frame has the comforting and satisfying knowledge that he has the Best Frame obtainable—one where every vital point of construction has been given very careful consideration.

• • •

The Real Cyclist is quick to appreciate any improvement in cycle construction; it is of vital concern to him.

EXCLUSIVE FEATURES OF THE GRANBY CYCLE

THE GRANBY RELEASE.—Finger adjustment Non-slipping. Instantaneous Location.

THE GRANBY SQUARED CHAIN STAYS.—5 per cent. Increased Lateral Rigidity. Extra Clearance for Chainwheel and Tyre.

THE GRANBY SLEEVE LINED BRACKET totally excludes all dust and dirt from the bracket bearings.

THE GRANBY RIGID SEAT LUG avoids slotting seat tube and lug at back.

THE GRANBY RELEASE (G) illustrated

Is so constructed that it is impossible for the wheel to slip under driving pressure.

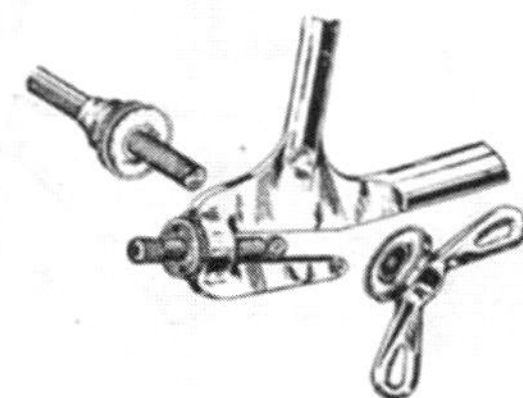

Assembly—The loose washer is screwed firmly against the hub cone as a lock-nut, annular groove facing outwards. The adjuster screws into the fork end, and the grooved washers of the device (one attached to the wing nut) clamp over the ball end of the adjuster when the wing nut is tightened. After adjustment by the finger, the adjuster is locked in position by the small lock-nut. The wheel can then be removed and replaced without disturbing the adjustment. AND IT CANNOT SLIP.

THE GRANBY SQUARED CHAIN STAYS

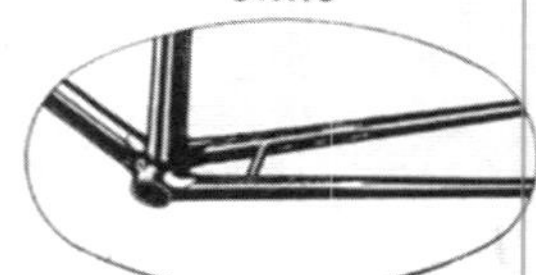

A great advance in lightweight construction. No dents or impressions, yet by this unique method plenty of clearance is obtained for 1⅞in. wheels and an increase in lateral rigidity.

THE GRANBY RIGID SEAT LUG

This conveniently places the seat bolt in front. The elimination of the usual back slot ensures rigidity of the seat tube. It is important to insert the seat pin at least 2¼ins. into the lug.

THE GRANBY BRACKET

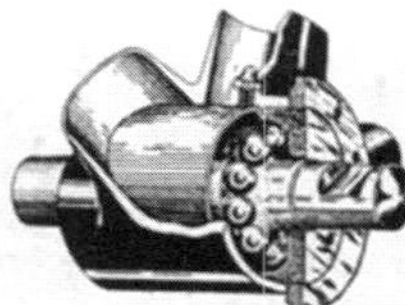

A very light alloy sleeve totally closes the ends of the tubes converging at the bracket. Oiling is effected by a lubricator which pierces the sleeve.

GRANBY - "Continental"

IN H.M. - "531" or CHROME-MOLY STEEL

A. E. MADGETT,
Cycle Agent,
DISS.

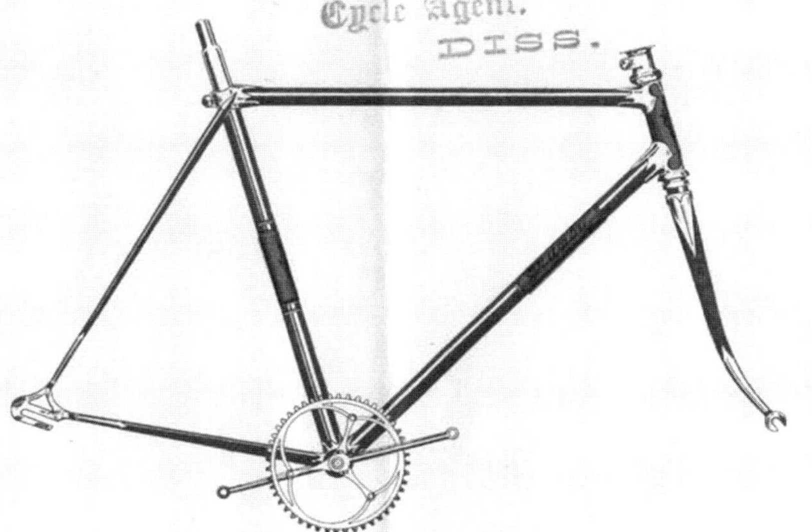

This frame is built by us from the best Continental Lugs which are cut out and tapered to a fine finish.

Continental Angles or to special requirements.

Front forks are Oval to Round section with forged steel crown, tapered seat stays and chain stays.

Solid steel fork ends.

IN ANY TWO COLOUR ENAMELS with Plated Crown

THE WORLD'S BEST BICYCLE

Continental Chain wheel and cranks in Nickel Chrome steel, four fluted	£6 : 2 : 6
In B.S.A. or Chater Lea fittings - - - - - -	£6 : 10 : 0
In Black Enamel Granby fittings - Williams C 1000 Chainwheel set	£5 : 2 : 6
In two colour enamel	£5 : 10 : 0

EXTRAS
Chrome Plated front and rear ends - - 7/6
Taper Tubes 5/-

GRANBY CYCLES

338, NEW CROSS ROAD, LONDON, S.E.14

Phone: TIDeway 3398

SPECIFICATION

Tubing All Harrison Frames are built of 531 Butted Tubing throughout including Chain and Seat Stays, and Fork Blades, the latter being Oval or Dee to round or all round with small diameter tips.

Lugs Only the best quality lugs obtainable are used and are all beautifully cut out with a different design for each model. Crowns may be solid or two plate type.

Interiors Head and Bracket fittings are of Brampton or Bayliss Wiley manufacture, except where otherwise stated. Lytaloy, Gnutti, etc., can be fitted to order.

Sizes All frames may be built to your own specification and angles and may be any size from 19½ in. to 25½ in. and of lady's design if required.

Fork Ends Stallard, Chater Lea, Cyclo, Clements ends are all available.

Attachments Brazed on fittings include Pump Pegs for 15in. or 18in. pumps and Lamp bracket. Mudguard eyes may be either on the stays or the ends. Brake and Gear stops are fitted on some models or to order and any other Gear fittings may also be fitted if required.

C/Wheel Sets May be fitted as available at extra charge.

Finish All frames are first bonderized and finally varnished and may be finished in any choice of colour with lining, panelling or Chromium to taste.

Standard finishes at the prices quoted are on page 10, or in a plain colour would cost less.

GUARANTEE

Every machine bearing our transfers, and purchased from us or our agents is built in our own works under my personal supervision. All reasonable care has been taken to secure the finest materials and workmanship possible and any complaint will be fully examined on return of part, carriage paid, and if fault is found, will be replaced or repaired free of charge. This does not apply to defects caused by accident, misuse, wear and tear or neglect, and only applies to parts manufactured by us.

Frames Chromium Plated all over cannot be guaranteed against interior corrosion, but every care is taken to ensure against this happening.

We do not hold ourselves responsible for any consequential damage or expense which may arise from the result of defective material or workmanship.

This guarantee is only valid to the original purchaser of the machine and providing it has not been let out on hire or repaired or altered by any other firm.

The right is reserved to alter any detail, at any time, on any model, if we consider it to be warranted, without previous notice.

2

CONTINENTAL SUPERBE.

Frame	73° head, 71° seat, 23" top tube, 41½" wheelbase.
Forks	Solid crown, oval to round blades, 2½" rake. Brazed on brake and gear stops.
Finish	As page 10.
Wheels	27" high pressure on Solite gear sided hubs. Butted spokes.
Gear	Benelux or Simplex 3-speed.
Chain	Coventry.
Pedals	Phillite or Webb.
C/wheel set	C. 34 Williams.
Mudguards	Britannial Celluloid.
Brakes	Strata, hooded levers.
Saddle	B. 17 N. on Strata alloy seat pin.
Handlebar	Strata alloy to choice.
Stem	Alloy G.B. 1¾" or 2¾"

3

KERMESSE.

Frame	72° head and seat, 22½″ top tube, 41½″ wheelbase.
Forks	D/round small tip solid crown.
Seat Pin	Strata alloy.
Finish	Red, Blue, Green or Orange Flam on Silver and lined.
Wheels	26″ H.P. chrome rims on light steel hubs, double sided for gear. Fitted with freewheel. The frame may be built to your specification, 15/- extra.
Chain	Coventry.
Pedals	Light steel.
C/wheel set	Williams C.34.
Mudguards	Brittanial celluloid or alloy.
Brakes	Webb with hooded levers.
Handlebar and Stem	Strata alloy to choice on steel stem.

4

METEOR.

Frame	73° head, 71° seat, 23″ top tube, 40½″ wheelbase.
Forks	⅞″ round or oval or D/round, 2¼″ rake, solid or two plate crown. Brazed fittings, pump pegs and lamp bracket only.
Finish	See page 10.
Wheels	26″ or 27″ Dunlop chromium H.P. rims, Solite hubs double sided for fixed or gears. Double butted spokes. High pressure tyres.
Pedals	Brampton B.8.
Chain	Coventry
Mudguards	Bluemels Airweight or Noweight.
C/wheel set	Williams C.34.
Brake	Front or rear Doherty or G.B. alloy.
Saddle	Brooks B 17 range on R.R. 56 seat pillar.
Handlebar	Alloy, pattern to choice.
Stem	R.O.H. Special to your requirements.

5

SUPER CIRCUIT.

Frame	74° head, 72° seat, 23″ top tube, 41″ wheelbase.
Forks	Oval to round blades, 2¼″ rake, solid or two plate crown. Brazed fittings include brake and gear stops.
Finish	See page 10.
Wheels	26″ or 27″ Dunlop H.P. chromium finish on Airlite Continental hubs. Double butted spokes. H.P. tyres.
Pedals	Brampton B.8, Phillite or Webb.
Chain	Coventry.
Mudguards	Bluemels Continental alloy or Noweight celluloid.
C/wheel set	Special light steel, 3 pin fitting.
Gear	Benelux or Simplex 3 or 4 speed.
Brakes	G.B. or Doherty alloy, hooded levers.
Saddle	Brooks B. 17 range on R.R. 56 seat pin.
Handlebar	Alloy. Maes, Pellisier, etc.
Stem	R.O.H. Special chromium plated steel, 2″ to 4″.

6

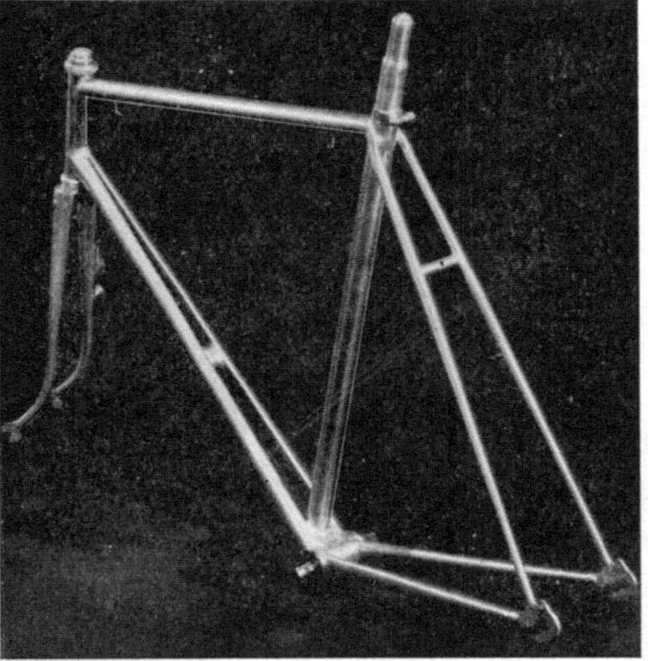

SHORTWIN.

A mechanically sound design for the short wheelbase enthusiast approximately 38-39 inches.

Bronze welded construction only.

The head is 73° and the design is such that the top tube length and seat tube angle give the equivalent of 23 ins. and 71° respectively.

With track ends the chainstays may be as short as 14½ ins. but 15½ ins. with forward opening ends will allow for 27s and Mudguards, and as the stays are of flat oval section they are internally webbed to ensure rigidity. Double taper seat stays are also fitted for this reason.

To obtain wheel clearance the seat tube is brought in front of the bracket shell and the normal down tube is replaced with two D section tubes and this assembly being boxed makes the bracket immensely rigid.

The forks may be ⅞ in. Rd., D. or oval to round brazed with solid crown.

7

LYTA.

Frame 73° head, 71° seat, 23" top tube, 41" wheelbase or to your specification.

Forks Oval to round blades, 2¼" rake, crown to choice.

Interiors Gnutti, Lytaloy or similar head and bracket fittings.

Finish Super electro, any colour, and Lined. Fork blades and rear stays ¾ chromium plated.

Wheels Conloy rims, Ultralite H.P. tyres, Airlite D/S hubs. Butted spokes.

Pedals Strata Quill alloy or to order.

C/wheel set Williams C. 1200, Gnutti, Durax or to order.

Chain Coventry.

Mudguards Bluemels Continental or Noweight.

Brakes Doherty or G.B. alloy, front or rear.

Saddle Ormond or Brooks B.17 range.

Handlebars Any shape alloy, Strata or RR56. Strata alloy or R.O.H. steel stem.

Professional Model with Benelux or Simplex 3-speed and two brakes. See price list.

8

CHARLTON TOURER.

Frame Brazed or welded. 72° head, 70° seat, 42" wheelbase.

Forks D/R solid crown. All fittings brazed to frame, including pannier.

Finish See page ten.

Wheels Dunlop chromium Endricks, Sprite tyres. Sturmey Archer 3-speed and Dynohub.

Gears 2 or 3 speed Cyclo or Cyclo double chainwheel set may be fitted at an extra charge.

Chain Coventry.

Mudguards Brittanial alloy with front and rear lamps attached.

Brake Cantilevers with brazed on fittings, or to choice.

Saddle Brooks B.73 or Dunlop Tourist.

Pedals Webb or Phillite.

Handlebars and Stem To choice.

9

STANDARD FINISHES.

No. 1 Finish. Any colour Flamboyant on Silver, lined or lugs picked out.

No. 2 Finish. Any colour Enamel or Lustre, Chromium crown and lined in contrasting colour.

No. 3 Finish. Any colour Enamel or Lustre, Chromium crown, coloured head tube and band on seat.

No. 4 Finish. Any colour Enamel or Lustre, Chromium crown and front and rear ends.

ADDITIONAL FINISHES AT EXTRA CHARGES.

Chromium Forks all over	20/0	extra
Finish 2 and 3...	12/6	„
Finish 4	7/6	„
Chromium Frame and Forks all over ...	60/0	„
Chromium Head or Head Lugs	15/0	„
Chromium Seat Lug	12/0	„
Chromium Crown and Front and Rear Ends ...	25/0	„
Finish 2 and 3	17/6	„
Chromium Chain and Seat Stays	52/6	„
Finish No. 4	42/0	„
Flamboyant on Silver	7/6	„
Flamboyant on Polished Nickel	42/0	„
Flamboyant on Polished Nickel with Chromium Plated Ends	57/6	„
Lining Finish 3 and 4	15/0	„
Coloured Head and Band on Seat, Finish 2 and 4	12/6	„
Continental Panelling ... ... from	12/6	„
Checker Bands	12/6	„
White or Crackle Finish, 2, 3, 4.	7/6	„
Lug Lining	12/0	„
Colour Bands ... ... from	5/6	„

R.O.H. HANDLEBAR STEMS for 2 in., 5½ in. **25/0.**

Curved 3½ in., 5½ in. **27/6.**

Fitted with Expander Bolt.

10

ORDER FORM.

R. O. HARRISON, Ltd., 23 Queens Road, Peckham. London, S.E.15
NEW CROSS 0391.

Name .... Amount of Remittance £ ....

Address ....

Model (see catalogue) Welded or Brazed ....

Frame Size .... Head Angle .... Seat Angle ....

Top Tube Length (Centres) .... Wheelbase (Approx.) ....

Bracket Height .... with .... Wheels.

Rear ends, track, forward opening, Osgear or Simplex type ....

Length of Chainstays (Centres) ....

Forks D/R ⅞in. R or Oval/rd. .... Rake or Offset ....

Crown Solid or 2 Plate ....

Brazed on Fittings for 15in. or 18in. Pump, Lamp Bracket,

Mudguard Eyes, Cable Stops, Gear Fittings ....

Rims Type .... Size .... Pedals ....

Hubs .... Saddle ....

Tyres .... Brakes ....

Gear .... Handlebars ....

Cog Sizes .... Extension ....

Wing Nuts or Track Nuts .... Mudguards ....

Finish ....

11

RIGIDE.

Frame	72° head, 70° seat, 22½ front and 23" rear top tube. Wheelbase 64" approx. Fitted with Williams chainwheel set.
Finish	Any colour enamel or lustre and lined.
Wheels	Dunlop Chrome Endricks, Sprite Tandem tyres, Airlite hubs.
Gear	Cyclo 3-speed, Benelux or Simplex.
Brakes	Cantilever.
Mudguards	Bluemel alloy or celluloid.
Saddles	Brooks Range.
Handlebars	Alloy or steel on R.O.H. steel stem.
Pedals	B.8 or to choice.

MEMBERS

12

HIGGINS

T. Higgins & Son started in business in 1933 at 281 Portland Road, South Norwood, London, SE25. The firm was established as high-class lightweight cycle makers, catering for the club cyclist and lightweight enthusiast. At this time, Frederick John Higgins was 18 years old, and his father, Thomas Henry Sides Higgins, would have been in his late forties. In 1937 they became a limited company with both father and son listed as 'Cycle Builders' in the company papers. To date no information has been found as to their prior involvement in the cycling world. However, father and son were clearly very knowledgeable in cycling and frame building matters.

The earliest known Higgins catalogue, printed between 1935 and 1937, lists a range of five bicycles and three tandems. It also advertised the availability of Accessories, Bags, Clothing, Oilskins, Racing Equipment, Shoes, etc. - in fact, 'Everything for the Clubman'.

The pre-war production total is believed to be around 700 cycles. The majority of these would have been bicycles, with a small number of tandems and tricycles. Before 1939, only a few tricycles were built by the firm. Each of these were individually designed, each evolving as the firm gained experience in tricycle building.

During the war years, 1939 – 1945, Fred Higgins and his father were engaged on war work, utilizing their brazing skills in the manufacture of radiators for military vehicles. With the shortage of frame building materials, it is unlikely that many, if any, cycles were built during these years.

By 1945, Higgins had moved to 214 Portland Road, South Norwood, where cycle production began in earnest after the war years. Initially, mostly bicycles were built, along with a few tandems.

By the early 1950s, their tricycles had been further developed and refined so that, with their axle design and use of lightweight frame tubing, the Higgins' tricycle was an exceptional machine which surpassed all other tricycles available at that time. The firm went on to become the leading builder of lightweight tricycles in the country for the next two decades.

Their tricycles included the 'Ultralite' and 'Light Roadster' models. Also produced, in very small numbers, was the Higgins 'K-Type' model. This was of the Kendrick design, having two front wheels linked to provide Ackermann type steering, and with the rear wheel being the driving wheel. The 'K-Type' was only listed in the 1953 Higgins Tricycle catalogue. Only two of these tricycles are known to have been built, both of which still exist.

In 1952, Higgins introduced their differential, which enabled drive to be transmitted to both rear wheels, either by single fixed or by multiple freewheel. This unit could also incorporate a drum brake, providing braking to both rear wheels. Fred's design and engineering skills were fully utilised as all the components for the differential were made entirely in his own workshop.

It is understood that after 1945, Fred Higgins did most of the frame building and manufacturing of specialist parts. However, as business increased after the war years, Higgins employed George Taylor as a frame builder/sprayer/machinist and Jack Dunn also as a machinist, especially on a capstan lathe. Jack also looked after the shop sales. Higgins did all their stove enamelling, offering a complete range of finishes and colours. In 1952, a local young apprentice in light precision engineering, John Farrow, was co-opted by Fred to assist in a part-time capacity, machining components for the Higgins differential. This was quite a compliment for John to be considered good enough to do this work.

By 1953, Higgins had reached their peak, having an established and proven range of bicycles. These comprised the 'Path Frame', 'Grand Prix', 'Ultralite', 'Plus Parfait', 'El Continenta' and the 'Time Trialist'. In November of that year, Higgins introduced a cleverly designed 'in-line' Sturmey Archer hub geared tricycle axle. This design obviated the need for a two-stage chain drive.

Their tricycle designs had now reached their final form, as had their tandems and tandem tricycles. Higgins also manufactured tricycle axle units to convert either a solo bicycle to a tricycle, or a tandem to a tandem tricycle. Many Higgins cycles were now being used for racing and record breaking, both at club and national levels. Higgins also had a strong North American market, where they were also used in competition.

Whilst the range of Higgins cycles suited most requirements, Fred Higgins was quite willing to build special models, providing that he considered that they were of sound design. Known examples of these are the 'Dunster Special' bicycle, designed by Les Dunster of the Calleva Road Club and a small-wheeled tricycle designed by Higgins for a disabled rider.

By the early 1960s, the UK cycle trade was in decline as cycling became less popular. This was partly due to the increasing affordability of the motor car, which enabled more families and people to buy a car. As a result of the difficult trading conditions, Higgins closed their retail shop on 30th August 1964. Frame production continued through to June 1966, when decreasing orders, particularly from the North American market, made the continued production of their frames uneconomic, with the resultant closure of the firm.

From 1945 to 1966 over 4,000 cycles were built by Higgins. Of this total, at least 2,000 are believed to be tricycles and tandem tricycles. Pre-war frame numbers are believed to have commenced at '100' and continued to around '800'. Post-war numbers commenced at '6000' and continued to '9999', which was reached by 1964. Higgins then adopted an 'A' series of numbers, from 'A1' to 'A83'.

The third edition of the 'Register of Higgins Cycles', which is a 36-page booklet and contains details of nearly 500 machines of all types, a short history of the firm together with many photographs and technical illustrations, is available from Chris Hewitt, 1 Coleswood Road, Harpenden, Herts. AL5 1EF, price £6.00 plus £1.50 p&p.

Chris Hewitt

Catalogue is a four page leaflet printed in blue ink and datad 1952. It was kindly lent by Chris Hewitt

1952

TRICYCLES

by

Higgins Cycles

WE offer these products, which are built with the finest materials available, with every confidence that none better are procurable. The life-long experience and policy of 'Quality First,' with no piece-work and its evils, make this possible. All enquiries are dealt with promptly and without obligation to purchase.

F. J. Higgins

TERMS OF BUSINESS

Deposits: Frames £2. Complete Machines £5. Balance due on notification of completion; **Carriage, Packing and Insurance** U.K.: Frame 10/-. Complete Machine £1

214 PORTLAND RD. · S. NORWOOD · LONDON S.E.25

TELEPHONE ADDISCOMBE 1480

The Higgins Trike

"The Bicycle" photo

Weight 5 lbs. complete

AXLE UNIT

A thoroughly tested and reliable unit to convert a solo machine to a tricycle. Will fit any make or size of frame.

PRICE, Complete with Hubs
£10 10 0 Ex works
Carriage and packing U.K., 5/-
Other width axle or finish may be had at extra charge

SPECIFICATION

Built and enamelled entirely in our own workshops with the finest materials procurable. Reynolds 531 tubing, alloy steel axles with tapered hexagon for hub drive, accurately machined. Hardened and ground cups and cones. Width overall 27½ ins. Drive is on nearside wheel only which has proved most successful. Lubrication is through Tecalemit nipples in Housing tubes. Adequate seatstay adjustment is provided for frames up to 24 ins. Longer stays are available if required without extra charge. Hubs are detachable and interchangeable and are available drilled either 32 or 40 holes. Supplied with drive axle to suit either fixed cog or multi-speed freewheel. Finished five coats durable stoved white enamel. Seatstays, seatstay clips, bolts and fixing spindle are cadmium plated.

Fitting Instructions:

NOTE—1. Lefthand fixing plate has smaller distance piece (brazed on) than righthand one.

2. Fixing spindle (11) has two plain nuts (10) and two tracknuts (12). Tracknuts (12) should always face against the rear forkends of the frame.

(a) Remove one wheel and place Axle Unit in rear triangle of frame with lefthand fixing plate **inside** lefthand rear forkend, and righthand fixing plate **outside** righthand rear forkend.

(b) Insert longer screwed end of fixing spindle (11) through left forkend and fixing plate, screw on plain nut (10) facing fixing plate—then screw on track nut (12) with serrations facing right forkend. When nuts are free on spindle centre insert spindle through right forkend and fixing plate. Fit outer nuts, track nut on left and plain nut on right. Screw inner nuts out and make a secure joint between each fixing plate and forkend. Width across forkends (inside) should be 4½ ins.

(c) Fit stays through clamps on axle housing, and other ends to seat cluster. Adjust length. Secure firmly. Stays may be shortened without detriment to Unit.

NOTE.—Our Axle Units are available with chainline to suit either fixed gear, 3 x 1 8, (or 4 x 3 32) freewheel. One model can be modified to the other simply by changing the drive axle.

The Famous **HIGGINS TRIKE**

SPECIFICATION

Weight : Complete Machine from 24 lbs. Frame only, 10 lbs.

Size to order. Angles 72/72, $2\frac{1}{4}$ rake, round fork tapered to $\frac{5}{8}$in. dia., BB height $9\frac{1}{2}$, $15\frac{1}{2}$ back (centres), 28 in. axle or **to your exact specification.** Reynolds 531 tubing throughout. Completely bronze welded to iliminate any mechanical joints. Eccentric bracket unit for chain adjustment (concentric for gear usage only on lugged model). Light steel hubs fitted on tapered hexagon, accurately machined. Alloy steel axles rotate on Hoffman ballraces. Hubs are detachable and interchangeable. Cup and cone axle bearings optional (same price). Higgins quality stove enamelled five coats. Williams C34 CW set, Credulux pedals. Elite chain, BW front hub, HP rims, tyres and tubes, alloy bend 531 light steel stem, Strata alloy front brake, B17 saddle, Bluemels pump and front guard, alloy seat pin or similar equipment.

Price - - £36 . 16 . 0 Plus Tax

Frame only, complete with head and BB interiors, seat pillar and hubs **£19 . 19 . 0**

Lugged Model (suitable for use with gears only) choice of 3 designs of lugs **£3 . 3 . 0**

Simplex Gear Fittings - - extra **15 . 0**

Large Flange Hubs	extra	**£1 . 0 . 0**
Alloy Hubs	,,	**£1 . 10 . 0**
Hub Brake to offset wheel	,,	**£2 . 10 . 0**
Coupled Compensated Rear Hub Brakes	,,	**£6 . 6 . 0**
Chrome Crown and Front Ends	,,	**12 . 6**
Box Lining	,,	**10 . 0**
,, ,, Double	,,	**£1 . 0 . 0**
White Axle Housing	,,	**5 . 0**

NOTE.—Bottom bracket eccentric sleeves are available in three patterns, light steel for fixed only, light steel (concentric) for gear only and alloy for use either with gears or fixed (flush nearside for gear, flush offside for fixed). Please state type preferred when ordering. Also whether 32 or 40 hole hubs required (hub brakes are available 40 hole only).

SPARES

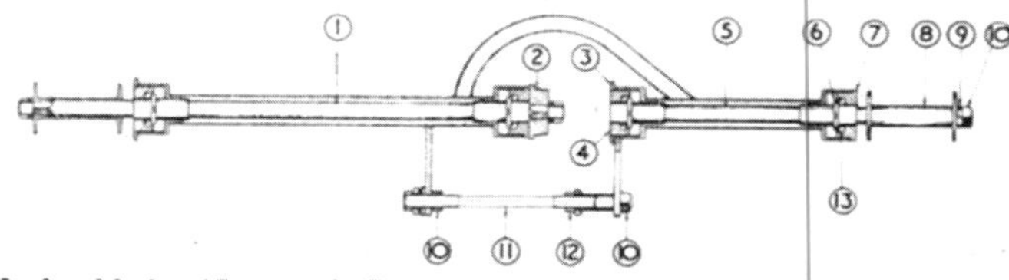

Axle Unit (Cup and Cone)

No.	Part	EACH
1	Drive Axle-fixed Cog ..	20 0
1G	,, for Muiti-freewheel	20 0
2	Sprocket Boss-fixed Cog ...	8 6
2G	,, for Freewheel only	8 6
3	Adjustable Cup Lockring	8
4	,, ,, ...	1 0
5	Idler Axle	17 6
6	Cone	2 6
7	Fixed Cup (LH thread) ...	1 0
8	Hub (32 or 40 holes) ...	15 0
8A	Alloy Hub (32 holes only)	30 0
8L	Hub, large flange steel (40 holes only)	25 0
9	Spring Washer	2
10	Nut	3
11	Fixing Spindle	1 9
12	Track Nut	10
13	$\frac{1}{4}$-inch Steel Balls ... ... Doz.	6
	Parts not illustrated :	
14	Stay	10 6
15	Stay Adjusting Clamp ...	2 9
16	Stay Adjusting Clamp Bolt	5
17	Seatbolt	9

Trike (Journal Bearings)

Parts not illustrated :

	EACH
Drive Axle (state length) ...	17 6
Idler Axle ,, ,, ...	17 6
Journal (ballrace)	13 0
Double Spring Washer	3
Journal Cover Washer	4
Sprocket Boss Spacing Washer	4
Idler Angle Flanged Nut	1 6
Long Sprocket Boss Nut	1 3
ECCENTRIC BB SHELLS :	
Steel (chrome) for fixed	10 0
,, complete...	21 0
*Steel (chrome) for gear ...	10 0
,, complete	16 6
Alloy for Gear and Fixed ...	10 0
,, complete	21 0
Brake Drum Hub (current model only)	30 0

*Please note that this Shell is concentric.

Wheels, built on standard rear hubs, No. 8, with 15/17G DB spokes

	per pr	Front to match on No. 9 BW Hub
Chrome Endrick, 26 x $1\frac{1}{4}$ or $1\frac{3}{8}$,	67/6	29/3
Chrome High Pressure, 26 or 27	75/-	33/-
San Gorgio, wide section 27 only recommended	78/-	34/6
,, ,, narrow section 26 or 27	82/6	36/9
,, ,, Sprint 27 inch only ...	92/-	41/6
Conloy Asp WO 26 or 27 ...	115/-	55/-
,, ,, Sprint	110/-	50/6

If rear wheels ordered with trike frame or axle unit in lieu of hubs normally supplied please deduct 30/-

Wheels with other makes of front hub and rims quoted on request.

Repairs, Service, etc.

One New Frame Tube	**30/-**	Clean off and Re-enamel any colour, fix transfers	**40/-**
Two New Frame Tubes	**50/-**	Dismantle, reassemble head, bracket, axle interiors	**15/-**
Three New Frame Tubes	**60/-**	Ditto, Complete Machine	**40/-**

New Front Fork unenamelled **45/-**

Dismantle and reassemble axle assembly (replacements extra) **10/-**

Return Carriage : Frame 10/-, Complete Machine 20/-

Puller Tool for removal of Hubs and Sprocket Boss **2/-**

Mudguards

Rear with Stays to clamp round axle housing. Made to special order only. Celluloid or Alloy ... ... per pair **50/-**

All other Repairs and Accessories quoted for on request.

Printed in England by Portland Press, S.E.25

53

The Balance in YOUR Favour

Higgins Cycles

LONDON

We offer these cycles, and Frames, all built entirely with Reynolds '531' tubing stays and forks, with every confidence that none better are procurable. The life-long experience and policy of 'Quality First,' with no piece-work and its evils, make this possible. All enquiries are dealt with promptly and without obligation to purchase. We also make Tandems, Trikes, and Trike axle units. List free on rcquest.

TERMS OF BUSINESS

Deposits: Frames £2. Cycles £5. Balance due on notification of completion; **Carriage and Packing:** Frames 5s. Trike and Tandem Frames 10s. Cycles15s. Hire Purchase facilities available to customers resident in London area. Quotations free on request.

(F. J. Higgins)

214 PORTLAND RD. · S. NORWOOD · LONDON S.E.25

TELEPHONE ADDISCOMBE 1480

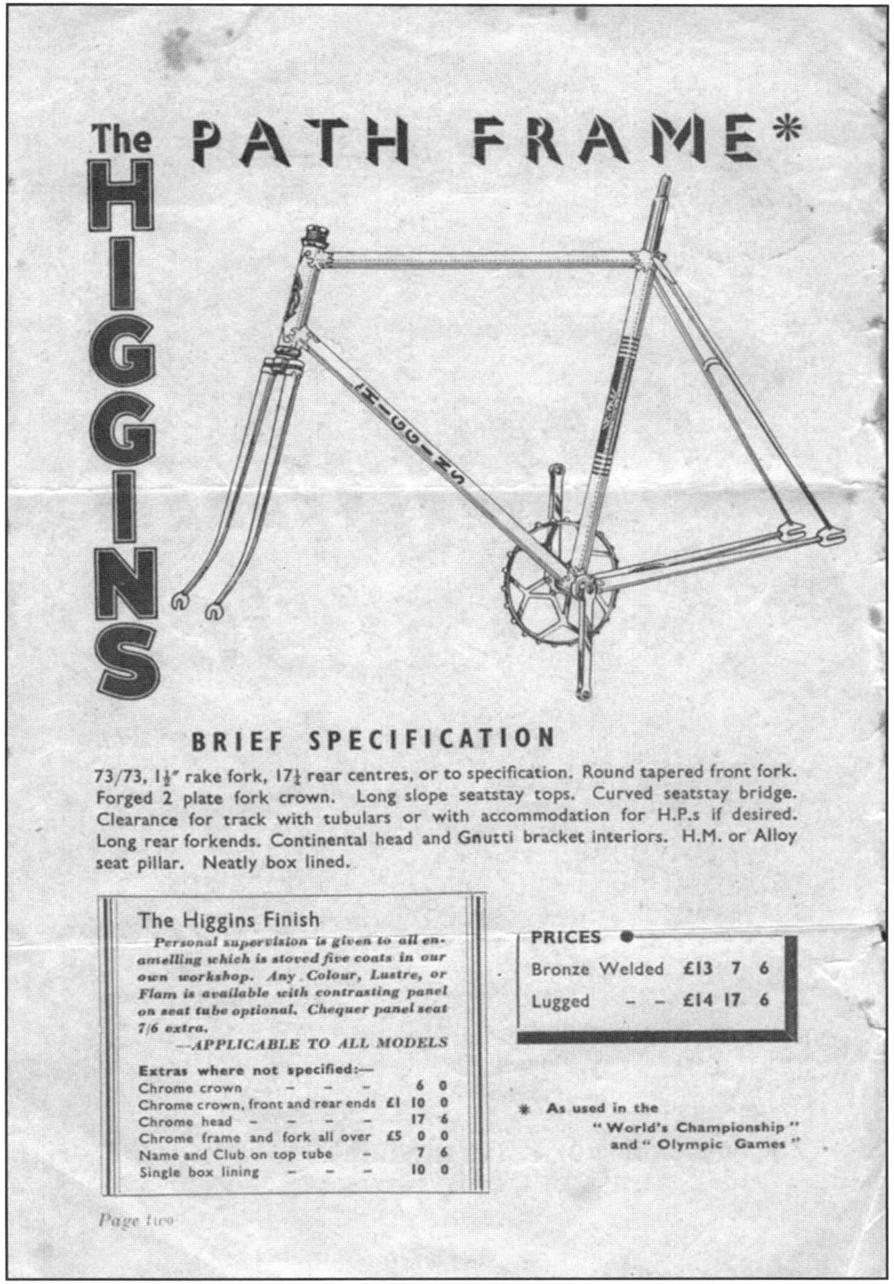

The HIGGINS PATH FRAME*

BRIEF SPECIFICATION

73/73, $1\frac{1}{2}$" rake fork, $17\frac{1}{2}$ rear centres, or to specification. Round tapered front fork. Forged 2 plate fork crown. Long slope seatstay tops. Curved seatstay bridge. Clearance for track with tubulars or with accommodation for H.P.s if desired. Long rear forkends. Continental head and Gnutti bracket interiors. H.M. or Alloy seat pillar. Neatly box lined.

The Higgins Finish

Personal supervision is given to all enamelling which is stoved five coats in our own workshop. Any Colour, Lustre, or Flam is available with contrasting panel on seat tube optional. Chequer panel seat 7/6 extra.

—APPLICABLE TO ALL MODELS

Extras where not specified:—

Chrome crown – – –		6	0
Chrome crown, front and rear ends	£1	10	0
Chrome head – – – –		17	6
Chrome frame and fork all over	£5	0	0
Name and Club on top tube –		7	6
Single box lining – – –		10	0

PRICES

Bronze Welded	£13	7	6
Lugged – –	£14	17	6

* As used in the "World's Championship" and "Olympic Games"

Page two

Weight of Frame approx 7½ lbs.

BRIEF SPECIFICATION

Size to order. 72/72 angles. 2¼ rake oval tapered fork. Forged fork crown. Fixed or loose clip seat clamp. Spearpoint stay tops or as "Path" model. Brazed on solid gear lever boss, roller on bottom bracket and eye on chainstay for Simplex. Brake cable eyes on top tube. Pump pegs for 15″ or 18″, with or without cradle for adaptor. Agrati rear fork ends with integral bracket for Simplex optional. Reinforcement tube to seatstay bridge for rear brake. Finish as page two. Box lined. Gnutti N.K. head and B.B. interiors Alloy seat pillar.

COMPLETE MACHINE

With 10-speed Simplex "Tour De France" gear. Gnutti double chainwheel set. Prior 5 freewheel. Gnutti quick-release hubs. Alp, Gloria or G.B. brakes. Conloy Weimann, San Gorgio or Mavic sprints. Dunlop or D'Allessandro tubulars.

Price—**£55 15 10**, inc. Tax

ALTERNATIVE MODEL

With single chainwheel. Simplex 5. Huret wingnuts. Strata or Phillips Alloy brakes. H.P. rims and tyres.

Price—**£38 14 2**, inc. Tax

PRICE

Complete Frames, less chain set
£13 7 6

A machine designed and successully used by the massed start and circuit riders. Available to your precise specification.

Page three

The Higgins 'Ultralite'

BRONZE WELDED
Weight of Frame approx 7½ lbs

BRIEF SPECIFICATION

FRAME—Size to order. 73/71 or to specification. Oval or round forks tapered to ⅝″ O. diameter. Brazed on lamp bracket boss, pump pegs, and mudguard eyes if desired. Brampton bracket and Continental head interiors, or Brampton headclip if preferred. WHEELS—Sivada hubs. Chrome H.P. rims (26 or 27). Choice of tyres. Huret wingnuts. GENERAL—Williams C34 chainwheel set. Brampton No. 20 pedals Alloy Bend on "531" light steel stem. B17 saddle. Bluemels guards. Webb, Phillips or Strata Alloy brakes.

A Light Machine weighing approximately 22-lbs., popular for all-round club riding, Time Trials, etc. Used and recommended by two former World's Champions on two Continents. Alternative specifications quoted on request.

PRICES

Lady's or Gent's Model
£28 10 9, inc. Tax

Frame only, less chainwheel set
£11 10 0

Lady's Model with extra stays to rear ends — **£1 1 0** extra

Page four

Weight approx 22 lbs

BRIEF SPECIFICATION

Size to order. 72/72 or to specification. 2¼″ rake oval fork tapered to ⅜″ O. diameter. 17¼″ rear. Extruded light steel lugs neatly cut away and finely finished. Brazed on fittings and Agrati rear ends with integral lug for Simplex gear. Brake cable eyes. Pump pegs for 18″ pump with cradle for adapter, optional. Reinforcement tube to seatstay bridge. Lining as illustrated 25/– extra. Continental head fittings. Alloy seat pillar. Gnutti double chainwheel set, and quick-release hubs. Simplex 8 or 10 speed gear. San Gorgio sprints. Pirelli, Hutchinson, or D'Allessandro tubulars. Alloy bend of "531" light steel stem. San Gorgio or Strata Alloy Brakes.

PRICES

£48 9 0, inc. Tax

4 or 5-speed Model
£45 11 1, inc. Tax

Or with H.P. rims and tyres
£43 4 0, inc. Tax

4 or 5-speed Model
£40 6 1, inc. Tax

Frame only, less chainwheel set
£13 17 6

We introduce you to a light, robust, but rigid frame of quality, incorporating the latest design of Italian lug-work, thus giving the machine a Continental character.

Page five

WHEELS

HUBS	BW 9/10 or Sivada DS			DS Phillite Alloy			Gnutti DS, OS, OS2			Prior Alloy OS2	Airlite DS, OS, OS2, WF			Excel-too LF OS2	Gnutti QR OS OS2	Airlite Continental DS, OS, OS2, WF			Camp-agnolo QR os, os2	Camp-agnolo QR LF OS2
Rims, Wired on	Ft.	Rr.	Pr.	Ft.	Rr.	Pr.	Ft.	Rr.	Pr.	Pr.	Ft.	Rr.	Pr.	Pr.	Pr.	Ft.	Rr.	Pr.	Pr.	Pr.
Chrome Endrick, 26 × 1¼ or ⅜ ...	27/8	30/4	55/–	31/8	36/4	65/–	34/6	41/–	72/6	71/–	39/–	50/–	86/–	90/–	98/6	51/6	60/6	109/–	108/6	134/–
Chrome HP, 26 or 27	31/8	34/4	63/–	35/8	40/4	73/–	38/6	45/–	80/6	79/–	43/–	54/–	94/–	98/–	106/6	55/6	64/6	117/–	116/6	142/–
Chrolux, HP, 26 or 27...	36/8	39/4	73/–	40/8	45/4	83/–	43/6	50/–	90/6	89/–	48/–	59/–	104/–	108/–	116/6	60/6	69/6	127/–	126/6	152/–
San Gorgio wide section 27	31/8	34/4	63/–	35/8	40/4	73/–	38/6	45/–	80/6	79/–	43/–	54/–	94/–	98/–	106/6	55/6	64/6	117/–	116/6	142/–
San Gorgio narrow section 26 or 27	35/5	38/1	70/6	39/5	44/1	80/6	42/3	48/9	88/–	86/6	46/9	57/9	101/6	105/6	114/–	59/3	68/3	124/6	124/–	149/6
Boaloy 26 or 27 ...	37/2	39/10	74/–	41/2	45/10	84/–	44/–	50/6	91/6	90/–	48/6	59/6	105/–	109/–	117/6	61/–	70/–	128/–	127/6	153/–
Conloy Asp. 26 or 27	50/8	53/4	101/–	54/8	59/4	111/–	57/6	64/–	118/6	117/–	62/–	73/–	132/–	136/–	144/6	74/6	83/6	155/–	154/6	180/–
Stainless Steel HP, 26 or 27	39/2	41/10	78/–	43/2	47/10	88/–	46/–	52/6	95/6	94/–	50/6	61/6	109/–	113/–	121/6	63/–	72/–	132/–	131/6	157/–
Rims, Sprint, 27″																				
San Gorgio... ...	38/–	40/7	75/6	42/–	46/7	85/6	45/9	51/3	93/–	91/6	49/3	60/3	106/6	110/6	119/–	61/9	70/9	129/6	129/–	154/6
Conloy	46/2	48/10	92/–	50/2	54/10	102/–	53/–	59/6	109/6	108/–	57/6	68/6	123/–	127/–	135/6	70/–	79/–	146/–	145/6	171/–
Fiamme			83/–			93/–			100/6	99/–			114/–	118/–	126/6			137/–	136/6	162/–
Weimann Wood Lined			90/6			100/6			108/–	106/6			121/6	125/6	134/–			144/6	144/–	169/6
Weimann Hollow ...			99/–			109/–			116/6	115/–			130/–	134/–	142/6			153/–	152/6	178/–
Weimann Criterium			97/6			107/6			115/–	113/6			128/6	132/6	141/–			151/6	151/–	176/6
Mavic or Record ...			113/–			123/–			130/6	129/–			144/–	148/–	156/6			167/–	166/6	192/–

Abbreviations: DS—Double Sided fixed. OS—Single Sided gear. OS2—One side fixed, one side gear. WF—Single Sided fixed. Ft—front. Rr—rear. Pr—pair. LF—Large Flange. QR—Quick Release.

Prices are for Double Butted 15/17G spokes. If 15G plain required, deduct 1/6d. per wheel.

Page six

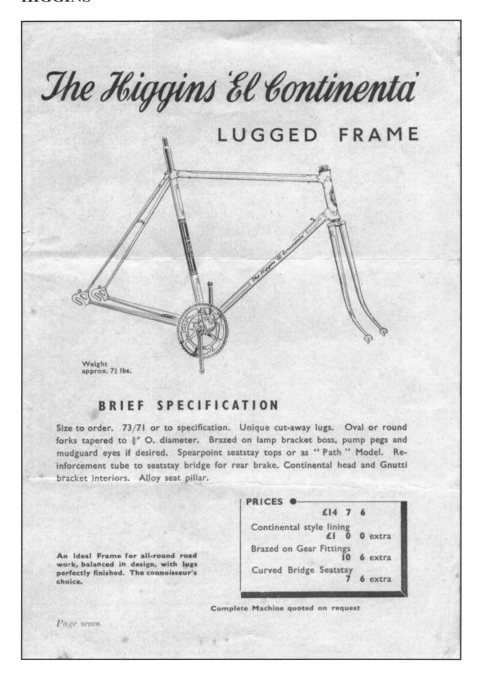

The Higgins 'El Continenta'

LUGGED FRAME

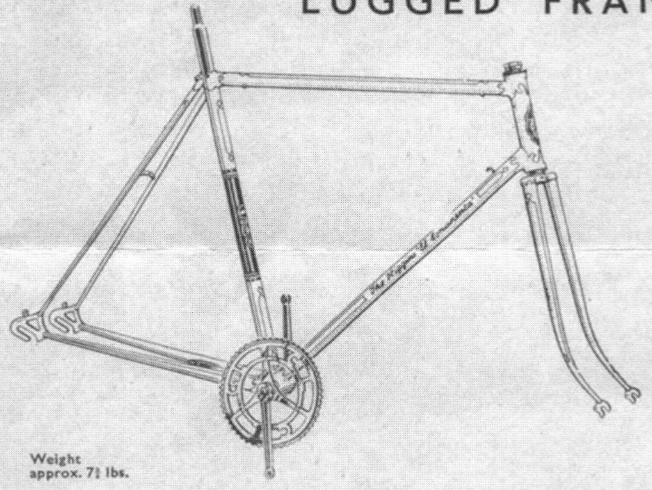

Weight
approx. 7½ lbs.

BRIEF SPECIFICATION

Size to order. 73/71 or to specification. Unique cut-away lugs. Oval or round forks tapered to ⅝″ O. diameter. Brazed on lamp bracket boss, pump pegs and mudguard eyes if desired. Spearpoint seatstay tops or as "Path" Model. Reinforcement tube to seatstay bridge for rear brake. Continental head and Gnutti bracket interiors. Alloy seat pillar.

An Ideal Frame for all-round road work, balanced in design, with lugs perfectly finished. The connoisseur's choice.

PRICES

	£14 7 6
Continental style lining	£1 0 0 extra
Brazed on Gear Fittings	10 6 extra
Curved Bridge Seatstay	7 6 extra

Complete Machine quoted on request

Page seven

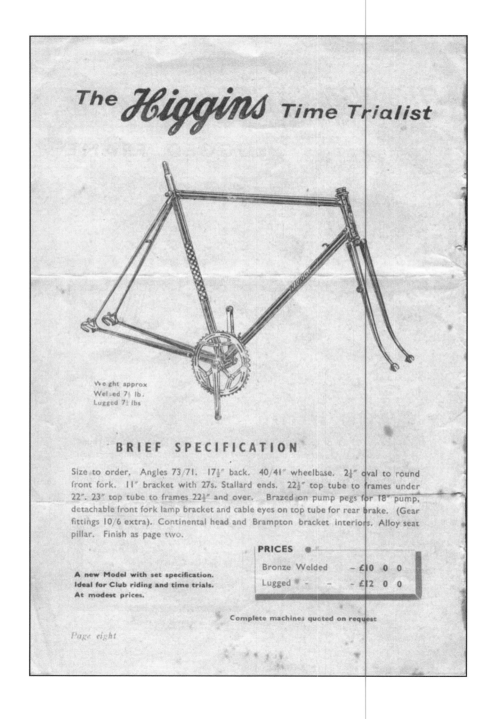

The Higgins Time Trialist

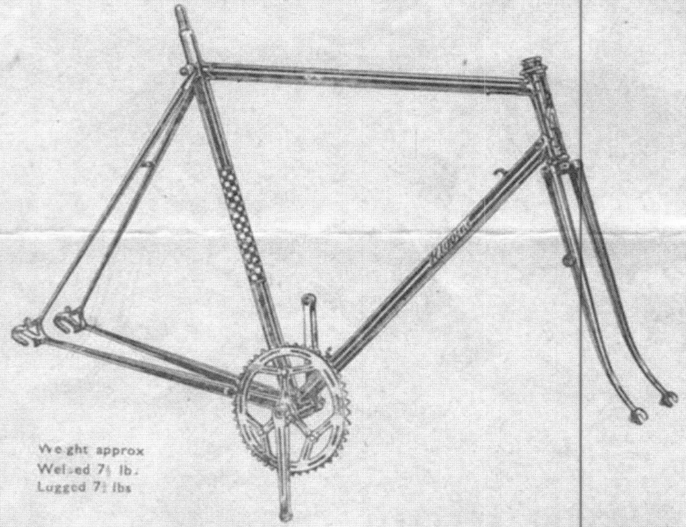

Weight approx
Welded 7¼ lb.
Lugged 7½ lbs

BRIEF SPECIFICATION

Size to order. Angles 73/71. 17½″ back. 40/41″ wheelbase. 2½″ oval to round front fork. 11″ bracket with 27s. Stallard ends. 22½″ top tube to frames under 22″. 23″ top tube to frames 22½″ and over. Brazed on pump pegs for 18″ pump, detachable front fork lamp bracket and cable eyes on top tube for rear brake. (Gear fittings 10/6 extra). Continental head and Brampton bracket interiors. Alloy seat pillar. Finish as page two.

A new Model with set specification. Ideal for Club riding and time trials. At modest prices.

PRICES

Bronze Welded	£10 0 0
Lugged	£12 0 0

Complete machines quoted on request

Page eight

MACLEANS

Don Maclean formed the company sometime prior to 1922, and may well have been assisted by his future partner, Harry Bailey.

V-CC member Nick Tithecott has a part of the packaging which once contained 2,000 "Jackson Rd" transfers; this bears the date December 1922 and may have been the first batch of formal transfers for the fledgling company. They were based at 39 Landseer Road prior to 1922 when the company moved to 2 Jackson Road, Holloway, London N7. In 1928 they acquired additional premises nearby in 366 Upper Street, which extends south of Holloway Road. From 1929 to 1933 they were using only the Upper Street premises.

Advertisements found in the 9th January 1925 and 14th August 1925 issues of "Cycling" magazine for the Featherweight Cycle Company's range of complete cycles, show the company trading at 366 Upper Street. This would indicate that Macleans took over the Lightweight Cycle Company and soon after incorporated the word "Lightweight" into their own title. By September 1926, an advert shows Macleans Featherweights being advertised.

In 1934 they moved a few doors up the road to occupy 362-3 Upper Street where they remained until the business was wound up in 1962 and passed into the ownership of Holdsworthy cycles. Holdsworthy produced small numbers of "Maclean" badged cycles throughout the 1960s; these being re-badged versions of their own range of frames, thus a 1960s Maclean frame could also be found with Claud Butler or Holdsworthy badges.

An undated sales catalogue describes the company as "Specialists in building to customers' detailed specifications". They were "Actual Manufacturers of high class Racing, Touring, Lightweight Cycles and Tandems". All their frames carried a 10-year guarantee.

In small print they also claimed, "We are the oldest firm in the lightweight cycle industry" and at the bottom of each page in the pre-war catalogues are written one-line statements relating to the way the business is run, such as: "Our Super Salesmen – Our Products" and, more to the point, "No Figureheads at Macleans – Only Mechanics!"

A former employee, Norman Penstone, who worked for the company between 1957 and 1961 said that the shop in Seven Sisters Road was only a retail outlet and that the frames were made in Camden Passage, Islington behind the main shop at 362-3 Upper Street, Angel. He lists the staff as:

Shop Owners – A Wolfe and Norman Taylor
Shop Manager – Joe Pearson
Mechanics – Alan Macher, Norman Penstone and Bob Badger
Temporary Mechanic – Cliff Nyman
Frame Builders – Fred Tarsley and John Marriott

He also remembers when Dick Swann arrived as manager in 1961. He brought in new technology – malleable cast lugs, and tried hard to get the owners to sell more lightweight equipment, but his words fell on deaf ears. Alan Macher was with "Macs" from 1952 until they closed – he is now retired and was living in Bournemouth in 2004.

Pat Hanlon had just left when Norman arrived in 1957, but he got to know her through Alan, who was a good friend of hers. She was recognised as the best wheel builder of her time.

A customer, G Keeley, owned a Maclean 50 years ago in the 1940s and remembers that Jack Lauterwasser, the great pre-war triallist, built frames in the Holloway Road workshop.

Another customer, Derek Waters, recalls that Macleans catered more for the tourist market; you would not see groups of road-race riders hovering outside the shop in the same way they gathered outside the nearby shops of Hetchin's or G W Lightweights (built by Len Glover).

The catalogue shown here is from 1938 and shows four cycles, two frames and three tandems which was probably the widest range of machines offered by the firm. A very much narrower range of models was offered in the post-war years.

The original Maclean transfer (probably an "off-the-peg" design) features an oval, hatched in blue, grading from dark to light from top left to bottom right. The oval is contained within a wreath border. At the bottom is a small ornamental panel. The words "D MACLEAN, 2 JACKSON RD. HOLLOWAY" are inscribed on five lines within the large, wreathed oval and the words "LONDON N7" on one line in the small bottom panel. It is believed that Harry Bailey removed the "D" from the company notepaper sometime after Don's death in the mid-20s.

The most commonly seen transfer, used on many restored cycles, features the transfer used in the 1928-33 "366 Upper Street" period. This transfer retained the oval wreathed border, but now contained the wording "MACLEAN'S LIGHTWEIGHT" on two lines – the latter word being curved downwards to fit. In the smaller bottom panel appears the words "366 UPPER ST. LONDON" on two straight lines. The oval badge is now surmounted by the splendid London coat of arms.

When the company moved to 362-3 Upper Street, the transfer changed again. The wreathed oval now contained a Fleur-de-lis coronet above the upward curving words "MACLEAN'S FEATHERWEIGHT" on two lines. The small bottom panel contained the words "362-3 UPPER ST. LONDON" on two lines. The crowning

London coat of arms was simplified by the removal of the Fleur-de-lis from the centre of the Cross of St George shield. It is still a very impressive badge, but not as stunning as the earlier versions from 2 Jackson Road and 366 Upper Street. No further head and seat tube transfers have been recorded to date.

There are no records of the evolution of the transfers used on each side of the down tube. It would appear that pre-war frames only had the simple word "MACLEAN" in silver or gold capital letters on each side of the tube.

After the war in the late 1940s the above transfer was replaced with the attractive "MAC - LEAN" transfer in large gold block capitals with a motif in between the two parts (where the dash is placed). This consisted of a round wreath with the letters "MAC" inside, on a red background. A pair of silver outstretched 'angel' wings radiate out from the central wreath. Above the wings is the word "FEATHERWEIGHTS" in small gold capital letters. Below, on two lines, are the words "362/3 UPPER ST" and "ANGEL N1" in small silver block capitals.

Also to be seen on a few cycles is a simpler transfer with the word "MACLEANS" in dark blue, or red, scrolled capitals, each letter with a white/black border on a plain white background, behind which is another elongated background in pale blue with a silver outer edge, tapering to a point at each end. This transfer is on both pre- and post-war frames.

At the time of writing there are no records or proven information regarding the numbering of frames, both pre- and post-war. However, there are adequate known numbers of *post-war* frames, which have bills of sale, that have allowed the verification of the numbering system used post-war. For the pre-war frames, there are few confirmed dates of manufacture or sale to be able to date any other frames from this period. The known numbers, listed below, indicate how difficult it is to attempt to construct a number dating pattern. Pre-war cycle numbers as provided to date – all 1930s?

DE517 - Restored, in black, by Holdsworthy Cycles
DE928 - On a frame now in Ottawa, Canada
EE212 - Thought to be 1934
EE430 - A tandem seen in an advertisement in 1983
EE498 - A tandem
EE871 - Double gents tandem, resprayed maroon
B798 - Spring 1937. Black, double gents tandem, bought new
B822 - An un-restored tandem
C461 - A tandem tricycle, advertised as c.1938
C484 - Unrestored
E267 - Family owners stated that it was bought in 1935/6
G664 - Unusual down tube transfers
M17 - A frame, renovated in the 1950s?
N1 - Original duck egg blue tandem
W105 - 1936/7?
W265 - 27th April 1938 bill of sale – a "Super Cycle" model
W798 - Bought new in 1939
W888 - Solo
W983 - Tandem, bought from original owner

There are adequate post-war verified numbers to be able to date frame numbers quite accurately. After the war, the company started to use a numbering system that started with the prefix letter "K" followed by a number, which did not go beyond 999. There are no records of four-figure numbers following the letter prefix. Once the numbers reached 999, the company went on to use the prefix "KA" followed in sequence over the years by "KB, KC, KD and KE". There are no known recorded letter combinations beyond "KE". The frame number is usually to be found at the top of the seat tube. On some frames, it is also stamped on the inside of the steerer tube. It can also be found under the bottom bracket or on the side of a rear fork end. Listed below are known and proven dated post-war frame numbers:

K23 - March 1946
KB 123 - 11th March 1950
KA26 - Before 14th January 1948
KB905 - 14th June 1952
KA57 - February 1948
KC978 - 1955
KA79 - April 1948
KD213 - 29th September 1956
KA574 - May 1949
KD573 - April 1958
KA699 - 9th May 1949
KD909 - May 1959
KB6 - 1950

It is important to mention the fact that there are cycles currently in use that carry "Maclean" transfers, both pre- and post-war, that are not Macleans. It is relatively easy to come by the transfers and put them on a frame that the owner thinks is a Maclean, but, if the frame does not carry the trademark form of letter/number, then it is not a Maclean.

Murray Maclean

Catalogue believed to be from 1938 was provided by Ray Nott. It is stamped on the front cover 'ALL PRICES INCREASED BY 5%'

1938

MACLEANS Featherweight CYCLES

SPECIALISTS IN BUILDING TO CUSTOMERS' DETAILED SPECIFICATIONS

Actual Manufacturers of High - Class RACING, TOURING, LIGHTWEIGHT CYCLES and TANDEMS

ALL PRICES INCREASED BY 5% (1/- IN THE £1)

Assembling, Brazing, Wheelbuilding Shops on the Premises

—

Official Repairers to C.T.C. and N.C.U.

362-3 Upper Street, Angel, London, N.1
(By Islington Empire)
Phone - - - CANONBURY 2434

Tottenham Sales and Service:
258 High Road :: N.15
Phone : Stamford Hill 4372

Filing and Lug Cutting Shop :
78 ISLINGTON HIGH STREET
(Rear of Main Premises)

ALL PRICES INCREASED BY 5%

FOREWORD

In presenting this Catalogue, describing our Super and Super Club models, we feel no introduction is necessary, because Club Cyclists throughout Great Britain have recognised that a Maclean Lightweight Cycle or Tandem represents all that is best in WORKMANSHIP, PERFORMANCE and HIGH STANDARD of FINISH, and last, but not least, the after delivery service given by ourselves.

The fact that we do a minimum of advertising, do not employ racing cyclists, or offer free machines (being unnecessary, as our cycles sell entirely on their own merits) nor give cash bonuses, and that we are the oldest, and one of the largest organisations specialising in built-to-order machines, is sufficient proof that the quality of our products is our best advertisement.

We have been copied by other firms for a number of years, but our experience, combined with the most up-to-date plant, enables us to still offer Tandems and Cycles years ahead of other makes.

Many firms use the catchpenny phrase of "weight," as a means of getting business, and many riders to-day are riding Cycles pounds heavier than they have been led to believe.

Don't forget it takes a long time to save the money for a first-class cycle, so make certain you get satisfaction, and not heartache.

Do not choose a cycle by an exaggerated advertisement.

The best way to choose a cycle is to select two or three favourite makers ; watch the riders with them on the road, then ask their opinion of the cycle, and the service given by the makers.

We frequently get machines of our manufacture in for re-enamelling and overhaul, that have had 12 or more years of continuous service.

To sum up, the Maclean is a personal job, ridden by amateurs who are not allowed to advertise their successes, so ask the man who owns one.

2

Quotations for Path or Road Machines to any Specification or Dimensions

FRAMES

Standard or Upright Head Models

Weight of Skeleton Frame, 4 lb. 7 oz.
Weight of Skeleton Forks, 2 lb. (with liners in blades).

Lighter Forks if required.

Wheelbase and bracket height to order.
Built to your detailed specifications, Reynolds or A. & P. double-butted tubing, no depressions in chain stays, our own design, allowing ample tyre clearance. Mudguard and reflector eyes (brazed on), also pump pegs and Chater Lea adjustable lamp bracket.
Forks with butted steering column, blades fitted with light steel liners, with solid machined ends (any pattern blades).
Enamel, Black or Colour. Chrome-plated crown, and front and rear ends. Williams C34 chain wheel and cranks. Path Frame, no extra. Any shape seat post.

£3-15-0 Less Chrome Ends **£3-5-0**

15/- with order, and 7 monthly payments of **10/-**

Extras on Standard Frames

Reynolds 531 tubing, or high manganese	10/-
Hiduminium seat post	2/6
Williams C1000 light chain wheel and cranks	2/6
Tapered Tubes, 531 tubing	15/-
Dureel Chain Wheel and Cranks	10/6

Special finishes, quotations according to requirements (see page 14).

Frames built with Chater Lea or B.S.A. fittings, **£4-15-0**

The Oldest Firm in the Lightweight Industry

3

Low Easy Payment Terms

CLUB MODEL No. 1

Standard or Upright Head

Weight of Skeleton Frame and Forks, 6 lb. 7 oz.

FRAME - To your specification. Bracket and wheel-base to order. Reynolds D.B. tubing. (This tubing has stood the test of time.) Chain stays, new rapid taper: no depression, ample tyre clearance. All lugs cut away, pinned, mitred, and properly brazed. Mudguard and reflector eyes, pump pegs and lamp bracket brazed-on, also chain rest. Any pattern rear ends to order.

FRONT FORKS - Stem butted where strain takes place. Light steel liners in each blade, solid machined front ends. (Any pattern blades.)

WHEELS - Perry lightweight chromium hubs. Double-butted spokes. Dunlop, Endrick or Westwood rims. Black or chromium. Size to order.

CHAIN WHEEL - Williams C34 or 5-pin.

COGS - Two fixed or fixed and free (Villiers).

CHAIN - Renolds, Elite, or Coventry.

PEDALS - Brampton, Phillips Vitesse, or Mark 10.

HANDLEBARS - Adjustable stem (any pattern), bend to order, chromium plated or celluloid covered, with long sponge grips.

BRAKE - Resilion cantilever (best grade), front or rear, or two Monitor or two Radnall Ring bearing.

Every Maclean Rider a Maclean Enthusiast

4

Our Advice—Join a Good Club

CLUB MODEL
(Continued)

Equipped with Sprints suitable for Racing, Extra

MUDGUARDS - Bluemel's Noweight with combined or separate extension, or Duplex. Black, White, or Transparent, with quick release stays.

TYRES - Palmer's Super, Dunlop, Ambra Superga, or Avon, etc.

SADDLE - Mansfield, Brooks C32, or Terry's.

LUBRICATION - Two force feed oilers to head. Tecalemit or standard to other bearings.

FINISH - All lugs scientifically cut away. Carefully filed and stove enamelled black or colour to choice. All usual parts chrome plated, and chrome plated front and rear ends.

EQUIPMENT - Bluemel's Noweight pump, prismatic reflector and rear white patch in accordance with regulations, and oil gun.

PRICE £8-0-0 **Less Chrome Ends £7-10-0**

Or **£1** with order, and 13 monthly payments of **12/-**, or **3/-** weekly, or Terms arranged.

Weight according to specification. (For extras see page 14.)

Club M built with Chater Lea or B.S.A. fittings **£9-15-0**, or **£1-5-0** down and 12 monthly payments of **16/-**.

Ask the Owner of a Maclean Featherweight His Opinion of same

5

Call and See Us. No Obligation

MAC SUPER MODEL
68°, 70°, 73° Head

Weight according to specifications

Lightest weight with wired-on Tyres, 21 lb. 6 oz.

FRAME - As described on page 7. Built to order.

WHEELS - Featherweight, Constrictor B.S.A. Hubs, Solite or Airlite. Dunlop H.P. or Endrick light gauge rims, double butted spokes.

TYRES - Dunlop High Pressure, Palmer's, Ambra Superga or No. 3's.

GEARS - Two fixed or free.

CHAIN - Elite or Renolds.

STEM - Reynolds' Hiduminium. Bend: Reynolds' Hiduminium, pattern to own choice.

BRAKE - Cantilever A quality, or to order.

FINISH - See Super Frame (page 7).

MUDGUARDS - Bluemel's, with separate or combined extension and quick release stays.

SADDLE - B17, Ormond, Terry, Flyer, etc.

PEDALS - B.O.A., Brampton solid centre, or Phillips Hiduminium.

EQUIPMENT - Bluemel's Noweight pump, prismatic reflector, and Tecalemit oil gun.

PRICE £11-10-0

Or **£2** deposit and 12 monthly payments of **17/6**, or by arrangement.

Extras

Fiamme or Constrictor Conloy Rims, **30/-** Conloy Pedals, **10/-**

Extra on frame finishes. See page 14.

The Value of a Cycle Lies in the Frame

6

Quotations for Own Specifications with Pleasure

SUPER FRAME

Upright Head. 68°, 76°, 73° Head to Order

Weight of Skeleton Frame, 4 lb. 2 oz. Weight of Forks, from 1 lb. 9 oz.

DESIGN - - To order. Built throughout with Reynolds high manganese aircraft tubing, or Reynolds 531, or chrome molybdenum. Double-butted. Height, wheelbase and bracket to order.

LUGS - - Hand-cut in our own shops. Special design. Chater Lea. Chain stays, rapid taper, to allow ample tyre clearance. Rear fork ends. Pattern as desired. Fitments brazed to frame as required.

FRONT FORKS - Design of blades to order, round or D to round. Head bearings and clip, Chater Lea, with Tecalemit nipple fitted to clip and head lug. Chain wheel and cranks, Williams Dureel alloy, or light steel.

SEAT POST - Hiduminium straight, or H.M., L., or curved.

FINISH - - Black or Colour, Silver, Gold, Green or Red Flamboyant or Lustra, with chrome-plated front and rear ends.

PRICE £5-10-0 Terms arranged.

Chater Lea Chain Wheels and Cranks, **10/-** extra.
For Special Finishes, see page 14.

FRAMES

We supply frames separately for customers to fit up with their own parts, but when doing this, will they, in fairness to us, see that the wheels are central on the hubs, as very often, we are told, the frame is out of track, and find that the wheels are the trouble. We will be only too pleased to test your wheels, while you wait, if you bring them along, so don't handicap a good frame with doubtful fitments. It spoils your machine and our reputation.

No Better Frame Ever Made

7

We Specialise in What We Sell

TOURING MODEL

FRAME - - Built to customer's own height and specification. Every lug correctly cut away. All essential fittings brazed-on.

FRONT FORKS - Pattern as desired, with solid machined ends, and Chater Lea adjustable lamp bracket, brazed-on. Steel liners in blades.

ENAMEL - - Best Stove-Black or Colour. All usual parts chromium plated.

THREE-SPEED - Cyclo derailleur, Osgear, Simplex gear, Sturmey-Archer, or new Cyclo unit hub.

BRAKES - - To order (if hub brakes, B.H.C. Solite recommended), or two cantilevers.

TYRES - - Dunlop, Palmer, etc.

RIMS - - Dunlop Endrick or Westwood, black or chromium. Size to order.

HANDLEBARS - Adjustable stem. Pattern as desired.

BEND - - Chromium or celluloid covered (shape to order), with long Shockstop grips.

MUDGUARDS - Bluemel's Noweight, with quick detachable fittings. Black, white, or transparent.

EQUIPMENT - Bluemel's Noweight pump, Tecalemit oil gun, prismatic reflector and rear white patch or rear lamp.

SADDLE - - Terry's or Mansfield, etc.

PRICE £9-10-0 CASH

Or **25/-** down and 12 monthly payments of **15/-**, or terms arranged.

Extra on Frame Finishes, see page 14.

This Model has proved Ideal for Continental Touring

8

LADIES' SPORTS MODEL

For those who need a Gent's Frame, we can build with a shorter top tube, if ordered

FRAME - Size to order. Wheelbase and bracket height to order. Any design tube, from head to seat tube, or twin tubes from head lugs to rear fork ends. All fittings brazed on.

FRONT FORKS - Any design. Blades with solid machined ends.

WHEELS - Lightweight hubs. Double-butted spokes. Dunlop Endrick rims, black or chromium (size to order).

TYRES - Dunlop, Palmer, etc.

CHAIN - Renolds, Elite, or Coventry.

HANDLEBARS - Adjustable stem (any pattern). Bend any shape to order. Chromium plated or celluloid covered.

BRAKES - Two A Resilion cantilevers or hub brakes, or to order.

MUDGUARDS - Bluemel's Noweight, with combined extension.

SADDLE - Terry's, Mansfield, etc.

FINISH - To order. Black or Colour.

£8-0-0 CASH

Or **£1** deposit, and 13 monthly payments of **12/-**, or **3/-** weekly

CROSS-OVER DRIVE

Or Double-Diamond Pattern if preferred

Short Wheelbase

Weight of Skeleton Frame, 10 lb. 5 oz. Weight of Forks, 2 lb. 9 oz. Double Diamond pattern, ½ lb. lighter.

FRAME - Built of Reynolds high-tensile tubing, that will stand the roughest roads of to-day. Chater lugs, bracket bearings and head bearings. Williams chain wheel and cranks. Lugs hand-cut. All essential fittings brazed-on.

WHEELS - Endrick or Westwood. Double cog hub. Double-butted tandem spokes.

TYRES - Dunlop, Palmer, etc.

BRAKES - Two A cantilevers, or to order.

MUDGUARDS - Bluemel's Noweight, with quick detachable fittings.

FINISH - Stove enamelled, Black or Colour. All usual parts chromium plated.

CHAIN - Renolds or Elite.

HANDLEBARS - To selection.

SADDLES - Terry's or Brooks.

£16-16-0 CASH

Or **£3** deposit, and 15 monthly payments of **£1**

FRAME ONLY, as above, complete with Chain Wheels, Cranks and Seat Posts **£10-10-0**

Terms arranged.

Extras on Tandem—Three-speed Hub, **£1-0-0** Derailleur types, **£1-10-0**

Chater Lea chain wheels and cranks **£1** extra.

TOURING TANDEM

Double Diamond, if preferred

FRAME - Built to order with Reynolds high-tensile tubing. All lugs cut away.

SEAT POSTS - Pattern to order.

WHEELS - Dunlop. Endrick or Westwood rims. Double-butted tandem spokes. Hubs to order.

GEARS - Cyclo Derailleur, Simplex, or Sturmey-Archer 3-speed, with hub brakes.

BRAKES - Fitted with British Hub Co. brakes, who were the pioneers of hub brakes (and we recommend), having gained their experience in the early days of motor-cycling—being now able to supply hub brakes from which all the early faults are eliminated. Rear brake fitted with cable-cum-rod for easy operation ; or Two A quality Resilion cantilevers if desired.

TYRES - Palmer or Dunlop, etc.

CHAINS - Renolds or Elite.

MUDGUARDS - Bluemel's Noweight. Black, White, or Transparent.

SADDLES - Terry's, Brooks C32 or B15, Mansfield 38N.

HANDLEBARS - Pattern to order, with adjustable clip. Chromium plated or celluloid covered.

EQUIPMENT - Bluemel's Noweight pump and prismatic reflector.

PRICE £16-10-0 CASH

Or **£2-10-0** with order and 15 monthly payments of **£1-0-8**

CLUB TANDEM

Weight of Skeleton Frame and Forks, 14 lb. 12 oz.

FRAME - Built with Reynolds high-tensile tubing that will stand racing and hard touring. All lugs hand-cut in our workshops. All essential fittings brazed-on.

FORKS - Heavily butted stem, solid ends, and liner in each blade. Brazed-on detachable lamp bracket.

WHEELS - Endrick or Westwood rims, double-butted tandem spokes. Size to order.

TYRES - Dunlop or Palmer.

CHAIN - Renolds or Elite.

HANDLEBARS - As selected (chromium or celluloid covered).

BRAKES - Two A cantilevers, or hub brakes.

MUDGUARDS - Bluemel's Noweight, with quick release fittings.

FINISH - Stove enamelled Black or Colour, all usual parts heavily chrome plated.

EQUIPMENT - Bluemel's Noweight pump, prismatic reflector, Tecalemit oil gun.

PRICE £14-14-0 CASH

Or **£2** deposit and 14 monthly payments of **£1**
Lady Back—no extra charge.

Short Wheelbase **£1** extra. B.H.C. Super Tandem Brakes **6/-** extra.

Complete Frame as above, fitted with Chain Wheel, Cranks and Seat Post ... ... **CASH** **£9-0-0**

Terms arranged.

All Goods Backed by Our Reputation

Skeleton Frame, 11½ lb. Forks, 2 lb 12 oz.

This pattern Frame optional on all Tandems

WE MANUFACTURE ANY DESIGN TANDEM OR CYCLE FRAME

This Model **£1-10-0** extra.

REPAIRS DEPARTMENT

Repairs to any make of Cycle or Tandem. Speed Gears, Hub Brakes, Wheel Repairs. Tandem Conversion and Repairs. Enamelling and Plating.

FOR RIDERS WHOSE HEIGHTS VARY

Sloping Top Tube if preferred

We have without doubt the Most Up-to-date Workshop in London

All work open to Customers' Inspection during the various stages of Construction

Extras on Club Model

VARIABLE GEARS

Sturmey—		Cyclo—	
2-Speed	16/-	Unit Type	30/-
2-Speed, Close Ratio ...	20/-	4-Speed	35/-
3-Speed. K. Close or Medium Ratio	20/-	Witmy 2-Speed	15/-
2-Speed, with Hub Brake ...	22/-	Osgear, Boss Type	24/-
3-Speed, with Hub Brake ...	26/-	Simplex Gear	30/-
Cyclo 3-Speed	25/-	Simplex Gear, with Octagonal Hub	45/-

SADDLES

Brooks B17	5/-	Mansfield Ormond	4/6
Brooks " Swallow "	10/-	Brooks Duralium	10/-

BRAKES

A Cantilever Brake	10/-	Radnall Ring Bearing	4/6
B ,, ,, ...	6/-	Monitor Brake	6/-

WHEELS, RIMS, TYRES, Etc.

Dunlop Tubulars	15/-	Conloy Rims, Constrictor ...	32/-
Tabucchi Maple Rims	15/-	Fiamme Rims	30/-
Fort Dunlop Tyres	5/-	Hiduminium Stem	5/-
High Pressure Rims and Tyres	5/-	,, Bend	5/-
Reynolds 531 Tubing	10/-	Major Taylor Extension ...	2/6
C1000 Chain Wheel	2/6	B.O.A. Pedal	2/6
Dureel Chain Wheel Set ...	10/-	Phillips Hiduminium Pedals ...	2/6

HUBS

Featherweight Hub	5/-	B.H.C. Airlite Hubs	12/6
Constrictor Hubs	5/-	Ambra Superga	14/-

FRAME FINISHES (CLUB MODEL)

Chromium-plating—		Flamboyant Finishes or Lustra, Green, Gold, Red, etc. ...	5/-
Fork all over	4/6	(All flamboyants on dull nickel.)	
Chain and Seat Stays ...	12/-		
Frame and Fork all over ...	25/-		

FINISHES

Chromium-plating—		**Tandem Extra Finishes**	
Frame all over	25/-	Flamboyant with Chromium ends	35/-
Chain and Seat Stays and Forks all over	12/-	Lustra Finish with Chromium ends	30/-
Head Lugs and Tube ...	6/-		

Quotations for Own Specifications with Pleasure

Each Cycle an Individual Job

Clothing, Accessories, Etc.

A FEW OF THE MANY LINES IN STOCK

CAPES - Extra light, diagonal opening, concealed inside zip fastener, with flap over same, full skirt, and shaped at shoulders to give ample elbow room, **10/9.** With button fastening, **7/9,** guaranteed non-sticking. Cheaper line, **4/9.**

LEGGINGS, **7/6** OILSKIN SPATTEES, **4/6**

DYNAMOS - Lucas, Bluemel's, Lucifer, etc., stocked. Special line—6 volts, with Head and Rear Lamp, fitted with stand-by battery, fully guaranteed, **14/6** complete.

SHOES - Ladies' or Gent's with full flap-over tongue, **7/9,** Black or Brown. Black and Tan, **10/6.** Special hand-stitched, **14/6.**

WHEELS - Perry Light Hubs, chromium plated, double-butted spokes, Endrick Light Gauge Rims, black enamelled, **12/-.** Fitted with Ambra Superga Covers and Tubes, **25/-.** Chromium-plated Rims, **2/-** extra.

PLUS FOURS - Ladies' or Gent's, **7/9** and **12/6.** Full cut and tailor-made. Double-seated.

BAGS - Special Club Bag, Leather, 13" × 8" × 5½", reinforced back cape straps, two side pockets, **8/-.** Other lines from **3/-** to **19/6,** all with heavier material than usually offered.

ZIP JACKETS - Best Waterproof Black Cloth, full zip fastener, **9/11.** Suede Cloth, **8/9, 12/9** and **17/9.** Cord Jackets, with full concealed zip, **12/9.** All made wider than usual across the shoulders than the standard lines usually offered.

HOSE - From **1/8** to **4/9.** Ladies' or Gent's.

SHORTS - Drill, Cord and Flannel, from **5/5.**

JACKETS - Cotton, **4/6** and **5/9.** GENUINE ALPACAS, Grey, Brown and Black, from **8/6.**

TOE CLIPS - All the best makes. Adjustable piano wire, **9d.** per pair.

Complete Stock of all Racing Accessories, Tubulars, Sprint Wheels, Hubs, Clothing. All the best makes. Advice and individual attention.

We are Lightweight Cycle Manufacturers, but also cater for every branch of the sport, stocking a wide range of everything that is needed by lady or gent., in either clothing or accessory, having separate department for each.

A Mail Order Department deals promptly with orders and queries, so if you are unable to call, write, and we shall be pleased to supply any information, without any obligation on your part.

Nothing is too much trouble. We can supply your requirements.

Absolute Privacy. All Easy Payments Financed by Ourselves

15

GUARANTEE.

A TEN YEARS' GUARANTEE IS ISSUED WITH ALL FRAMES MANUFACTURED BY US. ALL CYCLES AND TANDEMS GUARANTEED MANUFACTURED ON THE PREMISES.

INSTALMENTS.—Absolute privacy. No third party. No enquiries made of employers.

DEAL FAIRLY WITH US AND YOU WILL FIND WE ARE MOST REASONABLE. AFTER-SALE SERVICE ALWAYS ACCORDED.

QUOTATIONS BY RETURN FOR ROAD OR PATH RACING MACHINES.

MACHINES BUILT TO ANY SPECIFICATION OR DIMENSION.

We are the oldest firm in the Lightweight Cycle Industry.

We offer a first-class machine at a competitive price because we have no heavy overhead expenses.

DEAL WITH US AND GET THE BENEFIT.

THE FOLLOWING GUARANTEE IS GIVEN WITH OUR CYCLES AND TANDEMS

We guarantee all Maclean Featherweight Frames and complete Cycles for Ten Years against defects of manufacture, and should any defect occur within the time, we replace the defective part gratis.

This Guarantee is subject to the conditions mentioned below.

With all machines and component parts herein specified we give a special guarantee instead of the guarantee implied by Statute or otherwise as to the quality of fitness for the purpose of cycling of goods supplied by us; any such implied guarantee being in all cases excluded. In cases of machines which have been used for "hiring out" purposes or in respect of which our trade or manufacturing number has been removed, no guarantee of any kind is given or is to be implied.

We guarantee, subject to the conditions mentioned below, that all precautions which are usual and reasonable have been taken by us to secure excellence of materials and workmanship.

This guarantee does not, of course, include tyres, rims, chains, saddles, variable gears, coaster hubs, etc., in respect of which we give the guarantee furnished by the makers, usually 15 months. And the purchaser shall not be entitled to claim any damage whatever save replacement of the defective parts. This guarantee does not apply to defects caused by wear and tear, misuse or neglect.

Angel N.1—By Islington Empire

16

MERCIAN CYCLES

Mercian Cycles commenced trading in 1946, when Tom Crowther and Lou Barker, two local clubmen formed a partnership and opened their first shop at 191 London Road, Derby. A combined name of Crow-Bar Cycles had been suggested, but a more suitable name of Mercian was settled on, being derived from the nearby Mercian Kings who had been buried in the nearby Repton Church in the 7th Century.

Shortly after opening, frames were being built in a small workshop in Castle Street, off London Road, and they later moved to a third floor workshop in Osmaston Mills in Bloomfield Street.

Lou Baker built some of the early frames and Tom Crowther ran the shop side of the business, along with his first wife, Ethel.

Initially they did not have enamelling facilities, but Bet Wilkins, who worked in the shop, would take the frames when they were built by train to Andy Bones in Nottingham and then collect them when they were enamelled. It was convenient that both shops were located close to the train stations.

In the early fifties frames were being made at a workshop at 2 Epsom Crescent, Ascot Drive, Derby and in 1964-5 the current workshops at Pontefract Street were built. Derek Land had worked as a frame builder for Mercian for many years, and was appointed Workshop Foreman. Rob Poultney worked as a sprayer from the mid-1970's and Stuart Wakefield as a frame finisher for a similar length of time and all are still currently with the company. The reputation of the quality of their finish was second to none.

Derek Wilkins, Bet's husband, never worked full time for Mercian, but worked nearby at Rolls Royce. Derek worked in his spare time cutting and filing lugs, including the decorative Vincitore pattern and was paid 2/6d (22p) for each set of lugs he completed!

Bill Holmes, the International Rider of the Hull Thursday R.C worked for Mercian for a while and several national records were held by amateurs riding Mercians.

The crack Nottingham Wheelers team, led by Gordon Ian, were riding Mercians and a 1955 advert in 'Courier – Sporting Cyclist' predicted the first 55 minute 25-mile Time Trial would be done on one of their machines. Dave Keeler rode a Mercian equipped with the early Campagnolo-Paris-Roubaix gear in his Lands End to John O'Groats ride.

In 1954 Ray Booty was riding a Mercian. The advert slogan was 'Everyone is going faster on a Mercian'.

With the racing success came the orders from further afield and America and Germany were countries, among others, that took a growing number of export models. The head badge incorporating 'The World Over' was introduced in the 1960's.

Tom Crowther left Mercian to set up his 'Tom Crowther Cycles' shop in the Midlands and the 1963 catalogue shows the directors as Ethel Crowther and Peter Riches. Peter had formerly been a frame builder with Hetchin's.

In 1965 the business was bought by Bill Betton, who had been working as a frame builder for some years for Mercian.

In 1971 the shop moved to larger premises at The Cavendish, Normanton, just off the Derby ring road. Jeff Bowler who had been working in the shop since 1967 was now the shop manager and Grant Mosley, the current owner, started in 1973.

Various shops throughout the UK were agents for Mercians and the Freewheel Catalogues of the 1980's showed various Mercian models. Frames were also built for other lightweight shops, including Sid Mottram in Leicester, Dentons in the North East, Swinnertons at Stoke and Uppadines in Doncaster.

Mercians ventured into co-sponsoring independent riders in the 1960's and local leading rider Derek Woodings rode for the Bantel/Mercian team with some success.

Tandems were introduced in 1978 and a Ladies mixte design has been available for many years.

The move to the present shop in Shardlow Road, Alvaston was made in 1984.

Bill Betton retired in 2002 and Grant Mosley and Jane Smith are the current Directors of the Company.

Mercian have long believed in traditional methods of construction, and have always used the open hearth method of brazing as they believe it reduces the possibility of overheating the tubing.

They have been loyal to Reynolds tubing over the years and were granted a Reynolds '753' licence to build in the early days of the lightweight tubing. They still build in Reynolds, including 631, 725, 853, 853 Pro Team and 953 stainless. Their most recent introduction is the Velocita which had a combination of Reynolds 853 and Dedaccia carbon fibre seatstays, chainstays and forks.

Over the years they have built a strong following of tourist and Audax riders, with the emphasis on quality of construction, a comfortable but responsive ride, and a traditional enamelling finish of the highest quality.

One of the current boosts to production of frames is the introduction of the Paul Smith (of fashion fame) Limited Edition, road and track machines which are finished with an extremely eye catching range of unique paintwork designs.

MERCIAN CYCLES

Mercian frame numbers and records are held by Mercian at Derby dating back to 1970. Earlier records were destroyed to make space at the workshop, some years ago.

Mercian frame numbers include the year of manufacture, but its position has varied over time. For at least part of the 1950's, the first two digits indicated the year, but this pattern was not followed consistently. From 1970 through to 1999, the year is the last two digits of the frame number. After 1999, the last four digits are the year of manufacture.

Chris Barbour, a Veteran-Cycle Club member in Boston, USA, has set up a Mercian Cycles' register and website in an attempt to reconstruct the lost records of earlier Mercian frames. Known frame numbers from the 1950's and 1960's are given below.

	1950's			**1960's**	
Year	**Frame No.**	**Model**	**Year**	**Frame No.**	**Model**
1950	22150	Super-Vigorelli road-path	1961	6191	Road-path
			1961	61685	Unknown
1951	5151	Vigorelli-road-path	1961	61831	Olympique
1953	4953	Unknown	1962	10862	Olympique
1954	36254	Vigorelli-road-model	1962	48262	Unknown
1955	29355	Road-path	1963	63125	Road-path
1956	56287	Unknown	1964	53964	King of Mercia
1957	37657	Super Vigorelli	1966	40166	Unknown
1959	5923	Olympic	1967	67443	Superlight track frame
1959	59557	King of Mercia			
1959	59574	Campionissimo	1968	68413	Professional
1959	59709	Unknown	1969	42369	Superlight

Mercian in Derby will supply details of post-1970 frames upon forwarding a fee to them, as considerable time is involved in searching the records.

Thanks to Mercian Cycles, Derek Wilkins and Peter Underwood for assistance with the compilation of these notes.

Granville Horton

Catalogue and Price List dated 1st September 1963 were kindly loaned by Granville Horton. They are printed in black on green paper

MERCIAN
CYCLES Ltd.

By courtesy of "Sporting Cyclist"

Directors:
E. D. Crowther
P. C. Riches

191 LONDON ROAD
DERBY
Telephone: 46304

Trade enquiries: 2 EPSOM CRESCENT, DERBY. Telephone 46786

We Cater for the Connoisseur

Introducing our latest range of Handbuilt Frames built by cyclists who are also experts at their occupation of frame building.

Built under the personal supervision of our workshop director, guaranteed handmade with no mass production methods used, from the very best materials obtainable today.

ALL FRAMES BUILT IN OUR OWN WORKSHOP

Used in Olympics, World Championships, National Championships and all Major Events all over the world.

KING OF MERCIA

The tried and tested Road-Racing Frame.

Designed from the pooled knowledge and experience of International Riders.

Only first quality '531' D.B. Tubing is used along with Solid Forged Fork Crown, Prugnat or Nervex Professional Lugs to choice. Wrap over Seat Stays.

Complete cycles supplied to order.

Frame Specification :

72° x 72° Parallel Angles, 2⅛" Fork Rake, or any practical design or measurements to order. Campagnola, Simplex or Plain Ends. All necessary cable eyes, pump pegs etc., brazed on.

Italia H.D. Set, Campagnola 29/6 extra.

T.D.C. Continental Bottom Bracket Set.

STANDARD FINISH :

One colour with contrast head and seat tube panel only.

ADDITIONAL BANDS etc., CHARGED EXTRA.

CHROME PLATING TO ORDER

THE NEW SUPERLIGHT

FOR TIME TRIALS and PURSUITING

All unnecessary ounces cut away and a new method of fitting seat stays to seat lugs, but leaving a perfectly rigid job that responds to every ounce of effort.

SPECIFICATION :
73° Head. 73° Seat.
10¾" Bottom Bracket Height.
1⅞" Oval or Round Forks (as preferred).
17" Chainstays.
Italia Head Fittings.
T.D.C. Continental Bottom Bracket Set.

FINISH : As 'King of Mercia' Models.
Campagnola Head Fittings are used at an extra charge [illegible]/-.

In Pursuit trim, total weight of machine using steel stem, steel cranks, 28 spoke sprints and silk tubs, can be got down to 16 lb. 12 oz.

For Time Trials with bell, brake and silk tubs, 17 lb. 8 oz.

The New Superlight

LUG DETAILS

The Lightest Frame built.
The Pursuiter's and Time Trialist's ideal.

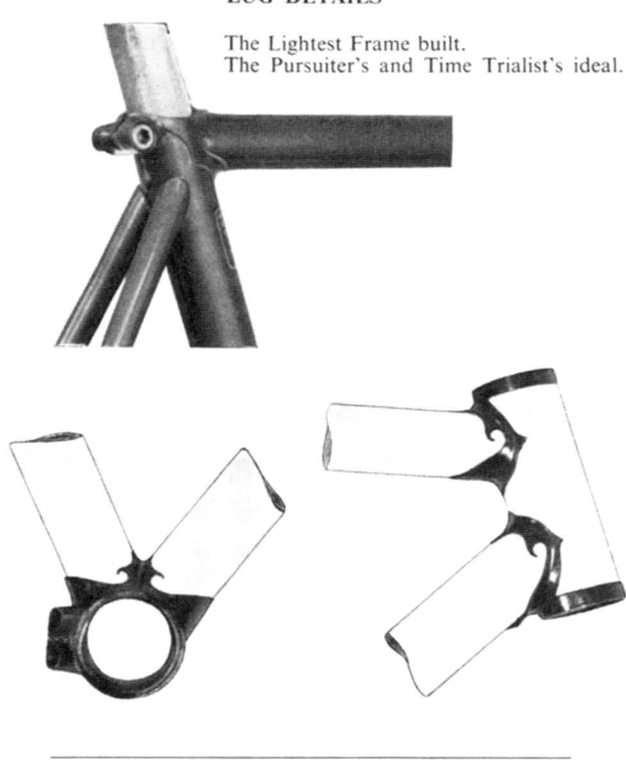

NEW SUPERLIGHT ROAD

FOR MASSED START and ROAD RACING

Built as a road frame, with Campag and all brazed-on fittings for those who prefer multiple gears.

THE CAMPIONISSIMO

Built with Nervex 'Serie Legere' Lug Sets, Reynolds '531' D.B. Tubing, Fork Blades, Seat and Chainstays, Dunlop H.P. Rims, Tyres and Tubes, Benelux Mark 7 Gears, Brooks B15 Saddle, Weinmann Q.R. Brakes, Williams C34 Chain Set, G.B. Bars and Stem.

FINISH : Any colour available with contrasting seat panel.

ADDITIONAL BANDS EXTRA

A good all round machine with only first class equipment used.

Specification : 72° Head, 72° Seat,
$2\frac{1}{8}$" Fork Rake,
$10\frac{5}{8}$" Bottom Bracket,
$17\frac{1}{2}$" Chainstay,
Brazed on Cable Eyes and Pump Pegs.
Lamp Boss fitted as standard.

Plain Rear Ends and no lever bosses to enable any Gear to be used.

5 Speed Benelux or Simplex	5 Speed Campag. or Simplex
10 ,, ,, ,, ,,	10 ,, ,, ,, ,,
Single Speed	

NO ALTERATIONS TO THE FRAME SPECIFICATION CAN BE ACCEPTED

Frame sizes: 21" — 24" only.

OLYMPIQUE ROAD FRAME

Built with Reynolds '531' D.B. Tubing, Fork Blades, Seat and Chainstays, and Nervex 'Serie Legere' Lugs.

Plain Dropouts and Gear Cable Eyes only, allowing choice of gear, etc.

FINISH : Any colour available with contrasting seat panel

ADDITIONAL BANDS EXTRA

T.D.C. Italia Head Set.
T.D.C. Continental Bottom Bracket Set.
Frame sizes 21" — 25" only.

Specification for Road Frame

21"—72° × 74°	21" T.T.	2¼" Fork Rake	17¼" C/Stays
22"—72° × 73°	21½" T.T.	2⅛" ,, ,,	17¼" ,,
23"—72° × 73°	22¼" T.T.	2⅛" ,, ,,	17¼" ,,
24"—72° × 73°	22¾" T.T.	2⅛" ,, ,,	17¼" ,,
25"—72° × 73°	23½" T.T.	2⅛" ,, ,,	17½" ,,

This Frame is designed solely for Road Racing and is fast, lively and handles perfectly at any speed, or on any surface.

NO ALTERATIONS TO THE FRAME SPECIFICATION CAN BE ACCEPTED

OLYMPIQUE TRACK FRAME

Standard Track Frame built for the Clubman, suitable for Track or Short Distance Time Trials.

Specification for Track Frame:

73° × 73°. 17" Chainstays. 10⅞" Bracket. Minimum clearance with 27" High Pressures.

ITALIAN STYLED SUPER VIGORELLI

Designed for fast short distance Time Trials and handles superbly on any hard track, and built with lugs designed to give increased rigidity to make a really responsive machine for the connoisseur.

SPECIFICATION :

73° Parallel
10¾" Bracket Height
1¾" Round Forks
16¾" Chainstays
Campagnola Head Set
Reinforced Track Ends
½" Wrapover Seat Stays
Prugnat Italian Lugs and Crowns

OR TO CUSTOMERS' OWN SPECIFICATION

ENAMELLED ANY COLOUR WITH CONTRASTING HEAD and SEAT TUBE PANEL

ADDITIONAL BANDS Etc., EXTRA

Chrome Plating extra

GUARANTEE :

We guarantee our frames for a period of 5 years against defect in material or workmanship.

W. Ball & Co., Printers, Rotherham

MERCIAN CYCLES LTD.

191 LONDON ROAD, DERBY

Telephone 46304

Trade enquiries: 2 Epsom Crescent, Derby. *Tel.* 46786.

PRICE LIST

1st SEPTEMBER, 1963

Prices subject to alteration without notice, but a month's notice will be given when possible.

Frames

	£	s.	d.
Super Vigorelli	17	8	0
Superlight Track	17	8	0
Superlight Campag.	18	18	0
Superlight Simplex	18	8	0
King of Mercia (Simplex or Plain Ends)	15	5	0
King of Mercia (Campag. ends)	16	5	0
Olympique Road	12	19	11
Olympique Track	13	5	0
Campionissimo	12	6	3

Complete Cycles
Campionissimo

Continued—

	Price			*P. Tax*			*Total*		
	£	s.	d.	£	s.	d.	£	s.	d.
5 Speed Benelux/Simplex	24	9	2 +	4	8	2 =	28	17	4
10 ,, ,, ,,	26	5	0 +	4	14	6 =	30	19	6
5 ,, Campag.	26	19	6 +	4	17	4 =	31	16	10
10 ,, ,,	30	1	3 +	5	8	6 =	35	9	9
Single Speed	21	9	5 +	4	0	4 =	25	9	9

MERCIAN CYCLES LTD.

191 LONDON ROAD, DERBY

Telephone 46304

1st SEPTEMBER 1963

Trade enquiries: 2 Epsom Crescent, Derby. *Tel.:* 46786

RENOVATIONS TO ANY MAKE OF FRAME

	£	s.	d.
Frame and Forks stove enamelled any colour	2	0	0
Frame and Forks Lustre or Metallic	2	2	6
Frame or Forks Flam or Silver	2	7	6
Coloured Head Tube		10	0
Coloured Band on Seat Tube		10	0
Extra Bands on Seat Tube ... each		2	6
Double Box Lining		15	0
Lugs Lined		12	6
Name and Club on Top Tube both sides		6	0
Small dents filled in where possible		2	6
Mask up and save chrome		2	6
Fork Crown, Front and Rear Ends, Front or Rear Dropouts ... each		2	6

Makers Transfers not supplied. We shall be pleased to fit these if supplied with order.

CHROME PLATING

	£	s.	d.
All Chrome Frame extra on price of Frame	4	0	0
Chrome Crown		10	6
Chrome Front Ends. Approx. 8″		12	6
Chrome Rear Ends. Approx. 8″	1	7	6
All Chrome Forks	1	7	6
Chrome Head Lugs	1	5	0
Chrome Front Dropouts		9	0
Chrome Rear Dropouts		15	6
All Chrome Seat and Chainstays	2	15	0
Chrome Seat and Chainstays to Bridge	2	10	0
Chrome Seat Tube Panel. Approx. 8″	1	0	0

Chrome Plating now accepted on Repairs and re-enamels but add 33⅓ per cent to above prices.

MERCIAN CYCLES LTD.

191 LONDON ROAD, DERBY
Telephone 46304

1st SEPTEMBER 1963

REPAIR CHARGES TO ANY MAKE OF FRAME

The prices include the use of '531' tubing, fork blades, seat or chainstays.

All frames to be completely stripped, no responsibility will be taken for fittings left in.

A charge of 4/- each will be made for stripping and reassembling head or Bottom Bracket fittings, including new bearings.

	£	s.	d.
New Bottom Bracket Shell	2	12	6
,, Top Tube	1	15	0
,, Down Tube	1	15	0
,, Seat Tube	1	17	6
,, Head Tube and Lugs	2	2	6
Top and Down Tube	3	5	0
New Top, Down, Head Tube and Lugs	4	5	0
1 pair Seat Stays including Mudguard Bridge	2	7	6
1 pair Chain Stays	2	5	0
1 pair Seat Stays and Dropouts	2	15	0
1 pair Chain Stays and Dropouts	2	15	0
Campag. or J.U.Y. 56 Ends extra		10	0
Complete new rear Triangle with Simplex, Benelux or Track Ends	4	12	6
Campag. or J.U.Y. 56 Ends extra		10	0
New Rear Dropouts only, Track Simplex or Benelux	1	12	6
Campag. or J.U.Y. 56 Ends	2	5	0
New Front Dropouts		16	6
New Campag. Front Dropouts	1	1	0
New Pair Forks	2	5	0
New Fork Blades with Dropouts	1	12	6
New Fork Blades with Campag. Dropouts	1	17	6
New Fork Column	1	1	0
New Pump Pegs, Brake or Gear Cable Stops, each		1	9
Simplex or Benelux Lever Boss		3	0
Campag. Gear Lever Boss		6	6
Campag. Gear Hanger brazed on		8	0
Mafac Criterium Brake Parts brazed on (supply own parts) per Brake		10	0
New reinforced Brake and Mudguard Bridge		8	6
New Bottom Bridge		5	6
Lamp Bracket Boss		2	6
Roller on Bottom Bracket		3	6
Tunnel on Bottom Bracket		3	0
Re Track Frame and Forks from		12	6
Re Track Forks from		7	6
Mafac Bridge on Seat Stay		7	6

PARAGON CYCLES

Andy Bone was born in the village of Skillington in Lincolnshire, on 10th October 1899, but when he was about seven he moved to Grantham. He joined the army in 1914 at the age of 15 years, and whilst serving in France he was shot in the arm and legs. On discharge he returned to Grantham, and was given a bicycle to help strengthen his legs.

He eventually got a job with Albert Oliver, a cycle manufacturer building Cromwell Cycles in Nottingham. He cycled from Grantham to Nottingham every day, a round trip of 48 miles, before eventually finding digs at Ockbrook, near Derby.

In the mid-1920's he became a founder member of the Grantham Road Club, and won their 50-mile Championship from 1924 to 1928. He also won the President's Cup for the 25-mile Championship from 1925 to 1927. These cups are still in the family's possession today. He also held the 12-hour record of 218.5 miles in the Notts. Castle Bicycle Club, as well as the Grantham Road Club record of 225.7 miles in 12 hours in 1928.

He borrowed £100 to start his own business on Alfreton Road in Nottingham, which opened on 10th February 1929. He moved to Heathcote Street near the centre of Nottingham for a short time, before moving to his final address at 18 - 20 Arkwright Street near the Midland Station in 1932. On 30th July 1947, he bought the freehold of 18 Arkwright Street and relinquished the tenancy of No.20.

In 1929 a tandem had been built and Andy and a friend did the Nottingham to London and back place-to-place ride in 17 hours 40 minutes, taking 3 hours and 20 minutes off the previous record. The 'Beamish' Dynamo kept blowing bulbs and at Barnet they had to purchase from a night watch man, a battery operated cycle lamp which he had on his bicycle. In the following years both the Nottingham to York and back and the Nottingham Skegness records were broken.

Just before Andy had opened his first shop in 1929, Noel Priestley, a fellow clubman, asked him if there was likely to be a job, as Noel worked at Rolls Royce in Derby, a 16-mile ride each way. He had been a couple of minutes late on one or two occasions due to punctures or headwinds and had been locked out and docked half a day's pay each time. Andy took him on as a temporary stopgap, but in fact Noel stayed on until 1975 when he was 64 and over four decades, Noel was to build most of the Paragon frame sets.

In the early days of Mercian of Derby, Mercian did not have enamelling facilities and Andy and Tom Crowther were good friends, so Mercian frames (who were at the time near the station in London Road, Derby) were put on the train and collected at the Midland Station in Nottingham. When the frames were completed they then made their return journey to Derby Station.

Andy was also a close friend of Claud Butler, who up to 1947, had his only shop outside of London at Greyfriar Gate, ¼ mile up the road from Andy.

Andy's son Desmond came into the business straight from school in 1955.

With the decline of the lightweight trade into the 1960's, Andy Bone had to diversify to survive, so lightweight motorcycles from the Continent and the Far East were sold, in addition to the cycle sales.

A major re-development scheme for the Meadows/Arkwright Street area was underway, and on 3rd February 1976 the doors closed for the last time, Nottingham City Council having carried out a compulsory purchase order.

Some 47 years after Andy had first opened up, his son Andrew Desmond Bone and Noel Priestley became redundant and Des started his own business at the top of Huntingdon Street on 3rd September 1975 selling motorcycles and accessories, becoming a Honda 5-star dealer. Noel joined Desmond at the Huntingdon Street premises until his retirement.

Riders who used Paragons in the early days included Ray Booty and Lloyd Binch. A small number of frames were made for another Nottingham shop under the Horace Rogers name.

At least three of the cards in the Players Cigarette Card Cycling Series were taken from models of the Paragon, including a Tandem, Track and Road Bike.

Frame numbers were stamped under the bottom bracket and it is believed that the first Paragon frame was numbered 101, but the earliest record we have is No.111 built in 1931, for which an original invoice still exists. This had a celluloid finish which was in vogue at that time.

Number 518 was one of the last built before the Second World War in 1939, and the next record we have after the war is frame no.1553 built around 1946, so a gap of 1,000 appears to have been bridged during the war years when building was at a standstill.

Frame No.1798, built in 1950, still retains its original but faded paintwork, and has been rebuilt by a V-CC member with an Osgear as fitted originally, and was featured in the November 2006 edition of 'Cycling Plus'.

Frame No.2249 built in April 1950 and still owned by the original purchaser Dave Drinkwater, has recently been re-enamelled in dark blue flam as original specification, but now has a 17" bottom gear. This machine has now covered over 120,000 miles.

The very last frame built was a 'Le Donington' model with Nervex Pro lugs, No.2289, in 1966 and it is still owned by a Nottingham CTC member, who had it renovated some years ago in black with gold lug lining.

PARAGON CYCLES

We have on the Paragon Register over 125 frame sets recorded, mainly with photographs. They have turned up in such places as Australia, New Zealand and North America.

I am indebted to Des Bone and Roger Spinks for their help in producing these notes.

Granville Horton

Catalogue Details
The 1937 Catalogue has a buff colour cover with red and black lettering, and was supplied by Granville Horton.

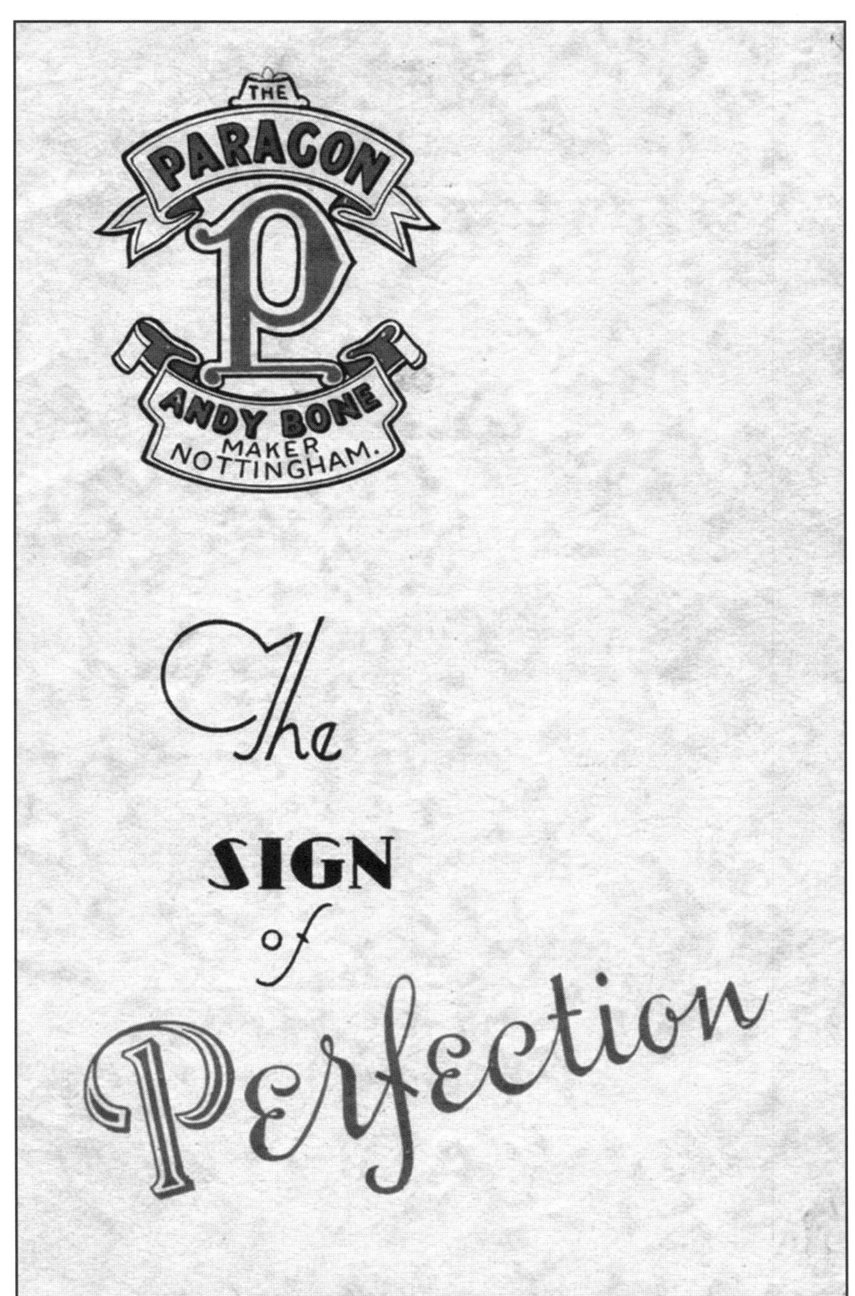

ANDY BONE

18-20, Arkwright Street,
NOTTINGHAM.
Phone 85392.

BUSINESS TERMS.

PRICES stated in this catalogue are for nett cash and a minimum deposit of £1 on frames and cycles, and £2 on tandems must be remitted with order, the balance of cash price to be remitted when the machine is ready for despatch.

ALL HIRE PURCHASE business is financed by myself, and customers are assured private and personal attention, and special rebates, which are printed on payment cards, are given to customers who settle their account before time stated.

CARRIAGE is paid to all parts of Great Britain to nearest railway station, and should any damage or loss occur in transit please notify the Railway Company and myself at once.

GUARANTEE.—All Paragon Cycles and Tandems are guaranteed for five years and a written guarantee is issued with every machine.

HOURS OF BUSINESS

MONDAY, TUESDAY AND WEDNESDAY : 8.30 a.m. to 8 p.m.

THURSDAY : Half-day, Close 1 o'clock.

FRIDAY : 8.30 a.m. to 8 p.m.

SATURDAY : 8.30 a.m. to 9 p.m.

INTRODUCTION.

THE popularity of PARAGON cycles and tandems has been increasing year by year. This is not surprising when they are compared with other machines of a similar price. The superiority and class is at once apparent. Look at the PARAGON and you will see what is meant by "superiority and class," the material, the workmanship, the finish and precision of assembly down to the smallest screw.

Reynold's High-Manganese and "531" alloy steel is used exclusively unless otherwise ordered. Chain and seat stays are all-round section of a special gauge and taper, these have more lateral rigidity and verticle resilience than oval, or "dee" section chain stays of equal weight.

All PARAGON frames are stage-built, that is, each joint is set and brazed separately. This method of building ensures that bottom-bracket and wheels are in perfect alignment. Lugs are cut out to beautiful but neat designs, and filed down to a reasonable thickness before brazing. This lightening before brazing process saves several minutes brazing time, thus eliminating possibility of burning the tubes. Frames built on these lines, with accurately mitred tube joints are absolutely superior in workmanship, as well as materials.

Special attention is given to the filing-up, and buffing of PARAGON frames, which are carefully scrutinised, and have to pass exacting tests before being passed for plating and enamelling. These tests ensure the accurate alignment of wheels, bracket, front and rear fork-ends, etc., thus riders will find no difficulty in centralising the rear wheel between chain and seat stays, which is a common fault with some makes.

All PARAGON frames and forks are hand-finished throughout, and although this is a more expensive method of production it is vastly superior to the mass produced article.

All enamelling, from glossy black, to the latest lustre, flamboyants, and "trick" finishes, are done on the premises, by an expert with the latest type spraying and stoving plant at his command.

Personal attention is given to all enquiries and orders. Instructions are carefully examined before building is commenced, and any feature that may prove detrimental to the design is first referred back to the customer for confirmation.

This catalogue is only intended as a guide to price, etc., and any model can be built up to your own specification, and I shall be pleased to quote you for any special requirement.

Any customer is welcomed to inspect his machine at any stage of its construction.

I assure you that your confidence will not be misplaced if you decide to entrust me with your order, my business has been built up on straight forward honest dealings, proved by the preponderance of PARAGON cycles sold in our own district, against all other makes.

All weights given in this catalogue are approximate according to specifications.

PHEON "A.M."

Weight, 3-Speed, 28 lbs.
Single Speed, 26 lbs.

SPECIFICATION.

FRAME	Any size to order. Reynold's High-Manganese butted tubing. Neat cut away, and tapered lugs. Brazed-on mudguard eyes, pump pegs, lamp bracket and chain rest, or to order. Tecalemit nipples to both head bearings and bottom bracket.
FRONT FORKS	"Dee" to round, round, gradual, or abrupt rake to order. Neat cut-out crown. Solid fork ends. Head clip fitting.
WHEELS	26ins. x 1¼ins. Dunlop Endrick chrome rims. British Hub Co.'s small-barrel front hub, and best quality black 15-17 gauge spokes. Carefully hand-built on the premises.
GEAR	The new Sturmey-Archer "A.M." (Medium Ratio) frictionless three-speed gear. Quote sprocket size, when ordering.
TYRES	North-British Rubber Co's black "Speedee" light racing.
CHAIN	Coventry ½in. x ⅛in. roller.
CHAIN WHEEL AND CRANKS	Williams' 3-pin detachable chrome 6½ins. cranks. Quote size of chain-wheel when ordering.
PEDALS	Brampton chrome rat-trap.
BARS AND STEM	Any pattern chrome bend to order, on 1in., 2in., or 3in. light steel extension.
SADDLE	Brooks' C32 on light steel straight chrome seat pin.
BRAKES	2 "A.B." Special side-pull chrome with waterproof cables.
MUDGUARDS	Bluemels "Featherweight" white or black celluloid Duplex fitting and quick release stays, etc.
FINISH	Any colour, best quality hard gloss enamel, on special rustproof base. Fork crown chromium plated.
EQUIPMENT	Bluemels white celluloid pump. Tecalemit oil gun, and reflector.

CASH PRICE (as illustrated) **WITH "A.M." 3-SPEED GEAR £8 15 0**

H.P. Terms : **£1** Deposit and 52 Weekly Payments of **3/6**—Total **£10 - 2 - 0**

CASH PRICE WITH SINGLE SPEED - - - - £7 7 0

H.P. Terms : **£1** Deposit and 52 Weekly Payments of **2/11**—Total **£8 - 11 - 8**

COMPLETE FRAME ONLY £4 0 0

PEERLESS

Pheon frame with slightly cheaper fittings—

CASH PRICE - - - - - - - £6 19 6

H.P. Terms : **10/-** Deposit and 52 Weekly Payments of **2/11**—Total **£8 - 1 - 8.**

POPULAR TOURIST

Weight as illustrated, 29½ lbs.

SPECIFICATION.

FRAME	Any size to order. Designed for pleasure riding and touring in any country. Built throughout in Reynolds Super H.M. butted steel tubing. Neat cut away and tapered lugs. Brazed on mudguard eyes, pump pegs, lamp bracket, chain rest, or to order. Tecalemit lubrication to both head lugs. Bracket fitted with oil retaining aluminium sleeve.
FORKS	Dee to round or ⅞in. round with full rake, or Reynolds Super Resilient, solid pattern fork ends. Head clip fittings.
WHEELS	26ins. x 1¼ins., or 1⅜ins. Dunlop chromium Endrick rims built on Perry Super hub brakes, 15-17 gauge spokes, or rim brakes if preferred.
GEAR	Cyclo Witmy 2-speed. Ratios fitted to choice.
TYRES	Dunlop and Sprite, Silver Sprite, Fort, Translucent, or to order.
CHAIN	Coventry best roller ½in. x ⅛in.
CHAIN WHEEL AND CRANKS	Williams C34 3-pin detachable chrome plated, 6½in. cranks or to order. Quote chain wheel size.
PEDALS	Brampton rat-trap or rubber.
BARS AND STEM	Any pattern bend on adjustable stem to choice fitted with Sponge rubber grips.
SADDLE	Brooks B66, B18, spring pattern, or to order.
BRAKES	Front and rear Perry Super brake hubs, or AB side-pull.
MUDGUARDS	Bluemels black or white celluloid, or to order, Duplex fitting with quick release stays.
FINISH	Best quality hard gloss black enamel on special rustproof base, or any colour to order. Chromium plated fork crown.
EQUIPMENT	Bluemels celluloid 15in. pump, reflector, Tecalemit oilgun.

CASH PRICE, WITMY 2-SPEED MODEL - - - £10 0 0

H.P. Terms : **£1** Deposit and 52 Weekly Payments of **4/1**—Total **£11 - 12 - 4**.

CASH PRICE, CYCLO OR STURMEY-ARCHER 3-SPEED £10 10 0

H.P. Terms : **£1** Deposit and 52 Weekly Payments of **4/4**—Total **£12 - 5 - 4**.

COMPLETE FRAME ONLY £4 0 0

SPECIAL PATH

Weight 18 lbs.

SPECIFICATION.

FRAME	Any size to order, built to specification with Reynolds Super "531" alloy steel tubing throughout. Chater Lea special fork ends with adjusters. Can be designed to individual requirements. Brazed on fittings to order. Bracket fitted with oil retaining sleeve. B.S.A. best quality fittings throughout.
FORKS	Special Path rake ⅞ins. round, Spearhead Crown, or to order.
WHEELS	Constrictor first choice rims, Solite wide flange race hubs, 15-17 gauge spokes, tied and soldered.
TYRES	Dunlop Path Tubulars to choice.
CHAIN	Coventry 1in. x 3/16in. block chain.
CHAIN WHEEL AND CRANKS	B.S.A. best quality 1in. x 3/16in. size to order.
PEDALS	B.S.A. best quality or to order.
BARS AND STEM	Any pattern on Major Taylor extension or to order.
SADDLE	Brooks Sprinter or Mansfield Ormond Sprinter on light H.M. pin.
FINISH	Any colour hard gloss enamel or A.B. lustre on special rustproof base, chromium plated crown and front and rear fork ends. Continental bands or club colours to order.

CASH PRICE WITH B.S.A. FITTINGS - - - £12 19 6

H.P. Terms : **£1** Deposit and 52 Weekly Payments of **5/5**—Total **£15 - 1 - 8.**

CASH PRICE, SPECIAL PATH A.B. FITTINGS - - £11 11 0

(As above specification but Williams chain wheel and cranks, A.B. head fittings, Webb solid centre pedals, etc.)

H.P. Terms : **£1** Deposit and 52 Weekly Payments of **4/9**—Total **£13 - 7 - 0.**

COMPLETE FRAME only B.S.A. Fittings £6 6 0 A.B. Fittings £5 5 0

LE DONINGTON

Weight as illustrated, 21½ lbs.

SPECIFICATION.

FRAME	Any size to order. Special design suitable for massed start and road events. Built to specification with Reynolds' Super "531" alloy steel tubing throughout. All lugs and crown individually hand-cut to special design, and specially filed to feather-edge. Brazed-on fittings to order. Tecalemit lubrication to both head bearings. Bracket fitted with Aluminium oilbath sleeve.
FRONT FORKS	Paris Brest D to round or oval to round with special Bastide pattern crowns, ⅝in. round pattern, or to order. Solid central pattern fork ends, head clip fittings.
WHEELS	Constrictor best quality reinforced sprint rims 26ins. or 27ins., built on British Hub Co.'s Airlight hubs (special derailleur pattern), 15-17 gauge spokes, tied and soldered.
GEAR	Simplex Professional Racing Derailleur, Cyclo Poly gear, Super Inax Derailleur, Osgear, etc., to choice. Gear ratios fitted to suit your individual requirements.
TYRES	Dunlop Nos. 3, 4, 5 or 6, Constrictor 50, or Tabucchi.
CHAIN	Reynold Elite roller, ½in. x ⅛in.
CHAIN WHEEL AND CRANKS	Simplex Durax, Thetic, or Williams' Dureel, 6½in., 6¾in., 7in. cranks, chromium plated, sizes to order.
PEDALS	Racing Duralumin 3¼ins. wide, or to order.
BARS AND STEM	Super Dura Pellissier, Aerts, Leducq, on 2in., 3in., 4in. AVA Duralumin stem, or to order. Grips or coloured tape.
SADDLE	Brooks B17 Flyer, Sprinter, or narrow, or Mansfield Hiduminium, Ormond, on Brooks new combination pillar.
BRAKES	Gloria or Bowden alloy brakes, front and rear, or Tabucchi alloy, or to order.
FINISH	Special cream hard gloss enamel with Sun Ray panels and lugs lined black, or any colour enamel or lustre with panel finish. Name panel on top tube. Chromium plated crown and front and rear fork ends.
EQUIPMENT	Spearpoint extension or Finn Super baffle (as illustrated), Bluemel pump, Tecalemit oilgun.

CASH PRICE (as illustrated) - - - - - **£15 15 0**

H.P. Terms : **£1** Deposit and 52 Weekly Payments of **6/8**—Total **£18 - 6 - 8.**

COMPLETE FRAME ONLY £6 6 0

SPECIAL ROAD-RACE

Weight as illustrated, 26 lbs.

FRAME	Any size and specification to order. Built throughout with Reynolds Super "531" alloy steel tubing. Special cut away to lugs and fork crown, which are specially filed to feather-edge. Brazed on mud-guard eyes, pump pegs, lamp bracket and chain rest, or to order. Tecalemit lubrication to both head bearings. Bracket fitted with oilbath sleeve.
FRONT FORKS	Paris Brest D to round, ⅝in. round, gradual or abrupt rake, to order. Spearhead cut away crown, solid central pattern fork ends, head clip fittings.
WHEELS	26in. x 1¼in. light steel Endrick rims, chromium plated, or Dunlop Special High Pressure rims 26in. or 27in., built on Solite Super hubs. 15-17 gauge spokes.
GEAR	Super Simplex, Osgear, Cyclo Ace with unit hub, or to order. Gear ratios fitted to suit your individual requirements.
TYRES	Dunlop Sprite, Silver Sprite, High Pressure Racing 26in. or 27in., or to order.
CHAIN	Renold Elite Roller ½in. x ⅛in.
CHAIN WHEEL AND CRANKS	Williams Super C1000 3-pin detachable 6½in. cranks, chromium plated. Quote size of chain wheel when ordering.
PEDALS	Solid centre Quill pattern, chromium plated, or to order.
BARS AND STEM	Chromium plated, Binda, Tour de France, Bailey, Anglo Continental, Highgate, or to order, on 1in., 2in., or 3in. light steel extension. Rubber Grips or Coloured Tape to choice.
SADDLE	Mansfield Hiduminium Ormond, Brooks Champion B17 range on Lightweight H.M. seat pillar or to order.
BRAKE	Special AB Lightweight side pull, Resilion Cantilever, or to order.
MUDGUARDS	Bluemels Noweight, white or black celluloid, Duplex fitting, with quick release stays, etc.
FINISH	Any colour best quality hard gloss enamel, AB Super Lustre, on special rustproof base, chromium plated crown and front and rear fork ends. Continental transfers, etc., to order.
EQUIPMENT	Bluemels celluloid 15in. pump, reflector, Tecalemit oilgun.

CASH PRICE, SINGLE SPEED MODEL - - - £10 10 0

H.P. Terms : **£1** Deposit and 52 Weekly Payments of **4/4**—Total **£12 - 5 - 4.**

CASH PRICE, 3-SPEED MODEL - - - - £12 12 0

H.P. Terms : **£1** Deposit and 52 Weekly Payments of **5/3**—Total **£14 - 13 - 0.**

COMPLETE FRAME ONLY £5 5 0

POPULAR CONTINENTAL

Weight, 3 Speed, 27 lbs. Single Speed, 25 lbs

SPECIFICATION.

FRAME	Anysize to order. Reynolds Super H.M. butted steel tubing throughout, neat cut away and tapered lugs. Brazed on mudguard eyes, pump pegs, lamp bracket and chain rest, or to order. Tecalemit lubricators to top and bottom head bearings. Bottom bracket fitted with special aluminium oil retaining sleeve.
FRONT FORKS	Paris Brest D to round, round, gradual or abrupt rake, neat cut away crown, solid central pattern fork ends, head clip fittings.
WHEELS	26in. x 1¼in. Dunlop Endrick chrome rims. British Hub Co's small barrel chromium plated racing hubs. Best quality black 15-17 gauge spokes. Carefully hand-built on the premises.
GEARS ON 3-SPEED MODEL	Super Simplex, Osgear, Sturmey-Archer AR ultra close ratio, or to order. Gear ratios to order.
TYRES	Dunlop Sprite, Silver Sprite, Speed, Translucent, etc.
CHAIN	Coventry best roller, ½in. x ⅛in.
CHAIN WHEEL AND CRANKS	Williams C34, 3-pin detachable, chrome, 6½in. cranks. Quote size of chain wheel, when ordering.
PEDALS	Brampton or Vitesse Chromium Racing rat-trap.
BARS AND STEM	Any pattern chrome bend to order, on 1in., 2in. or 3in. light steel extension.
SADDLE	Brooks Racing B15 on light steel chromium plated seat pin.
BRAKE	Front and rear AB special chromium side pull, with best waterproof cables, one brake only fitted on single speed model.
MUDGUARDS	Bluemels Featherweight white or black, Duplex special fitting with quick release stays.
FINISH	Any colour best quality hard gloss enamel or AB special lustre finish, on special rustproof base, front forks chromium plated all over.
EQUIPMENT	Bluemels 15in. celluloid pump, reflector, Tecalemit oil gun.

CASH PRICE, SINGLE SPEED MODEL - - - £8 5 0

H.P. Terms : **£1** Deposit and 52 Weekly Payments of **3/4**—Total **£9 - 13 - 4.**

CASH PRICE, 3-SPEED MODEL - - - - £10 0 0

H.P. Terms : **£1** Deposit and 52 Weekly Payments of **4/1**—Total **£11 - 12 - 4.**

COMPLETE FRAME ONLY £4 5 0

SPECIAL TANDEM.

SPECIFICATION.

FRAME	Size to order, upright racing design, built throughout with Reynolds Super H.M. or "531" tubing and lightweight fittings. All lugs hand cut to special design, and filed to feather-edge. Brazed on mudguard eyes, pump pegs, lamp bracket, chain rest, or to order. Double diamond, as illustrated, or central tube design to choice.
FRONT FORKS	D to round, oval to round, or to order.
WHEELS	26in. x 1¼in. or ⅜in. Dunlop chrome Endrick rims, built on specia Tandem hubs with 12-14 gauge spokes. Carefully hand-built.
GEAR	Sturmey-Archer, as illustrated, with hub brakes, Cyclo, Poly, Simplex, Tri Velox, or to order. Gear ratios to choice.
TYRES	Dunlop Special Tandem tyres, or to order.
CHAINS	Renold Elite roller ½in. x ⅛in.
CHAIN WHEEL AND CRANKS	Williams Special Tandem Set, chromium plated, detachable 3-pin chain wheels, 6½in. cranks.
PEDALS	Solid centre Quill pattern, or to order.
BARS AND STEMS	Any patterns to order on 2in. or 3in. special tandem extension, chromium plated.
SADDLES	Brooks B17 Champion, B17N, or to order.
BRAKES	Hub brakes, or Resilion cantilever, or to order.
MUDGUARDS	Bluemel's Noweight, black or white, special Duplex fitting, quick release stays.
FINISH	Any colour best quality hard gloss enamel or AB super lustre on special rustproof base, chromium plated crown and front and rear fork ends.
EQUIPMENT	Bluemels 15in. celluloid pump, reflector and Tecalemit oil gun.

CASH PRICE, WITH SPECIAL LIGHTWEIGHT FITTINGS £18 18 0

H.P. Terms : **£3** Deposit and 52 Weekly Payments of **7/3**—Total **£21 - 17 - 0.**

COMPLETE FRAME ONLY £10 10 0

CASH PRICE, POPULAR MODEL - - - - £16 19 6

Chromium plated Fork crown and fittings, B15 saddles, Brampton pedals, Cyclo or Sturmey-Archer gears, Featherweight guards, Renold chains, etc.

H.P. Terms : **£3** Deposit and 52 Weekly Payments of **6/5**—Total **£19 - 13 - 8.**

EXTRAS.

	£	s.	d.
Cycle Frame and Forks chromium plated all over (Special, Le Donington, Path)	1	5	0
Popular Model, chromium plated all over	1	7	6
Pheon Model chromium plated all over	1	10	0
Seat and Chain Stays chromium plated all over (Special, Le Donington, Path models)	0	10	0
Seat and Chain Stays chromium plated all over (Pheon and Popular models)	0	15	0
Tandem Frame and Forks chromium plated all over ...	2	10	0
Chromium plating Pheon Forks all over	0	5	0
Chromium plating Special, Le Donington, Path models, Forks all over	0	3	6
Chromium plating Rear Fork Ends of Pheon or Popular models	0	7	6
Chromium plating Head Tube and Lugs all models	0	5	0
AB Special Lustre Finish on Pheon models	0	5	0
Dunlop Special High Pressure Rims and Tyres on Popular models	0	5	0
Dunlop Special High Pressure Rims and Tyres on Pheon model	0	12	0
Cycle Frame built with taper tubes	0	5	0
Hiduminium Seat Pillar in place of light steel	0	2	6
Brooks B17 Champion saddles on Popular model	0	5	0

Any other alteration to specifications quoted on request.

Frame Repairs and Renovations to any make of Cycle or Tandem carried out on the premises at competitive prices for real high-class work.

Estimates sent free of charge.

Any make of Cycle or Tandem renovated as new. Estimates Free.

Special quotations to approved Cycle Traders.

GEAR TABLE.

Teeth on Chainwheel.	Teeth on rear Sprocket.	26-in. Steel.	26-in. Sprint.	27-in.
	12	92·7	90·9	94·1
	13	85·6	83·1	87·4
	14	79·5	77·2	81·0
	15	74·2	72·7	75·7
	16	69·5	67·5	70·8
42	17	65·4	63·6	66·7
	18	61·8	60·6	63·0
	19	58·0	56·8	59·6
	20	55·6	54·0	56·7
	21	53·0	51·9	54·0
	22	50·5	49·1	51·1
	12	97·1	94·4	99·0
	13	89·2	87·1	91·3
	14	83·2	80·9	84·8
	15	77·7	75·5	79·2
	16	72·8	70·8	74·2
44	17	68·5	66·6	69·8
	18	64·7	62·9	66·0
	19	61·3	59·6	62·5
	20	58·3	56·6	59·4
	21	55·5	53·9	56·4
	22	53·0	51·5	54·0
	12	101·6	98·7	103·5
	13	93·7	91·1	95·5
	14	87·0	84·6	88·7
	15	81·2	78·5	82·1
	16	76·1	74·0	77·6
46	17	71·7	69·6	73·0
	18	67·7	65·8	69·0
	19	64·1	62·3	65·4
	20	60·9	59·2	62·0
	21	58·0	56·4	59·1
	22	55·4	53·8	56·5
	12	106·0	103·0	108·0
	13	97·8	95·0	99·7
	14	90·8	88·2	92·5
	15	84·8	82·4	86·4
	16	79·5	77·2	81·0
48	17	74·8	72·8	76·2
	18	70·6	68·6	72·0
	19	66·9	65·0	68·2
	20	63·6	61·8	64·8
	21	60·5	58·8	61·3
	22	57·8	56·1	58·1

MAL REES

Maldwyn Claude Rees was born in 1909 in Chepstow and first became interested in cycling as a 17-year-old. Previously he had been a runner and rugby player and was a young man of good education, having attended Newport High School.

By his own account, his first cycling club was the Newport and Risca Wheelers (later Newport & District). He was a club rider and time triallist.

He moved to the South London area about 1930 and joined the Dale Park CC. During this period he worked for various companies within the cycle trade, including Holsworth, F W Evans and M G Selbach. He eventually settled in Hayes, West London where, in 1939, he was a founder member of the Middlesex Road Club along with Arch Harding, Jack Jackson and Tich Waller.

Mal Rees Cycles was founded in 1946 at 83 Coldharbour Lane, Hayes. The first shop manager was Alan Emery a member of the Middlesex Clarion and a strong advocate of the BLRC. V-CC member, Bill Foster, worked for Mal Rees in the late 40s and remembers his job included travelling to Hobbs of Barbican by train, collecting finished frames and, on his return to the shop, fixing the Mal Rees transfers.

In 1951 Ken Lingard joined the business as manager. During this period, frames were being built within the shop by Bill Perkins, known as Perky Bill, the main frame builder, assisted by Ron Rowlands. I have no knowledge of any catalogues or model types produced at this time and know of only two machines from the years 1949 to 1953. It was eventually decided, on safety grounds, that frame building should be discontinued at the shop – the working area was very restricted and the shed at the rear of the shop was being used for storage purposes.

In 1954 Ken Lingard negotiated contracts with Bill Hurlow whom he had known for some years and was already repairing frames for the business, and Wally Green. Bill Hurlow built Rameles using one of his own lug cutout designs (Amersham and Chalfont models) and Wally Green produced the competitively priced Chiltern model to combat Claud Butler and other cycle dealers' cheaper models. This machine was fitted with all-British equipment to keep the price as low as possible. The number of hand-built frames during the period Ken Lingard was involved with the business was quite low, Ken estimates an average of around fifteen a year, including the Chiltern model built by Wally Green.

The frame numbering system from 1952 onwards was a four or five digit number, mainly under the bottom bracket, but sometimes found on the rear drop-out. The number system is as follows:

1st digit = number of frame built that month
2nd digit (from October, 2nd & 3rd) = month
3rd and 4th (from October, 4th & 5th) = year
Example: Frame No: 3359 = third frame built in March 1959.

On the earlier models, up to 1955, the system was reversed.

A catalogue was produced using Johnny Helm's cartoons, for which he received a Rameles frame as payment, (Rameles is an anagram of Mal Rees). I have been informed that from this time on all the catalogues followed the same format and contained the same four models. Ken Lingard left Mal Rees in 1964, the shop still being situated at 83 Coldharbour Lane, Hayes.

In 1967, Mal Rees sold the business to work as a sports journalist and photographer, Malcolm & Sue Nichols took over and during their time moved the shop to 13 Coldharbour Lane, the old Co-op grocery. The shop ceased to exist during the 1980's.

Mal Rees died in 1983 and was cremated at the Breakspear Crematorium, Ruislip.

Peter Stray

Catalogue was provided by Peter Stray and is undated. It is very well produced and has a coloured cover.

MAL REES
CYCLES
83 COLDHARBOUR LANE, HAYES
MIDDLESEX · HAYES 2402

DESIGNED FOR MAL REES CYCLES BY GLENN STEWARD.
PRINTED BY DITCHLING PRESS LTD, HASSOCKS, SUSSEX.
BLOCKS BY WINGRAVE PROCESS ENGRAVING CO., LTD, NEW CROSS, S.E.15.
PHOTOGRAPHS BY MAL REES, ARTHUR WRIGHT AND COURTESY OF 'SPORTING CYCLIST'.
SPECIAL 'BAZ' CARTOON BY JOHNNY HELMS.
EXTRACT FROM 'CYCLING' BY COURTESY OF TEMPLE PRESS LTD, BOWLING GREEN LANE, E.C.1.

WITH THE ISSUE OF THIS CATALOGUE (PRICE SIXPENCE) PREVIOUS EDITIONS ARE CANCELLED.

dear Reader

I address myself to the experienced cyclist and the potential enthusiast alike, with 35 years of experience in the trade and sport to put at their disposal.

In these days, although it is possible to obtain a ready-made, factory built, imitation lightweight cycle using expensive components, there is still a great demand for the CRAFTSMAN-BUILT bicycle, one constructed of the finest materials available and individually designed for each and every customer.

For the real enthusiast, nothing but the best is good enough and it is just for these cyclists that we cater.

Our sport frowns on the use of racing and record breaking

successes (when done by amateurs) to advertise a brand of cycle or equipment, but we hope we may be forgiven if we point out that we have had the honour to provide bicycles and tricycles, built to specification for holders of National R.R.A. records, Competition records, Championships and to countless road and track 'stars'.

We would like to stress that every frameset is guaranteed to be of the highest standard obtainable, and that there is no special treatment meted out to fast men which is not available and provided for the newcomer acquiring his first real bicycle.

Sincerely Yours,
MAL C. REES

the Chiltern

A lively machine hand-built by cycle-enthusiast craftsmen from Reynolds '531' tubing with Nervex 'Continental' lugs to the angles most suited to the sizes of the frame and designed for use with multi gears.
Frame sizes: 19½" with 26" wheels. 21", 22", 23" or 24" with 27" wheels.
Wheels: Dunlop Sprite tyres and tubes fitted to Dunlop Special lightweight steel rims on Bayliss Wiley hubs for use with gears or fixed sprocket.
Chainset: Williams C.34 with detachable single or double 3/32" chainrings.
Gear: Benelux Mk. VII double roller.
Transmission: Benelux 5-speed freewheel with Brampton 3/32" chain.
Brakes: G.B. Coureur Plus Alloy with coloured cables to bare wire stops under top tube.
Handlebars: G.B. Hiduminium alloy 'Maes' or 'Olympic' 15/16" with G.B. alloy stem to suit frame size. Plastic handlebar tape to match colour scheme.
Saddle: Lycett L.15 Swallow (cutaway) with chromium-plated frame.
Pedals: Brampton No. 20 Racing pattern.
Mudguards: Dover or B & T to match colour scheme.
Finish: Any colour of glass-hard enamel or metallic lustre with contrasting seat panel. Lugs finely lined with contrasting colour.

The Chiltern 'Super 60'

This superb new model is fundamentally a counterpart of the well tried CHILTERN model but is provided with additional frame sizes of 22½" and 23½" and while most of the components are as used on the Chiltern the cycle is enhanced by the addition of the New Benelux 'Super 60' gear and the highly finished Weinmann 'Vainqueur 99', centre pull action brakes with quick release and lever hood rubbers.

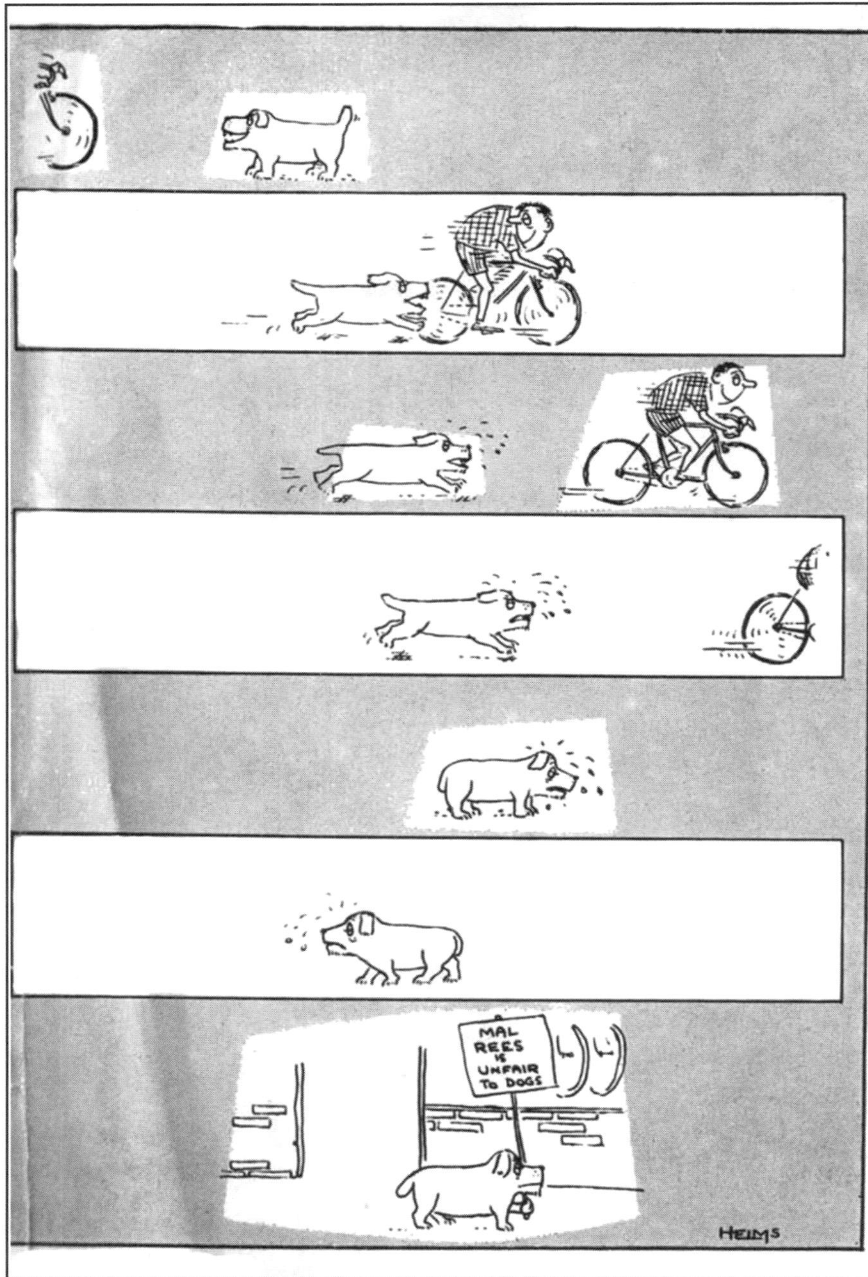

Pace Setting

It seemed an obvious choice to make when the new Mal Rees Chiltern Super 60 arrived at our office—I would put the machine through its paces in the range of hills from whence the bicycle obtained its name, the Chilterns. The Chiltern Hills are an 800ft. range north-west of London, stretching some 50 miles across the Home Counties. The northern boundary town is Dunstable, while to the south the boundaries are Reading and Windsor. Within these limits is a beautiful range of winding valleys, beech-woods and commons, pleasant farming country and new dwellings built by those daily refugee travellers from London offices. Bold routes like the A40 and A41 cut through it; narrow, grit-covered paths and tracks climb its ridges. Obviously the testing ground could not be more complete.

So it was with some anticipation of pleasure that I headed into the hills on the Chiltern Super 60. The bicycle did not fail me. Its performance ably matched the attraction of its namesake: it looks colourful like the countryside; but it is clean cut and serviceable like the trunk roads.

Let me emphasize that the bicycle is quite the liveliest I have tested for some time—it leaps away at the slightest suggestion of effort in the legs, climbs hills with an ease that amazed me and it descends, corners and stops with all the stability of a London bus. Although it has been designed and built with a more general market in mind, I would recommend it to the racing enthusiast. The embryo fast-man with his pedantic ideas on equipment might prefer other fittings than those provided but it would be an unnecessary choice: less mudguards and, as it stands the bicycle would be ready for time trialing or road racing.

The Benelux Super 60 gear which contributes to the name together with a 14-16-19-21-24 block and 46-tooth chainwheel provides ratios of 54, 61.7, 68.2, 81, and 94.5in. Recently introduced by the Cyclo Gear Company, it functions on the parallelogram principle—pull the lever back for bottom; push it forward for top.

I thoroughly enjoyed riding this bicycle, which weighs just 28lbs., and other staff men who rode it in a wide range of conditions and various spheres of our pastime enjoyed a stimulating experience.

Extract from CYCLING
Nimrod road test, the Chiltern Super 60

the Rameles

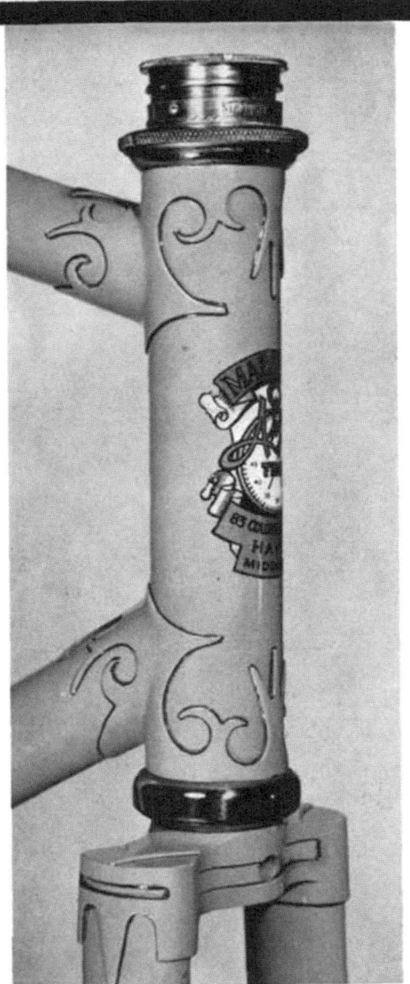

Distinctively designed and executed with all the care and precision which we lavish on our work, the hand-built, hand-cut-lugged Rameles has a new and unique cut-out which is at once graceful and very efficient. The elaborate and intricate pattern of the cut-out is not primarily with the purpose of saving weight, although of course it does; its object is to provide the longest feathered edged support for the tube.

To give an example, an uncut lug provides a support (lug to tube) of an amount equivalent to the circumference of the tube, and in such case the head tube of $1\frac{1}{4}''$ would have a lug edge of $3\frac{3}{4}''$ approx., but in the case of our Rameles cut-out the actual length of the lug to tube edge is in excess of 15″ which is an increase of efficiency of some FOUR TIMES.

We build with Reynolds '531' Butted tubing throughout, and to our customers' requirements; there is no standard specification for this model.

Front forks may be round or oval to round with a drop-forged crown of high grade steel. Chainstays Round/oval/round or to choice. Top seat stay eyes may be flat, fluted or may be wrapped over the top of the seat lug if so desired.

Finish in any shade of Glass-Hard Enamel, Metallic Lustre or Flamboyant finish with lugs picked out and contrasting seat panel to choice.

the Chalfont

The Chalfont model provides a neat, graceful and strong cut-away of the lugs which has become extremely popular in recent seasons.

The appearance though plainer than the Rameles set is is quite distinctive, is strong at all the vital points and is greatly enhanced when completed with the special care that we give to the final file-and-polish stage of production.

Built with Reynolds '531' alloy steel tubing by cycling-enthusiast craftsmen, tracked up constantly throughout each stage of production to produce a responsive frame which will retain its alignment no matter how great the stress imposed by an energetic rider.

Forks may be Round, or Oval to Round. Fork crown of High Grade Steel, drop forged. Ultra rigid rear triangle with chainstays in Round/oval/round and using ⅝in. or 9/16in. seatstays. Top eyes may be flat, fluted, or wrap-over as desired.

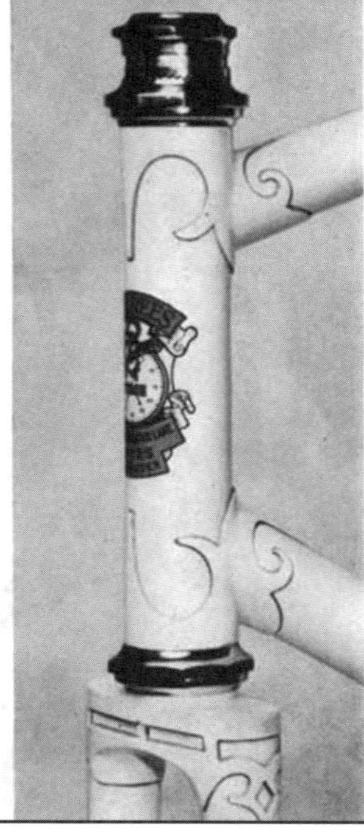

Any type of rear fork end, with or without gear hanging attachment (Campagnolo extra).

Any fittings brazed-on to customers' choice, pump pegs, gear cable channel, gear or brake cable stops or lamp bracket bosses.

the Amersham

The Amersham is a frame built to individual specification using a well filed, cleaned up version of the Nervex Professional Lug set. We would ask our readers to beware of copies of the Amersham model which use a similar set of lugs but which are in the main mass produced and 'cheap'.

Reynolds '531' double butted tubing.

Round forks or Oval to Round.

Fork crown of highest grade drop forged steel.

Rigid rear triangle using Round/oval/round chainstays and either ⅝" or 9/16" seat stays with flat, fluted or wrap-over top seat stay eyes.

All models have a reinforced, curved, rear seat bridge of special gauge tubing giving tremendous support for bolt fixing rear brakes. Any type of rear fork end may be used with or without gear hanging mechanism. Campagnolo ends however are extra. Brazed on fittings: pump pegs, gear cable channel, gear or brake cable stops, lamp bracket bosses, etc., to customers' choice.

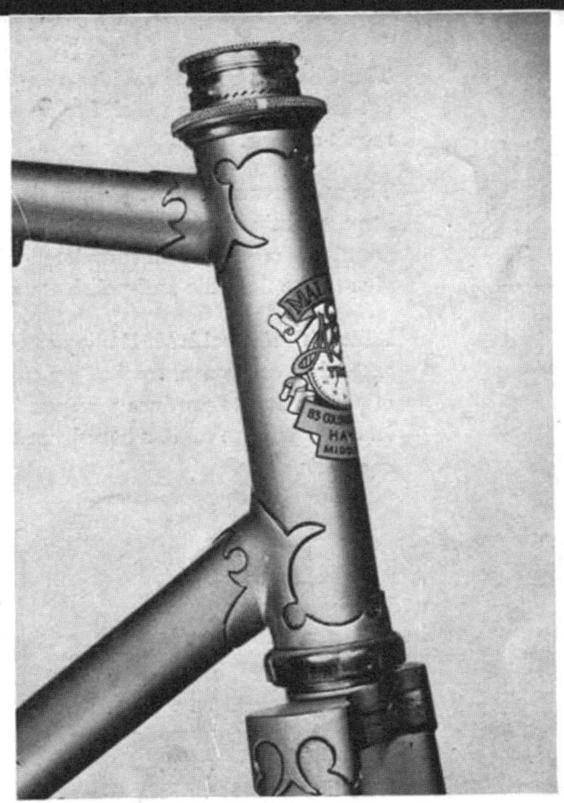

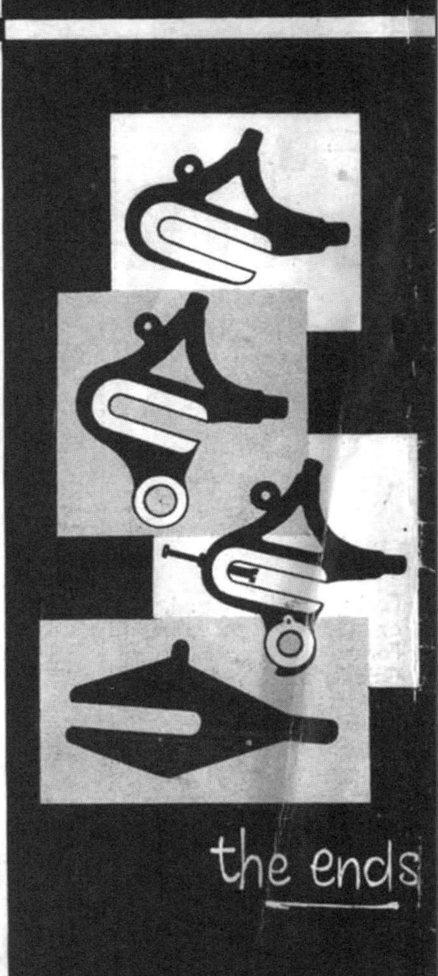

When ordering a new frame it is necessary to specify correctly the type of drop-out required. Illustrated on the right are four very popular types. The Agrati, without gear hanger, the Agrati-Simplex, for use only with Simplex gears, the Campagnolo, for Campag' users only, and last but not least the path-end made from 5/32in. steel plate with long slot for maximum chain adjustment.

SAXON CYCLE ENGINEERING COMPANY

The Saxon Cycle Engineering Company is today probably best known for their popular Twin-Tube lightweight bicycle, which was produced for only a few years towards the end of the Company's life. The twin tube was typical of the innovative designs that had come from Saxon since their beginning in the early 1920s.

The earliest advert for Saxon appeared in 'Cycling' on February 15th 1923 introducing the Saxon as 'tempered like a sword' and built to modern scientific engineering practices. Lightweight club machines, tandems, track racing bicycles and track racing tandems were offered, all made with BSA, Chater-Lea or Brampton fittings and Reynolds' butted tubes.

The address of the company was 123 Holloway Road, London N7. Not a lot is known about the people involved with the Saxon Company but it is thought that the company was founded in 1923 by S J Campaigne and a Mr Barnmore who had a connection with Bertrand Cycles. In the early adverts placed in various cycling publications and in catalogues, F W Kiddie, H H J Cadell and G B Chance were other names mentioned. S J Campaigne, born in Salford, Manchester on 22nd August 1885, had a good career in marine, refrigeration, agricultural, motor and electrical engineering and was an Associate Member of the Institution of Mechanical Engineers in 1922. It is not known if he had a cycling background and it seems he had left Saxons by 1929 because W J Bailey, the World track racing champion, had become chief engineer then.

Saxon put great emphasis of the process of manufacturing their bicycles. The frames were jig assembled, drilled and pinned and all joints in one particular spot were brazed simultaneously. The completed frames were then tempered as described in the 1924 catalogue "with the old method of brazing a frame the greater portion of the tubes remained cold whilst the lugs and ends of the tubes became red hot ... this leaves the frame hard and soft in places and renders it liable to snap or bend at these various points. This is practically impossible with the Saxon method, because the frame is raised to one uniform heat throughout and then passed through specially prepared oils which equalise the carbon in the steel, rendering in one perfect unit of temper".

The first Saxon lightweights had simple cut out lugs and a plain fork crown which was soon to be replaced with a fork crown with cut outs to match the frame. Frames were made from the Reynolds double butted tubes (19/22 gauge) with tapered rear stays brazed to the seat lugs. Models offered were the Clubman's Model "A" (and ladies sports model), and the Clubman's Model "C". These were all offered at £8.8s.0d and a Track Model, which could be specified with forward facing or ordinary slotted drop out, was £9.17s.6d (5 shillings extra if made to special measurements). The rear fork ends were either forward facing drop out Model A or the Model B which had the more familiar type slotted fork end and was favoured by those who prefer the old draw bolt method or hollow spindle hub" (Chater-Lea made a hub of this description as did Bastide who offered this type of hub before the First World War using a modified BSA hub).

Saxons made with BSA fittings throughout cost £12.0s.0d, if a Meredith hollow spindle hub was specified, it cost 5 shillings extra, with Chater-Lea fittings, the price was £11.12s.6d. Saxon also listed Tandems, including a double gents racing tandem at £24.10s.0d.

Saxon advocated the idea of having as small a bike as possible, a 21 – 22" frame being suggested as the optimum size for rigidity and lightness. The Little Low Lightweight Bicycle was available in black, purple, Indian red, dark green, Royal blue, light saxe blue or grey.

Saxon grew quickly and in November 1924 they opened their new head office and showroom at 190 Pentonville Road, Kings Cross, London, keeping the 123 Holloway Road site as their North London branch. In the same year, S J Campaigne introduced his patented Saxon Rigid Narrow Section Steel Rim in 26 x 1 1/4" or 26 x 1 3/8" and the Patent cone locking device for their hubs. The rim resembled the Westwood pattern, but the rolled over edges of the rim were brazed to the base, so making the rim solid.

The hub, which was milled from a single piece of steel, had its adjusting cone made with a serrated surface on which a serrated washer was locked on to it by a normal hub lock nut. This was designed to eliminate the problem of the cones becoming unadjusted in use. This hub, which won the CTC's Silver Plaque Award in 1926, was standard on all Saxon bicycles up to 1939.

1926 saw the introduction of "annular" bearings in hubs and the bottom bracket as a special option on offer at £3.10s.0d extra on the price of the bicycle. Ash lined forks were also introduced in the same year. The forks had a removable top plate of ash wood with a V cut out at the bottom end inserted into the top of each fork leg after they had been enamelled. This was instead of the usual practice of brazing a steel liner inside each fork leg, and it was thought that the ash liner was more resilient and good insurance against fork breakage. The unbreakable fork was improved in 1928 by having a steel liner fitted as well as the ash insert. Also in 1926 Saxon moved to their new works and showroom at 15 – 19 Arcola Street, E8. This was a large modern building and it still stands today and is used for small business units.

Saxon introduced their own centre pull brake and special lever in 1927 which was similar to the Bowden centre pull brake. The Saxon brake was offered on all models as front or rear, or both, as in the case of the Saxon all-weather bicycle which combined Bowden brakes with roller levers on the handlebars.

SAXON CYCLE ENGINEERING COMPANY

In 1928 Saxon acquired the ownership of Moon Cycle Company of 5 Stoke Newington Road, London, N16 and their branches at 68 Goldhawk Road, W12 and 58 Well Hall Road, SE9, which with 123 Holloway Road became Saxon showrooms where you could buy or order Saxon Bicycles and a large selection of cycling clothes, shoes and accessories. With the acquisition of Moon Cycle Company, Saxon introduced their Saxon Moon lightweight bicycle as a medium priced machine at £8.0s.0d. It had a fixed specification and could be bought in black, purple, pale blue or cane coloured enamel with plated fork ends and fork crown. Interestingly Saxon offered cadmium plating instead of the usual nickel plating offered by other cycle companies at that time. Saxon also offered a flamboyant finish on the Saxon Club and Saxon Super Club in amber, ruby, emerald or sapphire with plated fork ends or whole front fork plated, at £11.0s.0d or £11.10s.0d for the Super Club.

In 1929 W J Bailey, the world champion track racing cyclist joined Saxon as Works Manager and he introduced some very nice bicycles for Saxon's 1930 catalogue including the Saxon Deluxe and Saxon Bailey Path models. Both these bicycles were made from Chrome Molybdenum tubing which Saxon claimed in their 1930 catalogue was the first time that this new steel alloy had been used in cycle construction. The Saxon Bailey Path bicycle combined both head clip with expander bolt handlebar stem with lugs cut matching the frame and the front fork crown cut out design had a long centre tongue extending down the outside of the fork for about 3". It was a very popular machine with both track men and road time trialists during the 1930s.

The famous Saxon Bailey resilient fork, which was standard on the Club and De Luxe models, was introduced for the first time in this catalogue. They were made with "D" to round section tubing, tapering from 1" from the fork crown to the round section being the last 6" of the fork blade and the rake of the forks occurs in this last 6". They became the standard forks fitted to all Saxons, except the Track models. By now the Club model had smaller, less exaggerated rear drop outs, was still offered with double butted tubing, but was cheaper at £9.0s.0d and the Saxon Moon was discontinued, and in its place a Saxon Sports, made with double butted tubes, was sold at £8.0s.0d.

The 1931 Saxon catalogue saw the introduction of Saxon's Cotterless Steel Cranks which were made especially for them by Williams. The Cotterless cranks were very similar to modern cotterless chainsets except that the square ends on the modern chainsets bottom bracket axle were triangular on Saxons. They also offered cross over drive for tandems at 30/- and 12/6 for solos. In the same catalogue, The Saxon Rational Model makes its first appearance. This was a diamond framed racing bicycle made from double butted tubing for ladies who wanted a rigid gents lightweight bicycle but found that the standard gents frame had a reach that was too long for them and so it was built with a shorter top tube length of 20 3/8" and wheelbase of 40". It could be ordered with the Club model or De Luxe model specification. With the Club specification the cost was £9.0s.0d.

Saxon during the 1930s offered two low priced good value lightweight bicycles called The Saxon Magna at £6.19s.6d. and The Saxon Sports at £8.0s.0d, but in contrast introduced, in 1935, an expensive lightweight solo bicycle with an impressive specification. The Saxon Paramount was built with Chrome Molybdenum double butted tubing and lugs cut out in the same pattern as the De Luxe and Saxon Bailey Path Racer. It came with hollow octagonal steel cranks and conloy sprint rims and Saxon special lightweight hubs. It had Duralumin handlebars and brakes and an Ormond Duralumin framed saddle. Saxon offered their own make of three-speed derailleur gear that had a handlebar mounted twist grip control. Saxon claimed that you could change gear under sprint with this derailleur. The bicycle was priced at a staggering £17.17s.0d!

Saxon made a range of very good Tandems, marketed as The Wizard, Cyclone and Wings of the Wind. Double gents frames could be ordered with twin lateral stays from the head to rear dropouts, or with a single lateral stay or open double diamond and were priced from £16.16s.0d. A special track racing tandem was also offered with single lateral tube and supports in the rear triangle made from either Chrome Molybdenum or High Manganese steel tubing for £20.0s.0d. They offered a triplet and in 1933 a special Family tandem with twin lateral stays and rear top tube an inch lower than the front top tube. It had special brazed-on attachments for the sidecar it came with. Saxon also made a one-off quad for Dublin University.

In Autumn 1936, Saxon moved their factory to Sidney Road, Homerton, London, E9 and on 13th October, they filed for registration of the design for the Twin-Tube Tandem (No.815768). The solo and tandem twin-tube were introduced with a Twin-Tube Triplet in October 1937. The Twin-Tube solo had its own design registration filed on 17th February 1938 with its own number 826293. These bicycles, instead of having one normal seat tube in the frame, had two smaller diameter tubes running parallel from a special cast bottom bracket with two little cast lugs to the special seat cluster. The rear wheel ran very close to the twin tubes and the mudguard would fit between the two parallel tubes. This made for a very short wheel base on the solo at 38 1/2", the tandem at 59" and the triplet at 80" which made them quite distinctive and easily recognisable. The Super Wings of the Wind Twin-Tube Tandem was offered in Reynolds 531 for £21.0s.0d and the triplet, made with Chrome Molybdenum, for £24.0s.0d. The twin tube cro-mo tubing offered by Saxon was supplied by Accles & Pollock from Birmingham. The solo was offered as the Saxon T.T Model made with cro-mo tubing and Saxon resilient front forks and supplied with Dunlop HP rims on Saxon hubs, Constrictor Boa pedals and Brooks saddle at £9.10s.0d. The T.T Race Model was also offered with the same fittings but with Reynolds Hiduminium R.R56 handlebars and stem and New Ormond or Brooks Champion saddle on a 10" Hiduminium R.R56 seat pillar for £11.0s.0d.

The Path Model had straighter "D" to round forks in Chrome Molybdenum and rear track fork ends, Constrictor laminated wood rims on Saxon lightweight steel hubs, steel handlebars and stem with expander bolt and head clip, for £12.10s.0d. A Super Path Model was offered in either single or twin-tube which was claimed to weigh 17lbs 10oz and was made from Reynolds 531. It is not known if 531 was only used on the single tubed frame. It had hollow steel cranks, 27" Constrictor wood rims and was priced at £15.10s.0d. The Saxon Paramount became a twin-tube model in 1938, was still priced at £17.17s.0d but now had Gloria Duralumin calliper brakes and Hiduminium R.R56 handlebars and stem.

The Saxon Club Model, which was Saxon's first bicycle, went through a total re-design in 1938. It had the same new cut out cast malleable lugs as the Twin Tube and was made from Reynolds 531 double butted tubing throughout. It was fitted with Reynolds R.R56 handlebars and stem and seat pillar. The Saxon De Luxe was also re-designed in 1938 with the same lugs and made with Reynolds double butted tubing throughout, sharing the same specification as the Club model except that the De Luxe was fitted with a Cyclo 3-speed derailleur gear as standard and sold for £12.12s.0d. The Saxon Bailey Path Model remained unchanged in design, except that Reynolds 531 could be specified as an alternative to Accles & Pollock's Cro-mo tubing and was offered at £12.10s.0d. The diamond framed ladies bicycle, the Saxon Rational, became the Saxon Enchantress in 1938 and it was based on the cheaper Magna and Sports models instead of the Club and De Luxe models. In the same year Saxon introduced some cheaper roadster models. The Tourist Model had full chain case and cable brakes with North Road handlebars, was made from Accles & Pollock tubing and sold at £6.19s.6d. The Roadster Model with rod brakes and the Saxon Light Roadster with a 1" drop on the top tube to the head were both sold at £5.10s.0d.

In 1939, Sidney Road was re-named Kenworthy Road and at that time Saxon employed 5 or 6 frame makers, 1 fork maker and 5 filers and the total workforce, including the office, was about 34 – 35. They produced about 80 solo frames and 5 tandems a week. Three travelling salesmen were employed, one for Scotland, one for the Midlands and one for the South.

The frame numbering system for Saxon has not yet been deciphered, but a list of known machines and their numbers is given in the following table.

1920's		1930's		1930's	
Frame No	Model	Frame No	Model	Frame No	Model
51936	Club	69003	De Luxe	89867	Club
60597	Club	73778	Ladies	90827	Twin Tibe
65019	Club	76624	Sports	91181	Twin Tube
		78201	Club	92063	Twin Tube
		79059	Bailey Path	92148	Twin Tube Track
		79060	Bailey Path	92640	Twin Tube Tandem
		88719	Twin Tube Tandem		
		89453	Twin Tube Track		

Saxon closed in November 1939 for reasons that are unknown with H H J Cadell as sole director. The Kenworthy Road site was totally destroyed during a bombing raid in the Second World War, but the Holloway Road and Arcola Street sites still exist today.

After the war Claud Butler re-introduced the twin tube design because he had bought the Saxon name and was named as copyright owner of the twin tube designs on the Design Registration documents, but his twin tube differed greatly from the pre-war Saxon. Sometime in the 1950s, the Saxon trade mark was sold to Norman Cycles, of Ashford, Kent and they made some Saxon bicycles.

Ben Sharp

Catalogue dated 1938 and lent by Ben Sharp is printed in two colours

ON ROAD & TRACK IN 1938
SAXON
Lightweight Cycles

DESIGNED FOR MAL REES CYCLES BY GLENN STEWARD.
PRINTED BY DITCHLING PRESS LTD, HASSOCKS, SUSSEX.
BLOCKS BY WINGRAVE PROCESS ENGRAVING CO., LTD, NEW CROSS, S.E.15.
PHOTOGRAPHS BY MAL REES, ARTHUR WRIGHT AND COURTESY OF 'SPORTING CYCLIST'.
SPECIAL 'BAZ' CARTOON BY JOHNNY HELMS.
EXTRACT FROM 'CYCLING' BY COURTESY OF TEMPLE PRESS LTD, BOWLING GREEN LANE, E.C.1.

WITH THE ISSUE OF THIS CATALOGUE (PRICE SIXPENCE) PREVIOUS EDITIONS ARE CANCELLED.

The Coming Season

We offer you "On Road and Track in 1938" with pride and enthusiasm, believing that you, as a keen cyclist, will find it full of interest. It describes a range of handbuilt cycles which, we claim, are in advance of any yet produced—in the brilliance of their design, in the perfection of their workmanship and in the luxury of their finish and equipment.

In addition this little book includes features which give some very useful information on your favourite Sport. W. J. Bailey, four times champion of the World, offers you invaluable advice on the best methods of training, based on his experience of racing in all parts of the world. We also describe very briefly how a Saxon lightweight machine is built and give you a few tips on the upkeep of a cycle.

Photos by courtesy of "Cycling" and "The Cyclist."

We hope that you will find "just the machine you want" from amongst those described in these pages. There are models for every purpose—solos range in price from £6 19s. 6d. to £17 17s. od. Tandems cost £16 16s. od. and there is a special new Triplet model, very moderately priced at £24 0s. od. There are also two new Roadster machines at £5 10s. od. If you are already a Saxon enthusiast, we need not tell you of the skill and care which goes into the building of each machine, of their perfect balance and rigidity, or of their reputation for sweet-running and long service. If you have not yet had experience of a Saxon, we would say "ask a pal who rides one." He will tell you of the joy of owning a machine *built to an ideal* by master-craftsmen.

Whatever model you decide upon, you can be sure that it will help you to derive the maximum of pleasure from your cycling, and make 1938 the jolliest and most successful season you have ever had.

Built to an Ideal—by Master Craftsmen

The cast lug and the brazed joint are still the most satisfactory method of cycle construction. A mechanic brazing a frame.

In these days of mass-production and gigantic output, it is an inspiring and refreshing experience to visit the Saxon Works. Here you can see the World's finest lightweight Cycles being built *individually* by master-craftsmen.

The photographs on this page illustrate four stages in the production of a Saxon Cycle. There are no moving belts at the Saxon Works, with automatons whose sole job is to tighten nuts . . . the same nut, each time . . . as you saw in Charlie Chaplin's " Modern Times." The Saxon staff are *artists*, who work with unerring skill and meticulous care.

Let us imagine that your order has just been received at the office ; we will trace its progress through the works. Firstly, all the particulars of your order are tabulated on a sheet—the model you have chosen, the size of frame you need, its colour, and the fittings upon which you have decided. This sheet is handed to our Works Manager, himself an old track man ; he superintends the production of your machine throughout.

First comes the cutting of the tubes for the frame to the required length ; the tubes are of the finest steel, made by the foremost tube manufacturers in the country. The frame is then fitted together with the best quality cast lugs, which are cut out *in our own works* to our special design. The tube-ends are mitred, so that they meet *flush in the lug.* This " mitring " of the tubes not only gives additional strength to the frame, it also allows us to cut away a larger proportion of the lug, thereby saving weight. Every joint is then carefully brazed. This is important, it ensures the greatest possible margin against " stress " in the frame.

After the frame has been tested for the accuracy of its size and angles and subjected to a final critical examination by our Works Manager, it is sand-blasted, filed and polished to give it a perfectly smooth finish for the enamel. It is then placed in our special Bonderizing Plant which preserves it from rust for all time. Then it is enamelled the colour you have chosen or finished in Electric Bronze or Flamboyant styles if you have ordered one of these finishes.

The frame is next moved to the Assembling Rooms for the final stage. Wheels, guards, chain-wheel, pedals, chain, handlebars, saddle and brakes are fitted carefully and accurately. These are all of the highest quality and specially selected by us from a wide range of different makes.

Your machine is now complete, as perfect in every detail as we can make it—bearer of a name famous both on road and track . . . ready to give you *years* of easy, trouble-free riding.

This illustration exemplifies some of the care and skill which goes into the production of every SAXON cycle. Here is seen a partly constructed frame being checked on the Drawing Board to ensure the perfect truth of its angles.

We removed in the Autumn of 1936 to our present greatly improved premises. The space and light available to each of our skilled mechanics is clearly demonstrated.

Our aim is not to see how many machines we can turn out—but how well we can make each individual cycle. A skilled mechanic is erecting a Tandem.

Page 2

Page 3

Training Hints

BY W. J. Bailey

(Four times Champion of the World.)

AS there is no winter racing it is obviously not necessary to keep in perfect trim the whole year round. As long as regular riding is indulged in during the off months, such as to and from business or on Club runs, it should suffice to keep the legs sufficiently in trim, and if physical and deep breathing exercises are also carried out, then a fair state of fitness should be maintained.

It is advisable to start training early in January, putting in as much steady riding as possible during the month in order to strengthen up the legs for the season. Employ a gear that is neither too large nor too small, one that you can just feel, but at the same time get round without undue effort.

In February, begin to make the rides harder, assuring that one or two rides during the week are real lively ones. As Easter approaches you will find that the legs are beginning to tone up if you have been putting in the riding. The object now, should be more in the nature of acquiring speed, and even though a track may be available, the short days will in all probability not permit of it being utilised.

Therefore until the longer days arrive, training will still have to be carried out on the road, and it is preferable to do this on a small circuit if possible, so that pushing for any great distance against the wind is avoided. On the track one has to accustom the legs to an ever changing action—pushing firstly along one side against the wind, and on the other pedalling fast with it on the back. Therefore to bring conditions as near to this as possible then a small circuit is the solution.

Do not indulge in hill climbing as too much of this will react adversely on speed. Do your training in company with others, but do not ride flat out from the start, ride steadily, gradually working up the pace over 15 to 20 miles, so that it can be made nice and lively at the finish by doing bit and bit alternatively.

Reserve two days of the week for sprinting. This will have to be carried out on a quiet stretch of road of a known distance. If tubulars can be employed for this, so much the better, as a larger gear can accordingly be used, but not so large that it cannot be got round with ease. Take it in turns to lead out the sprints. Do not exceed three of these. Start from a given point and sprint "all out" to where it has been decided to finish, a distance not more than 250 yards, putting all you have into your effort. Let the one who wins the sprint start farther back in the "string" in the next sprint in order to extend him more. Do not stand about afterwards, but keep moving, as colds contracted at this period set you back considerably in your training.

Jumping should also be practiced, preferably in company with another rider so that progress can be noticed. Roll up to a given mark together with the feet strapped to the pedals, and then on a signal stamp on one pedal and pull up for all you are worth with the other alternatively until your feet begin to "rev." quickly, all the while holding your machine firmly to assure that you do not sway from side to side. The effort should only be for 75 to 100 yards, until you feel the legs moving. Do not overdo it, three or four jumps are sufficient.

When you can get on to the track, then do spins with other riders of 5 to 10 miles, starting at a moderate pace, riding lap and lap, gradually working up the pace towards the finish, making the last mile as fast as possible. If you have nobody to train with, then ride for—say 15 miles steadily, and then have a real good push over the last few laps. You will derive more benefit from this than trying to go "all out" by yourself for 5 miles. Furthermore you will be able to repeat it daily without any ill effects.

Cut down the work on two days in the week and indulge in sprints. When summer comes and it begins to get hot, then ease in the hard riding and concentrate on the "snappy" stuff.

FROM SATISFIED SAXON USERS

Durban, Natal, S.A. 21/7/37.

I shall be very glad if you will kindly send me a set of Saxon transfers. I am having my nine year old Saxon re-decorated. She's still going strong too, believe me. I have loaned this old "bus" to South African Champions and they've put up some times on it equal to those performed on new machines. In fact, I hold the record from Maritsburg to Durban (May 31st, 1935—56 miles in 2 hours 27 minutes). Over this course there are some of the worst hills in S.A.

Well, here's wishing you further success and thanking you in anticipation.—Yours sincerely.

Dundee, Angus. 24/2/37.

Would you please send me three transfers for my Magna, which I am doing up for the Spring.

I am proud of my machine, which was the only one in the Club two weeks ago. Now there are five, two Sports and three Magnas. **This is my third cycle since I started and it is by far the best.**

Dewsbury, Yorkshire. 12/6/37.

Ref. Saxon "Magna" No. 82633. I bought the above machine six weeks ago, since when I have had the opportunity of giving it a real test over our Yorkshire roads—and hills.

I would like to say how entirely satisfied I am with the machine, which is one of a series I have owned over the last 20 years. **It is by far the best cycle I have had,** and I am sure you will be glad to hear of the satisfaction it is giving.

Gorleston-on-Sea. 22/10/36.

Kindly send your Catalogue. **My 1928 Model is still going strong and good for some "thousands," yet!** I like to know of any improvements made.

Yours faithfully.

A WELL-KEPT MACHINE ADDS to the PLEASURE OF CYCLING :—

Many cyclists seem to think that a machine needs no attention and grumble when it lets them down "just at the wrong moment." Here are a few tips on how to keep your cycle in perfect running order :

- Oil your machine every two months or one thousand miles, whichever comes first.
- Go over all the nuts and bearings regularly and see that they are tight and properly adjusted. Brake levers are particularly liable to work loose through vibration. If a brake lever falls off the handlebars while you are riding the machine, it may cause a serious accident.
- Keep the tyres properly inflated.
- When you have been out in the rain, dry off the chromium plated parts with a soft duster or chamois leather. *It is a mistaken idea that chromium plating will not rust.*

Chingford, E.4. 10/6/37.

I feel it is my duty to say a few words in praise of your Short Wheelbase Tandem "The Wings of the Wind."

I have given it a real try-out—280 miles in two days. As a very fast Touring mount it is ideal. I found the steering very steady and the short-base takes the dreaded drag out of all hills.

Two fast comfortable positions can be obtained without that freakish frame distortion that other makers seem to delight in. It is as you claim a real Short Wheelbase scientifically obtained—a mount that one is proud to own!

Haynford, Norwich. 9/6/37.

I should like to add a word of praise for the performance of my Saxon "Club" model. I have had it for four years, and have used it for racing, touring and riding to and from business. **It's the liveliest cycle I have ridden** and everyone else who have ridden it say the same. I would not swop it for a new one of a different make, even now.

Guildford. 26/9/37.

I should be glad if you would let me have transfers to fix on my Saxon Cycle No. 64752 which I am repainting.

This Cycle has served me for 10 years hard cycle riding and is still as good as new mechanically.

Thanking you, Yours truly.

Strangford, Co. Down. 23/7/37.

I wish to acknowledge receipt of Saxon Path Frame and would like to thank you for your promptness, also for the fine job of work you have done. I have been riding another make during the past few weeks and **I find the liveliness and responsiveness of the Saxon really remarkable.**

I have won over one hundred prizes, including five Cups and the County Championship on my previous Saxon. — Yours sincerely.

4 *inventions* USEFULNESS- of OUTSTANDING -*introduced by Saxon....*

THE NEW TWIN-TUBE SHORT BASE FRAME

Registered Design No. 815768

This new Twin Tube Frame represents one of the greatest advances in cycle design in recent years. It allows for the unusually short wheel-bases of 38 in. for solo machines and 59 in. for Tandems, *without cramping the position of the rider or affecting the balance or steering of the machine.*

As you will see from the two photographs, the usual single seat tube is replaced by TWO parallel tubes. The rear wheel is moved up so that it runs between *these two tubes* thereby saving as much as 3½ in. on the wheelbase of a solo machine.

This frame is based on really sound Engineering principles and has proved its worth on road and track. It was included in our programme for the first time last season, on the "Wings of the Wind" Tandem. One of the leading cycling journals wrote of this model : *"It represents a great advance in Tandem frame design. Probably nothing just as unusual on "twicer" frames has been put on the market in the last ten years."*

Encouraged by its success Saxon Designers have adapted this frame for solo machines. Three models include it in their specifications — the Twin-Tube Road Race model (Page 11), the Twin-Tube Path model (Page 13), and the Paramount model (Page 16).

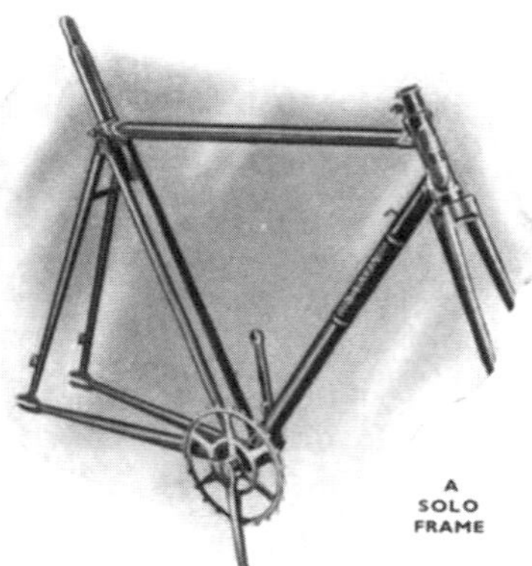

A SOLO FRAME

THE TANDEM FRAME

THE SAXON CONE-LOCKING DEVICE

Winner of the C.T.C. Plaque

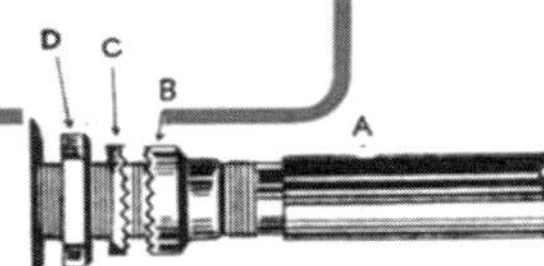

One of the simplest yet most efficient labour-saving devices ever invented for the benefit of the Cyclist. It permits of the finest adjustment of bearings and banishes cone trouble for ever.

As will be readily understood from the diagram, the finest adjustment is possible with these cones. A novice can adjust by hand to within 1/650th part of an inch, which is not possible with any other type of hub on the market. If properly adjusted you will experience no further trouble with moving cones or fitted cups and cones.

A SPINDLE.

B Adjustable cone with serrations on the face.

C Serrated washer. This slides along the two flats on the spindle and its teeth or serrations engage in the corresponding serrations on the cone.

D Nut which screws along spindle and engages up against "C," so that neither "C" nor "D" can under any circumstances move one way or the other.

THE SAXON OIL-BATH BOTTOM BRACKET

A simple yet unique invention. An aluminium sleeve is inserted in the bottom bracket, completely sealing axle and bearings : in this a Tecalemit nipple is fitted, so that when the cylinder is packed with grease or oil, the bearings and axles are continuously running in an oil bath.

THE WORLD-FAMOUS "SAXON" RESILIENT FRONT FORKS

These Forks were introduced by "SAXON" in 1929 and were the first Resilient Front Forks ever made. Most other firms now fit "Resilient" forks, but those made by "SAXON" remain supreme. They have just the right amount of resilience, plus immense rigidity and strength.

All "SAXON" models, with the exception of the two Path models, are fitted with these Forks. They add immeasurably to the pleasure of cycling, absorbing all shock and making rough roads smooth. They are ONE REASON why "SAXON" Cycles are such a joy to ride.

£6 . 19 . 6 CASH

EASY PAYMENT TERMS
10/- Deposit and
64 weekly payments of **2/6**.

SAXON "POPULAR" MODEL

An ideal machine for the young rider who wants an inexpensive lightweight cycle. It is individually handbuilt—like our most expensive machines, and will stand up to *years* of hard, intensive riding.

SPECIFICATION

FRAME. Accles and Pollock tubing, upright design, 41½ in. wheelbase. Finest pressed steel cut-out lugs and taper seat and chain stays. Rear stays brazed to side of seat lug. Forward drop-out fork ends. Pump pegs, cable guides, etc., brazed-on to frame. Cotterless type bracket fitted with "SAXON" aluminium Oil Bath (see page 7).

FRONT FORKS. The world-renowned "SAXON" Resilient Front Forks (see page 7), with best quality butted blade and detachable lamp-bracket on brazed-on boss. Straight or any make of blades to special order ; no extra.

HUBS. "SAXON" Light Racing Double Cog. Free-wheel 2/- extra.

RIMS. Endrick 26 x 1¼ in., chromium plated.

TYRES. Palmer Sports, 26 x 1¼ in.

CHAINWHEEL AND CRANKS. Williams.

MUDGUARDS. "SAXON" celluloid, black with white panel, or white, and built-in reflector, made by Bluemels. "SAXON" fittings and spring clips, fitted to brazed-on eyelets on rear stays and front forks with quick release wing nuts.

BRAKE. Rear calliper brake, chromium plated.

HANDLEBARS. Black Celluloid covered Shallow Highgate.

SADDLE. Brooks B.22.

EQUIPMENT. "SAXON" 1938 Large Touring Bag, Bluemels' Pump and Reflector.

FINISH. Best Black Enamel with Blue Head. Rims, Crown Plate and usual bright parts chromium plated. Lustre finishes in Ruby, Green, Blue or Silver, 12/6d. extra.

For extra cost of fitting Gears, see page 24.

SAXON "MAGNA" MODEL

The 1938 edition of the most famous moderate-priced Saxon model. Handbuilt throughout, fully equipped and smartly finished, it is the machine *par excellence* for the young clubman. There are many ten-year-old "Magnas" on the road to-day, which are running as sweetly as when they were new.

SPECIFICATION

FRAME. Upright design—41½ in. wheelbase. Accles and Pollock tubing. Malleable cast lugs, straight tapered rear and chain stays : rear stays brazed to side of seat lug. Forward drop-out fork ends. Mudguard eyes and pump pegs brazed to frame. Cotterless type bracket fitted with "SAXON" Aluminium Oil Bath.

FRONT FORKS. The Renowned "SAXON" Resilient front forks with best quality butted blade and detachable lamp bracket on brazed-on boss. Fork ends finished in "SAXON" quality Chromium Plate as illustrated. Straight or any rake of blades to special order. No extra.

HUB. Special "SAXON" all British Racing Double Cog, with thin barrels and chrome steel cones. Locknuts to both hubs with wing nuts and two fixed cogs. Chromium finish. Freewheel 2/- extra.

RIMS. Endrick's 26 x 1¼ in., Chrome.

TYRES. Palmer Sports.

PEDALS. Tubular Light Racing, Chrome finish.

CRANKS. Williams' 6½ in. with 46 x ½ x ⅛in. 5-pin chain wheel. Chromium finish.

MUDGUARDS. Bluemels' "Noweight" duplex, black with white panel, or white, with built-in reflector. "SAXON" fittings and spring clips, fitted to brazed-on eyelets on rear stays and front forks with quick release wingnuts.

EQUIPMENT. "SAXON" 1938 large Touring Bag. Bluemels' Pump (white) and Prismatic Reflector.

BRAKES. Calliper, front and rear.

HANDLEBARS. Shallow Highgate Bends, Chromium Plated.

GRIPS. "SAXON" Sponge.

CHAIN. Renolds'.

SADDLE. "SAXON" or Brooks' B.11.

FINISH. Enamelled in Brilliant Black with Silver Head, Front Fork Ends and all bright parts Chromium Plated, including Bars. Rims Chromium Plated. Flamboyant on nickel box, **12/6** extra. Cellulose colour to choice, **5/-** extra. Silver finish, **9/-** extra.

For extra cost of fitting Gears, see page 24.

£7 . 15 . 0 CASH

EASY PAYMENT TERMS
10/- Deposit and
73 weekly payments of **2/6**.

SAXON "SPORTS" MODEL

One of the most popular of last season's models, and this year its specification has been made still more attractive. Chromium Plated spokes give it an especially smart finish. The "Sports" is a perfect combination of honest workmanship and "good looks."

SPECIFICATION

FRAME. Accles and Pollock tubing. Upright Design, Malleable Cast Lugs. 41½ in. Wheelbase, straight tapered rear and chain stays, forward drop-out fork ends. Mudguard eyes and pump pegs brazed to frame. Cotterless type bracket fitted with "SAXON" Aluminium Oil Bath. "SAXON" Resilient front forks with Chromium Plated front fork ends. Detachable lamp bracket on brazed-on boss. Tecalemit oiling.

HUBS. Special Racing double cog, one fixed and one free, with thin barrels and chrome steel cones, and "SAXON" cone locking device (see page 7). Lock nuts to both hubs with wing nuts and two fixed cogs.

RIMS. Endrick, 26 x 1¼. Rims and Spokes Chromium Plated.

TYRES. Dunlop Sprite.

PEDALS. Brampton Racing.

CRANKS. Williams' C'34 6½ in. with 3-point 46 x ½ x ⅛ chain wheel.

BRAKES. Two Monitor Super cam.

MUDGUARDS. Bluemels' "Noweight" Black with White Panel, or White. Stays fitted to frame with easily detachable wing nuts. Built-in Reflector on rearguard.

HANDLEBARS. Shallow Highgate, or Continental, Chromium Plated.

GRIPS. "SAXON" Sponge Rubber. Black or Red.

CHAIN. Renolds.

SADDLE. "SAXON" Famous Racing Saddle. The best racing saddle on the road; or Brooks' "B.15."

FINISH. Best Black Enamel with Rims, Spokes, Front Fork Ends, Fork Crown, Bars, and usual bright parts Chromium Plated. Flamboyant on nickel base, 12/6 extra. Cellulose Finish, 5/- extra. Silver finish, 9/- extra.

EQUIPMENT. Bluemels' Pump, Rear Reflector, Tecalemit Oil Gun and "SAXON" 1938 Large Touring Bag.

For extra cost of fitting Gears, see page 24.

£8 . 10 . 0 CASH

EASY PAYMENT TERMS
12/6 Deposit and
64 weekly payments of 3/-.

£9 . 10 . 0 CASH

EASY PAYMENT TERMS
£1 Deposit and
14 Monthly payments of 15/-.

"T.T. ROAD RACE" MODEL

This model promises to be one of the outstanding machines of 1938. It incorporates our New registered Twin-Tube frame (see page 6), which allows for a wheelbase of 38½ in. *without straightening up the head or affecting the steering.* It weighs under 25 lbs. and is smartly finished in Delf Blue with red, white and blue bands on down tubes. Here is a real high class racing machine, most inexpensively priced.

SPECIFICATION

FRAME. Chrome Molybdenum tubing, with our special TWIN-TUBE frame (Registered Design No. 815768), the greatest advance in cycle design within recent years, allowing a 38½ in. wheelbase. New type cut-out and filed lugs. Tecalemit Oiling.

FRONT FORKS. The famous "SAXON" Resilient Front Forks (see page 7), with best quality butted blade.

HUBS. "SAXON" De Luxe Double Cog.

RIMS. Dunlop high pressure, 26 x 1¼, Chromium Plated. Spokes Chromium Plated.

TYRES. Dunlop high pressure.

PEDALS. Constrictor Boa.

CRANKS. Williams' C.1000 chainwheel and cranks.

MUDGUARDS. Bluemels' Lightweight transparent.

BRAKE. Calliper, front or rear.

HANDLEBARS. Bailey, Chromium Plated.

GRIPS. Special Blue Flexible celluloid handlebar sleeves to match frame (as illustrated), or John Bull sleeves.

CHAIN. Renolds.

SADDLE. "SAXON" or Brooks' B.11.

EQUIPMENT. Bluemels' Pump and Reflector.

FINISH. Delf Blue Cellulose, with red, white and blue bands on Down Tubes, and red Head. Head Lugs, Crown, Handlebars and usual bright parts Chromium Plated.

27 in. Wheels and "10-Spot" Brake, 2 6d. extra.

For extra cost of fitting Gears, see page 24.

£10 . 10 . 0 CASH

EASY PAYMENT TERMS
£1 Deposit and
15 Monthly payments of **15/6.**

SAXON "CLUB" MODEL

Ideally suited for those who need a machine which they can use for club riding *and* road racing. Its tubing and fittings have been specially selected for their lightness and strength. More races are won on "SAXONS" than on most other makes put together.

SPECIFICATION

FRAME. "531" tubing, upright design with new type cut-out and filed lugs. 41½ in. wheelbase. Tapered chain and rear stays, rear stays brazed to seat lug. Forward drop-out fork ends. Mudguard and reflector eyes, pump pegs, chain rest and brake cable guides brazed on. Tecalemit Oiling.

FRONT FORKS. "SAXON" Resilient Forks (read Article on page 7), built with best quality blades, small crown, and with solid steel fork ends. Brazed on mudguard eyes and detachable lamp bracket if required.

BOTTOM BRACKET. Cotterless, fitted with "SAXON" Aluminium Oil Bath.

WHEELS. Dunlop special lightweight rims, Chromium Plated. Spokes, Chromium Plated. "SAXON" De Luxe Double Cog hubs with Cone Locking Device.

TYRES. Dunlop High Pressure.

CHAIN. Renolds'.

CRANKS. Williams' C.1000 chain wheel and cranks.

PEDALS. Constrictor Boa, Chromium Plated.

SADDLE. "SAXON" or Brooks' B.15 on 10 in. Hiduminium R.R.56 seat pillar.

HANDLEBARS. Renolds' Hiduminium R.R.56, Continental, Highgate, or Bailey patterns, on 2 in. extension.

GRIPS. "SAXON" or Constrictor Sponge Rubber.

BRAKE. Resilion Cantilever, front or rear.

MUDGUARDS. Bluemels' "Noweight", black with white panel, or white. Built-in reflector. Spring clips fitted instead of straps, and stays fitted to frame with easily detachable wing nut fastening.

EQUIPMENT. Tecalemit Oil Gun, Bluemels' Pump, Prismatic Reflector.

FINISH. Cellulose colour to choice, or best quality black enamel with Chromium Plated Head Lugs, Crown, Front and Rear Fork Ends and usual bright parts.

Sturmey-Archer A.R. 3-speed **24**/- extra. Other Gears—see page 24.

TWIN-TUBE PATH MODEL

Another model with our new registered Twin Tube frame (see article on page 6). Here is an ideal Track machine—where lightness, strength and rigidity are combined in perfect proportion. The fittings are of luxury standard and it is finished in smart Delf Blue, with red, white and blue bands on down tube.

SPECIFICATION

FRAME. Chrome Molybdenum tubing, upright design, with our special TWIN TUBE Frame (Registered Design No. 815768) allowing a 38 in. wheelbase. New type cut-out and filed lugs. Tecalemit Oiling.

FRONT FORKS. "SAXON" Path, "D" to round blades, specially drawn from Chrome Molybdenum tubing.

HUBS. "SAXON" De Luxe single cog.

RIMS. Constrictor wood.

TYRES. Constrictor No. 2 grass, or No. 1 thread.

PEDALS. Constrictor Boa.

CRANKS. Williams' C.1000 Chain wheel and cranks.

HANDLEBARS. Bailey, Chromium Plated, with "Kromo" extension.

GRIPS. John Bull sleeve.

CHAIN. Renolds' block chain, 3/16 x 1 in.

SADDLE. Brooks' sprint.

FINISH. Delf blue Cellulose with red, white and blue bands on Down Tube, and red Head. Handlebars, Head Lugs, Fork Crown and usual bright parts Chromium Plated.

£12 . 10 . 0 CASH

EASY PAYMENT TERMS
£1 . 5 . 0 Deposit and
14 Monthly payments of **18/9.**

SAXON "DE LUXE" MODEL

A real luxury model which will appeal to the Connoisseur. Note its generous specification. This machine is finished in the colour of your choice, in Electric Bronze or Flamboyant styles. A machine you will be proud to own—NOW, *and in ten years time.*

SPECIFICATION

FRAME. "531" Tubing, upright design with new type cut-out and filed lugs, 41½ in. wheelbase. Superb tapered chain and rear stays. Rear stays brazed to sides of seat lug. Tecalemit Oiling. The following parts brazed on frame: Mudguard eyes, pump pegs, chain rest, and brake cable guides.

FRONT FORKS. "SAXON" Resilient Front Forks (read Article on page 7), "D" to round, with special solid fork ends, quick release, detachable lamp bracket if desired. Front and rear fork ends, Chromium Plated.

BRACKET. Cotterless type, fitted with "SAXON" Aluminium Oil Bath.

RIMS. Dunlop High Pressure, Chromium Plated.

HUBS. Front, "SAXON" De Luxe; rear, Cyclo. Fitted with our cone locking device which was awarded the C.T.C. Plaque (see page 7).

GEARS. Cyclo three-speed.

HANDLEBARS. Renolds' Hiduminium R.R.56, Continental, Highgate or Bailey patterns, on 2 in. extension.

TYRES. Dunlop High Pressure.

SADDLES. Brooks' B.17 on 10 in. Hiduminium R.R.56, seat pillar.

BRAKES. Monitor Super cam, front and rear.

CHAIN. Renolds.

GRIPS. "SAXON" Sponge Rubber.

PEDALS. Constrictor Boa, Chromium Plated.

MUDGUARDS. Bluemels' "Noweight" white, or black with white panel. Built-in reflector.

CRANKS. Williams' C.1000 chain wheel and cranks.

EQUIPMENT. Bluemels' Pump, Prismatic Reflector and Tecalemit Oil Gun.

FINISH. "SAXON" Electric Bronze, or Flamboyant. Colour to choice. Usual bright parts Chromium finish. Chromium Plated Front and Rear Fork Ends, Head Lugs, Rims and Crown.

£12 . 12 . 0 CASH

EASY PAYMENT TERMS
£1 . 5 . 6 Deposit and
14 Monthly payments of 19/-.

Page 14

£12 . 10 . 0 CASH

EASY PAYMENT TERMS
£1 . 5 . 0 Deposit and
14 Monthly payments of 18/9.

SAXON-BAILEY PATH MODEL

This machine is designed *for speed* by W. J. Bailey—four times champion of the World. All the knowledge and experience of England's greatest rider is reflected in its build and specification. It is unusually responsive—a machine which will *help* you to win.

SPECIFICATION

FRAME. W. J. Bailey's upright design, Chrome Molybdenum Tubes, Malleable lugs *beautifully cut out.* Solid rear ends with adjusters. Size to order.

FRONT FORKS. "SAXON" Path, "D" to round blades, specially drawn from Chrome Molybdenum tubing.

WHEELS. 27 in. "SAXON" Light Steel De Luxe Hubs. Constrictor round reinforced Wood Rims.

TYRES. Constrictor No. 2 Grass Cotton or No. 1 Thread.

PEDALS. B.S.A. Boa.

SADDLE. Brooks' Sprinter or Mansfield New Ormonde.

CHAIN. Renolds' 3/16 in. or 1/8 in. Block.

CHAINWHEEL and CRANKS. Williams' C.1000.

HANDLEBARS. Bailey or any type of bars to choice on forward extension, with expanding bolt and head clip. Chromium Plated.

FINISH. "SAXON" Electric Bronze with lugs lined Gold, or Cellulose Enamel to choice, with red, white and blue bands on Down Tube.

Any other specification to Special Quotation.

Page 15

£17 . 17 . 0 CASH

EASY PAYMENT TERMS
£3 . 12 . 9 Deposit and
13 Monthly payments of £1 . 5 . 3

SAXON PARAMOUNT Model

The World's finest lightweight cycle—built regardless of cost for the man who knows that it *pays* to buy the best. Specification includes our new Twin Tube frame (38½ in. wheelbase), or the usual single seat tube frame (41½ in. wheelbase). A machine of outstanding quality—pre-eminent in workmanship *and* performance.

SPECIFICATION (MODEL "A")

WEIGHT Under 23 lbs.

FRAME and FORKS. Built of "Chrome Molybdenum" tubing with our special and unique design of cut-out lugs. Neat taper chain and seat stays. Tecalemit Oiling. Choice of our new TWIN TUBE Frame (see page 6), allowing a 38½ in. wheelbase, or usual single seat tube frame, 41½ in. wheelbase. Mudguard eyes, pump pegs, cable guides, reflector eye and Derailleur gear bracket brazed to frame. "SAXON" Resilient Front Forks: "D" to round, with our special solid fork-end quick release. The fork crown is of particularly strong and neat design. Rear Fork-ends are of special design, to allow standard hubs to be used with Derailleur gear.

BRACKET. Cotterless type with "SAXON" Aluminium Oil Bath.

CHAIN WHEEL and CRANKS. This is a unique production, being all steel, yet weighing slightly less than the alloy sets. The cranks are Hollow and of Octagon Section, giving great strength. The chain wheel is all steel, rigid, yet of very light design.

PEDALS. Constrictor Boa, Chromium Plated.

RIMS. Conloy Sprint rims, built with double-butted spokes—tied and soldered.

GEARS. Another "SAXON" Speciality. Three-speed Derailleur with unique features. Gears can be changed at "full sprint" without slackening of effort or removing the hands from the bars. No complicated jockey-pulleys to hinder wheel removal and replacement.

HANDLEBARS. Renolds' Hiduminium R.R.56 on 2 in. extension, also in R.R.56

TYRES. Dunlop Special Silk, or to choice.

HUBS. Special "SAXON" all Steel light hubs, with "SAXON" Cone-locking device.

SADDLE. New Ormond Hiduminium or type to choice.

BRAKES. Two special Duralumin calliper brakes.

CHAIN. Renolds'.

GRIPS. John Bull sleeve or sponge rubber.

EQUIPMENT. Bluemels' Pump, Bluemels' Spearpoint Extension, Prismatic Reflector and Tecalemit Oil Gun.

FINISH. "SAXON" Electric Bronze, Flamboyant in Red, Green, Blue or Amber. Cellulose or Stove Enamel in Black or Colour to choice. Usual bright parts Chromium Plated.

Paramount Wired on Tyre (Model "B")

This Model is fitted with Bluemels' "Noweight" Guards, and Dunlop High Pressure Tyres and Rims, but in every other detail is similar to Model "A".

£15 . 15 . 0 CASH

OR A DEPOSIT OF £3/2/6 and
13 PAYMENTS of £1 2 6.

"CYCLONE" TANDEM

Those cyclists who prefer a *long base* Tandem, will choose the "Cyclone." It has a wheelbase of 64 in. or 67 in. and is an established favourite amongst experienced riders. We have specialised in Tandems ever since the days when Tandems were a rarity and the supremacy of the "Cyclone" is the result of our unique experience.

SPECIFICATION

WHEELBASE. Standard Wheelbase 67 in. Short Wheelbase 64 in. When ordering please state which wheelbase you desire.

FRAME. Super quality tubes throughout. All lugs neatly cut out. Drop-out Front Fork Ends, latest improved TRI-VELOX Drop-out Rear Fork Ends, allowing wheel to be removed without interfering with the gear. Pump pegs, reflector and mudguard eyes are brazed to frame. Tecalemit Oiling.

FORKS. "SAXON" Resilient, or any other pattern.

WHEELS. 26 in x 1⅜ in. Chromium Plated Endrick Rims.

TYRES. Palmer Paramount. The best tandem tyre on the road.

MUDGUARDS. "SAXON" duplex with detachable fittings, made by Bluemels. Built-in Reflector on rearguard, black with white patch or white.

GEARS. Tri-Velox, Cyclo or Sturmey-Archer three-speed.

SADDLES. Brooks' B.22.

HANDLEBARS. Shallow Highgate or North Road, Chromium Plated.

GRIPS. "SAXON" Sponge.

CHAINS. Renolds' or Coventry.

PEDALS. Tubular Racing.

BRAKES. Two Hub brakes with special large drums.

FINISH. In Brilliant Black Enamel. Handlebars, Rims and usual bright parts Chromium Plated. Colour 7/6 extra.

EQUIPMENT. Bluemels' Pump, Reflector, Oil Gun and Tool Bag and Spanners.

Twin Lateral Stay Design to special order—no extra. Lady Back Models 5/- extra.
Special Quotations for Tandems Built to Customer's Own Specification.

£16 . 16 . 0 CASH

EASY PAYMENT TERMS
£2 Deposit and
14 Monthly payments of £1 . 6 . 7

"WINGS OF THE WIND" TANDEM

This model, incorporating our special Twin Tube frame (see page 6), was introduced for the first time last year and proved *outstandingly* successful. It has the unusually short wheelbase of 59 in., yet allows a supremely comfortable position for both riders. The "Wings of the Wind" is faster, more responsive and entirely different from any Tandem you have ever seen.

SPECIFICATION

WHEELBASE. 59 in.

WEIGHT. Under 57 lbs., fully equipped as illustrated.

FRAME. Double Gent's. Super quality tubes throughout. Special TWIN TUBE Frame (Registered Design No. 815768). All lugs neatly cut out. Drop-out Front Fork Ends. TRI-VELOX Drop-out Rear Fork Ends, allowing wheel to be removed without interfering with the gear. Pump Pegs and Mudguard Eyes brazed to Frame. Tecalemit Oiling.

FORKS. "SAXON" Resilient.

WHEELS. 26 in. x 1¼ in. Chromium Plated Endrick Rims.

MUDGUARDS. "SAXON" duplex with detachable fittings. Black, white patch, or White with built in reflector. Made by Bluemels.

TYRES. Palmer Paramount. The best tandem tyre on the road.

GEARS. Tri-Velox, Cyclo or Sturmey-Archer three-speed.

SADDLES. Brooks' B.22.

HANDLEBARS. Shallow Highgate, front; North Road, rear, Chromium Plated.

GRIPS. "SAXON."

CHAINS. Renolds' or Coventry.

BRAKES. Two Hub brakes with special large drums.

FINISH. In Brilliant Black Enamel. Chromium Handlebars and Rims. Colour 7/6 extra.

EQUIPMENT. Bluemels' Pump, Reflector, Oil Gun and Tool Bag and Spanners.

£16 . 16 . 0 CASH

EASY PAYMENT TERMS
£2 Deposit and
14 Monthly payments of £1 . 6 . 7

£24 . 0 . 0 CASH

EASY PAYMENT TERMS
£3 . 12 . 0 Deposit and
16 Monthly payments of £1 . 10 . 0.

SAXON "TRIPLET" Model

We have introduced a new Triplet Model this year, built on the same lines as the "Wings of the Wind" Tandem. It has a wheelbase of only 80 in. Its equipment is unusually generous, yet it is yours for 2/6d. weekly per rider.

SPECIFICATION

FRAME. Accles and Pollock tubing, with our special registered design TWIN-TUBE frame, allowing an 80 in. wheelbase. Specially reinforced front forks as illustrated. Pump pegs, reflector and mudguard eyes are brazed to frame. Tecalemit Oiling.

RIMS. Endrick 26 x 1¼ in. Chromium Plated.

TYRES. Palmer Paramount.

PEDALS. Tubular Rat-trap.

CRANKS. Williams' chain wheels and cranks.

BRAKES. Two Hub brakes with special large diameter drums, giving ample braking surface, with additional Calliper to rear wheel.

HANDLEBARS. Shallow Highgate or North Road, Chromium Plated.

GRIPS. "SAXON."

CHAIN. Renolds'.

SADDLES. "SAXON" or Brooks' B.11.

MUDGUARDS. "SAXON," black with white patch, made by Bluemels.

GEARS. Sturmey-Archer, K.T. or K.T.C. three-speed.

FINISH. Best Black Enamel, with all usual bright parts Chromium Plated.

SAXON "TOURIST" MODEL

£6 . 19 . 6
CASH

EASY PAYMENT TERMS
10/- Deposit and 64 weekly payments of 2/6.

3-Speed Model (Sturmey-Archer K)
£8 0 6
or 12/- Deposit and 64 weekly payments of 2/10.

A machine much favoured by business and leisurely riders. It runs sweetly, looks good and LASTS. The fittings are remarkably complete, for such an inexpensive model.

"TOURIST" SPECIFICATION

FRAME and FRONT FORKS. Accles and Pollock Tubing and the renowned "SAXON" Resilient Front Forks with best quality butted blades and frame tubes of highest grade steel. Cotterless type bracket fitted with "SAXON" Aluminium Oil Bath.

HUBS. Special "SAXON" all British Double Cog, Free wheel, with thin barrels and Chrome steel cones. Lock nuts to both hubs with wing nuts. Chromium finish.

RIMS. Endrick's 26 x 1¼ in. Chromium Plated.

TYRES. Palmer Sports.

PEDALS. 4 in. Solid Rubber. Chrome fittings. Adjustable bearings.

CRANKS. Williams' 6½ in. with 46 x ⅛ 5-pin chain wheel.

MUDGUARDS. "SAXON" celluloid with "SAXON" fittings and spring clips. Black with white patch. Made by Bluemels.

EQUIPMENT. Oil Bath gear-case, "SAXON" 1938 large touring bag, complete with tools, oil can and spanner. Bluemels' Pump, Prismatic reflector.

BRAKES. Two Calliper, front and rear.

HANDLEBARS. Celluloid covered North Road Upturned on Chromium Plated Adjustable Clip.

GRIPS. Constrictor Short.

CHAIN. Renolds'.

SADDLE. Lycett Aero A.2.

FINISH. The Frame is Rustproofed by Bonderite Process and Enamelled brilliant Black, all bright parts Chromium Plated.

SAXON "ENCHANTRESS" MODEL

The "Enchantress" is specially designed for those ladies who wish to ride a diamond frame. Its short top tube (20 in.) and 40½ in. wheelbase allow for a really comfortable position.

It is built with the same specification as the "Popular," "Magna" or "Sports" models. Prices according to list price of model chosen.

THE "ROADSTER" MODEL

SPECIFICATION

FRAME. 22 in. or 24 in.

WHEELS. 28 in. x 1½ in.

REAR HUB. "SAXON," with Free wheel.

BRAKES. Two Roller Lever.

SADDLE. Best quality 3 Coil.

FINISH. Black, lined Red and Gold, and Chromium Plated.

EQUIPMENT. Inflator, Tool Bag and Tools, Rear Reflector, white patch on Rear Guard.

SAXON "S.X." ROADSTER MODELS

£5 : 10 : 0

(or 5/- Deposit and 51 weekly payments of 2/6d.)

LADIES' MODELS 5/- EXTRA
If on Easy Payments two extra weekly payments of 2/6d.

ROADSTER 22 in. Frame.
LIGHT ROADSTER 21 in. Frame.

Sturmey-Archer three-speed K.S., K.S.W., or K. 21/- extra.
Oilbath Gearcase 12/6 extra.

The "LIGHT ROADSTER" MODEL

SPECIFICATION

FRAME. 20 in. or 22 in, with Top Tube 1 in. drop.

WHEELS. 26 in. x 1⅜ in. Westwood.

REAR HUB. "SAXON" with Free wheel.

BRAKES. Two Roller Lever.

SADDLE. Best quality four wire.

FINISH. Black, lined Red and Gold, and Chromium Plated.

EQUIPMENT. Inflator, Tool Bag and Tools, Rear Reflector, white patch on rear Guard.

"SAXON" Accessories are renowned for their quality and value. We cannot spare the space in this Catalogue to list other than a few items of our stock—for we carry everything needed by the Racing and Touring Cyclist. Send a p.c. for particulars of our full range.

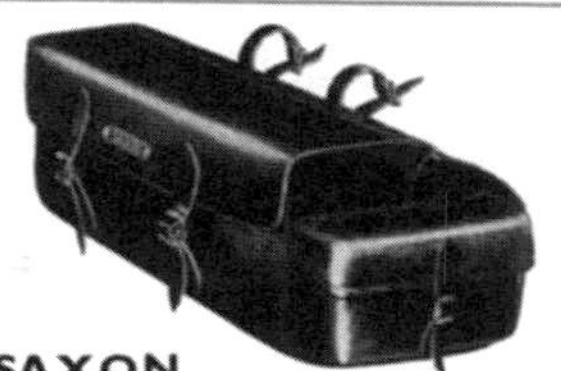

SAXON "POPULAR" TOURING BAG

Size: 12 x 9 x 7 inches.
Made in High Quality Leather Cloth **4/6**

SAXON SPECIAL TOURING BAG

Size: 14 x 8½ x 9 inches.
Made in High Quality Leather Cloth **9/6**

SAXON TANDEM BAG

Size: 14 x 9 x 9½ inches.
Made in Black Chrome Hide **23/6**

In Black or Brown Four-fold Waterproof Leather Cloth **16/6**

SAXON "HOLD-EVERYTHING" TOURING BAG

Size: 13 x 10 x 7 inches.
Made in Black Chrome Hide **17/6**

In Black or Brown Four-fold Waterproof Leather Cloth **14/-**

SAXON SHOES

IN MEN'S & WOMEN'S SIZES

C.3 10/-

Made in Box Hide Tan Leather with Black Caps and Pedal Patches, Flap Tongue, English Bend Soles, Rubber Top Piece to Heel.

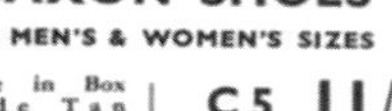

C.5 11/-

Made in Best Semi Box all Tan Leather with Pedal Patches. Ankle strap with buckle fastening, Flap Tongue, English Bend Soles, Solid insoles.

C.19 12/6

Made in Best Chrome Box Calf Tan Leather with Black Caps and Pedal Patches. Strap and Buckle fastening. Best quality bottoms throughout.

C.9 13/3

Made in best full Chrome Box Hide Dark Tan Leather throughout. Cap and Pedal Patches, Flap Tongue. Best English Bend Soles. Solid Insoles.

Some Famous Accessories

• CONTINUED •

SAXON SADDLE

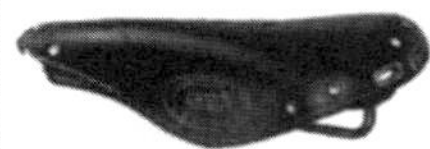

This saddle is the best value on the market. It is made from best quality Butt Hide and retains its shape indefinitely. **12/6**

SAXON BADGES

6d.

Gold Lettering on Blue Background.

Wear a "Saxon" Badge and be proud of your cycle.

SAXON OILSKINS

In spite of being extensively copied, these are still the favourites of discriminating Clubmen. Fully guaranteed and all seams proofed.

In Black or Gold :—

Ponchos ...	7/–, 9/6 and 10/6
Leggings	5/6, 7/10 and 9/7
Spats	6/3
S'Westers ...	1/9 and 2/6

SAXON ADJUSTABLE TOE-CLIPS

Original Vanderstuyft Toe Clips were first introduced into this country by us. The SAXON Pattern CLIPS are an exact replica, and are now made in England.

Vanderstuyft Pattern

	per pair
Chromium Plated ...	2/6
Nickel Plated ...	1/8
Straps ...	1/6

THE "J.P" PATENT SHOCK-ELIMINATING STEM

Chromium Plated { Solo 20/- each
Tandem 22/- each

FRAMES

CASH AND EASY PAYMENT PRICES

The Construction of these frames is as individual specifications of the relative models. Weight is reduced to the minimum which is consistent with strength and rigidity. All frames as listed are complete with Front Forks, Head fittings, Chain Wheels and Cranks, and Seat Pillars. For complete specifications of Frame and fittings see the specifications of the relative Models. In the case of Paramount or De Luxe Frames, if any gear brackets are desired to be brazed on special instructions must be included in your order.

MAGNA. Finished in Best Stove Black enamel, Silver head, and front ends Chromium Plated. **£3 12 6.** Cash or a first payment of **16/–** and 9 at **7/6**.

SPORTS. Finished in Best Stove Black enamel, Front ends Chromium Plated, and fork crown Chromium plated. **£3 17 6.** Cash or a first payment of **16/–** and 9 at **8/2**.

CLUB. Finished in Cellulose colour to choice, or Black enamel, Head Lugs, Crown, front and rear Fork ends Chromium Plated. **£5 5 0** Cash or a first payment of **£1** and 9 at **11/3**.

TWIN TUBE ROAD RACE. 38½ in. wheelbase. Finished in Delf Blue Cellulose, with Red head or Cellulose colour to choice. Chromium Plated Head Lugs and Fork Crown, red, white and blue bands on seat tubes and down tube. "SAXON" Resilient front Forks. **£5 10 0** Cash or a first payment of **£1** and 10 at **10/8**.

DE LUXE. Finished in Electric Bronze or Flamboyant, Head Lugs, Crown and front and rear ends, Chromium Plated. **£6** Cash or a first payment of **£1** and 10 at **12/–**.

TWIN TUBE PATH. (Exactly as illustrated on page 6.) 38 in. wheelbase. 71° Angles. Finished in Delf Blue cellulose, with Red head and Cellulose colour to choice. Chromium Plated Head Lugs and Fork Crown, red, white and blue bands on seat tubes and down tube. "SAXON" Special Path Forks. **£5 10 0** Cash or a first payment of **£1**, and 10 at **10/8**.

SAXON-BAILEY PATH MODEL. Finished in Electric Bronze or Flamboyant colour to choice, Chromium Plated Special "SAXON" Path Crown and Path Forks. **£5 10 0** Cash, or a first payment of **£1**, and 10 at **10/8**.

PARAMOUNT. TWIN TUBE Design 38½ in. wheelbase or single seat tube, 41½ in. wheelbase. Finished in Flamboyant colour to choice, or Electric Bronze. Chromium Plated front ends, Crown, and Head Lugs. "SAXON" Resilient front Forks. Special Light "SAXON" Nickel Chrome Chain Wheel set with hollow Cranks. **£6 12 6** Cash, or a first payment of **£1**, and 11 at **11/–**.

Gears

	£	s.	d.
Sturmey-Archer " K " 3-speed gear ...	1	1	0
" " " K.B." " " ...	1	7	6
" " " K.B.C." " " ...	1	7	6
" " " K.S." " " ...	1	1	0
" " " K.S.W." " " ...	1	1	0
Tri-Velox 3-speed gear without hub brake ...	1	12	6
" " " with hub brake ...	2	3	0
Cyclo 3-speed gear ...	1	5	0
" SAXON " Thumb-and-Finger-Tip-Control Derailleur Gear (Foreign) ...	1	17	6

CONDITIONS :—We give below prices for some of the more usual repairs. It will be appreciated that it is impossible to enumerate every type of repair that we may be called upon to execute, but we are always pleased to quote for any job you may require. Please note that all cycles or parts sent to us for repair, whether under guarantee or not, must be sent carriage paid, and no goods will be accepted by us unless this condition is complied with. All goods, whether accompanied by a covering letter or not, must be labelled with the owner's name and address. Failure to do this involves us in a great deal of trouble, and leads to complications and delays.

If repairs are required to any part of a cycle, it is recommended that only the part concerned be sent to us, and not the whole bicycle, as this saves carriage and labour charges. It will be noticed that, in front fork repairs, we quote only for new head stems. We definitely do not recommend that new fork blades be fitted under any circumstances, as we consider that such vital parts as the front fork blades should be tampered with as little as possible.

	Popular Magna Sports	Club T.T. Road Race T.T. Path De Luxe Bailey Path Paramount
Fitting New Head Stem to Forks ...	4/-	6/-
" New Top or Down Tube ...	7/6	11/3
" New Top and Down Tubes ...	12/6	18/9
" One New Seat or Chain Stay ...	5/-	7/6
" Two New Seat or Chain Stays ...	9/-	13/6
" New Seat and Chain Stays and Rear Fork Ends ...	15/-	22/6
Taking down and re-assembling Bicycle ...	10/-	10/-
Supplying New Front Forks (Black) ...	12/6	15/-
Supplying New Front Forks in Coloured Enamel ...	13/6	16/-
Supplying New Front Forks in Electric Bronze or Flamboyant ...	15/-	17/6
Re-enamelling Frame and Fork Black ...	10/-	10/-
Re-enamelling Frame and Fork Black with Chromium Plated Front and Rear Fork Ends ...	22/-	22/-
Re-enamelling Frame and Fork in Colour (Lugs lined 2/6 extra) ...	12/6	12/6
Re-enamelling Frame and Fork in Colour with Chromium Plated Front and Rear Fork Ends ...	28/-	28/-
Re-finishing Frame and Fork in Flamboyant or Electric Bronze ...	17/6	17/6
Re-finishing Frame and Fork in Flamboyant or Electric Bronze with Chromium Plated Front and Rear Fork Ends ...	32/6	32/6
Building Endrick or Westwood Rim on to own hub—Front or Rear Chromium Plated ...	5/7	
Building Constrictor Sprint Rim on to own hub—Front or Rear ...	15/-	
Building Conloy Sprint Rim on to own hub—Front or Rear ...	18/9	
Building Dunlop High Pressure Chromium Plated Rim on to own hub ...	6/9	
Chromium Plating Front Fork Ends ...	5/-	
Chromium Plating Rear Fork Ends ...	12/6	
Chromium Plating Front Forks all over ...	9/-	

Gear Table

COGWHEEL Number of TEETH	COG Number of TEETH	DIAMETER OF WHEEL 26 in.	27 in.	28 in.
44	13	88.0	91.3	94.8
	14	81.7	84.8	88.0
	15	76.2	78.5	82.1
	16	71.5	74.2	77.0
	17	67.2	69.8	72.4
	18	63.5	66.0	68.4
	19	60.2	62.5	64.8
	20	57.2	59.4	61.6
46	13	92.0	95.5	99.0
	14	85.4	88.7	92.0
	15	79.7	82.1	85.8
	16	74.7	77.6	80.5
	17	70.3	73.0	75.7
	18	66.4	69.0	71.5
	19	63.0	65.4	67.8
	20	59.8	62.0	64.4
48	13	96.0	99.7	103.4
	14	89.1	92.5	96.0
	15	83.2	86.4	89.6
	16	78.0	81.0	84.0
	17	73.4	76.2	79.0
	18	69.3	72.0	74.6
	19	65.7	68.2	70.7
	20	62.4	64.8	67.2
52	13	104.0	108.0	112.0
	14	96.5	100.2	104.0
	15	90.1	93.6	97.0
	16	84.5	87.7	91.0
	17	78.5	82.3	85.6
	18	75.1	78.0	80.8
	19	71.2	74.0	76.6
	20	67.6	70.2	72.8

THE PRICES IN THIS CATALOGUE DO NOT APPLY TO THE IRISH FREE STATE.

Guarantee

WE give the following guarantee with all goods supplied, in place of any guarantee implied by law, statute, or otherwise, as to the quality or fitness of the goods for the purpose for which they are supplied.

We guarantee, subject to conditions named below, that all precautions which are usual and reasonable have been taken by us to secure excellence of materials and workmanship. This guarantee shall be in force from the date of delivery by us of the goods, and the damages for which we make ourselves responsible under this guarantee are limited to the replacement of any part which may have proved defective. This guarantee shall not apply to defects caused by wear and tear, accident, misuse, or neglect. It only covers new goods and does not apply to the productions of other manufacturers, such as tyres, etc.

Should any defect be alleged in material or workmanship after purchase of a pedal bicycle from us or our accredited dealers, we undertake on the immediate return of the part which is alleged to be defective to our Works carriage paid, to examine the same and should any fault be found by us on examination to be solely due to defective material or workmanship, we will repair the defective part or supply a new part in place thereof, free of charge. We do not undertake to bear the cost of any work involved in reinstating a repaired or inserting a new part.

Bicycles used for hiring out purposes are not within the scope of this guarantee.

CONDITIONS OF SALE

We do not appoint agents in the legal sense for the sale of our cycles or other goods. We assign to Cycle Dealers who carry on business on their own account areas in which they have the exclusive or other right to sell goods purchased from us at our catalogue prices and they are not allowed to make any allowances. A Saxon Dealer purchasing from us, or a Subdealer purchasing from him may, on our behalf (as our agent for this purpose only) give the guarantee printed above. Any such dealer is not without our express authority to advertise, incur any debts or transact any business whatsoever on our account, nor is he authorised so as to bind us, to give any warranty or make any representation on our behalf, or to sell subject to or with any conditions other than those contained in such guarantee.

The prices and specifications given in this catalogue are subject to alteration at any time without notice.

SAXON CYCLE ENGINEERING Co., Ltd.

SIDNEY ROAD, HOMERTON, LONDON, E.9.

Telephone: AMHerst 4782/3. Telegrams: SAXCYK, HACK, LONDON.

E STEPHENS

Stephen Edwin Mitchell (known as Ed or Eddie) was born on 26th January 1902 in Highbury, North London. His father, also Stephen, was a master builder and Eddie expected when he left school at the age of thirteen that he would work for his father. However, this did not work out and Eddie found work with the Grandex Cycle Company at 138 Gray's Inn Road, London, WC1 and then the Hearn Cycle Co. Ltd., at 254 Gray's Inn Road.

In the early 1920's, Eddie negotiated the purchase of premises at 28 Newington Green Road, Islington, London N1 and set up as a cycle manufacturer and retailer. He chose to call his business 'E Stephens' as there was already a 'Mitchell' in the cycle trade. The shop had a cellar, complete with forge for brazing, which was used as the work shop for cycle manufacture.

A handwritten draft of the 1926 E Stephens catalogue described Eddie as the Manufacturer of B&S Lightweight Cycles, Tricycles and Tandems. Cyclists' clothing was also listed. B&S stood for Beatrice (his wife) and Stephen.

Eddie moved his business from Stoke Newington and opened a new shop in January 1938 at 136 Chase Side, Southgate N14, about five miles away.

In over thirty years as a manufacturer Eddie designed and built all his own machines. He was also an inventor of components and tools. His main interest was in building lightweights for touring and racing. During the 1930's he exhibited regularly at The Lightweight Show, organised by J E Holdsworth and held annually at the Royal Horticultural Hall, Westminster. The strap line in his catalogues and advertisements was 'A Clubman Knows A Clubman's Wants'. This was certainly true as Ed was leading member of the Southgate CC and later of the North Road CC.

As a manufacturer Eddie did not overwhelm his customers with choice. However, catalogue models were indicative rather than absolute and each machine was built to the customer's requirements. The 1926 catalogue offered his own design 'B&S' road frame (gents and ladies) with a stock size of 20 1/2", which could be built up with Brampton, Chater Lea or BSA fittings, either as a frame or as a complete machine. A roadster and tandem were also offered, again with the choice of fittings. By 1929 a tricycle and path racing model had been added. The tricycle was described as 'Designed for a noted tricycle exponent'. This was presumably Les Meyers, a Southgate CC member and friend of Eddie's, who in August 1929 took the End-to-End tricycle record.

By 1934 two versions of a 'Special' cycle were added to the catalogue which were lighter than the earlier road frame design and had higher specifications. Sturmey-Archer and Cyclo gears were also available as extras.

After the move from Stoke Newington to Southgate in 1938, a new catalogue continued to offer the original 'B&S' road frame design but without the choice of fittings. It was also available as the 'Cyclo' model. A slightly higher specification 'Club' model was offered, also appearing as the 'AM Sturmey' model. For the first time the 'Special No.2' model was offered with a choice of 26" or 27" wheels. This also applied to the new 'Continental' model, which had continental cutaway lugs and continental rake to the forks. Equipment, however, remained solidly British.

In the post-war period, only typed sheets for the different models and specifications were issued, including a new cheaper range of 'Southgate' models. The Stephens 'Club', 'Special' and 'Continental' models continued to be offered, together with the tandem and tricycle. A new massed start design was offered, called the 'Chelmsford'. However, after a short post-war revival, sales for all models dwindled. Prices had more than doubled compared with pre-war.

The Sales Ledgers show the rise of the manufacturing business, reaching a peak in 1935, and then the dramatic decline in the early 1950's. The following table shows the number of **Stephen's** models built, taken from the Sales Ledgers.

Year	No.	Year	No	Year	No	Year	No
1925(part)	7	1934	86	1943	33	1952	3
1926	59	1935	120	1944	40	1953	7
1927	51	1936	84	1945	34	1954	4
1928	38	1937to Oct)	40	1946	34	1955	1
1929	43	1938	missing	1947	17		
1930	47	1939	32	1948	34		
1931	63	1940	13	1949	51		
1932	30	1941	34	1950	47		
1933	40	1942	40	1951	18		

The following table shows the number of **'Southgate'** Models built.

Year	No	Year	No	Year	No
1945	5	1948	59	1951	18
1946	21	1949	29	1952	5
1947	31	1950	5	1953	3

The catalogue prices remained steady throughout the 1920's and 1930's. Only in the post-war period did prices rise steeply. The Club/Popular model remained in the range throughout, changing equipment as the years went by and reducing the options for fittings. The popularity for buying frames only decreased post-war. The Special models with High Manganese tubing were popular in the 1930's and were genuine lightweights. Both used Constrictor hubs with either Endrick steel or Constrictor-Bastide sprint rims. The latter version weighed 18lbs all on. The Continental model, introduced around 1939, weighed 19lbs including a Cyclo Super Inax three-speed derailleur, and was the first to offer alloy bars but still keeping a steel stem.

Eddie used different numbering systems at different times for his machines. The earliest ledger shows that from June 1925 to December 1932, he used a continuous sequence beginning with 0137 and ending with 0471. In 1933 the sequence continued but with the 0 dropped and 33 added as a suffix. The first number was 47233 (January 1933) and the final one 84237 (October 1937).

Some pages may have been lost as the next ledger begins in 1939 with 88139 and finishes with 1170 in 1946. In 1942 he had stopped adding the suffix identifying the year, a wartime economy? In 1945 'Southgate' models were recorded for the first time with the year as a suffix, eg. 41245.

The final ledger continued the 'Stephens' models sequence, beginning with 1172 in October 1946 and a final entry of 1408 in February 1955. There was a change to the numbering of the 'Southgate' models with the first two digits indicating the year. In August 1946, 4665 was the first number entered and the final one was 5303 in October 1953.

Machine numbers may be found on the head lug of the frame and on the fork crown. 'Southgate' models have 'S' as a prefix.

Eddie was a founder member of The Lightweight Manufacturers' Association (later The Lightweight Cycle Manufacturers' Association) and was Chairman in 1935. This was set up to obtain trade terms for components for the lightweight manufacturers.

Eddie retired, with reluctance, from the cycle trade in June 1956 and died in August 1973 aged 70.

Roger Bugg

Catalogue kindly loaned by Roger Bugg is undated but bears the Newington Green address putting it prior to 1938.

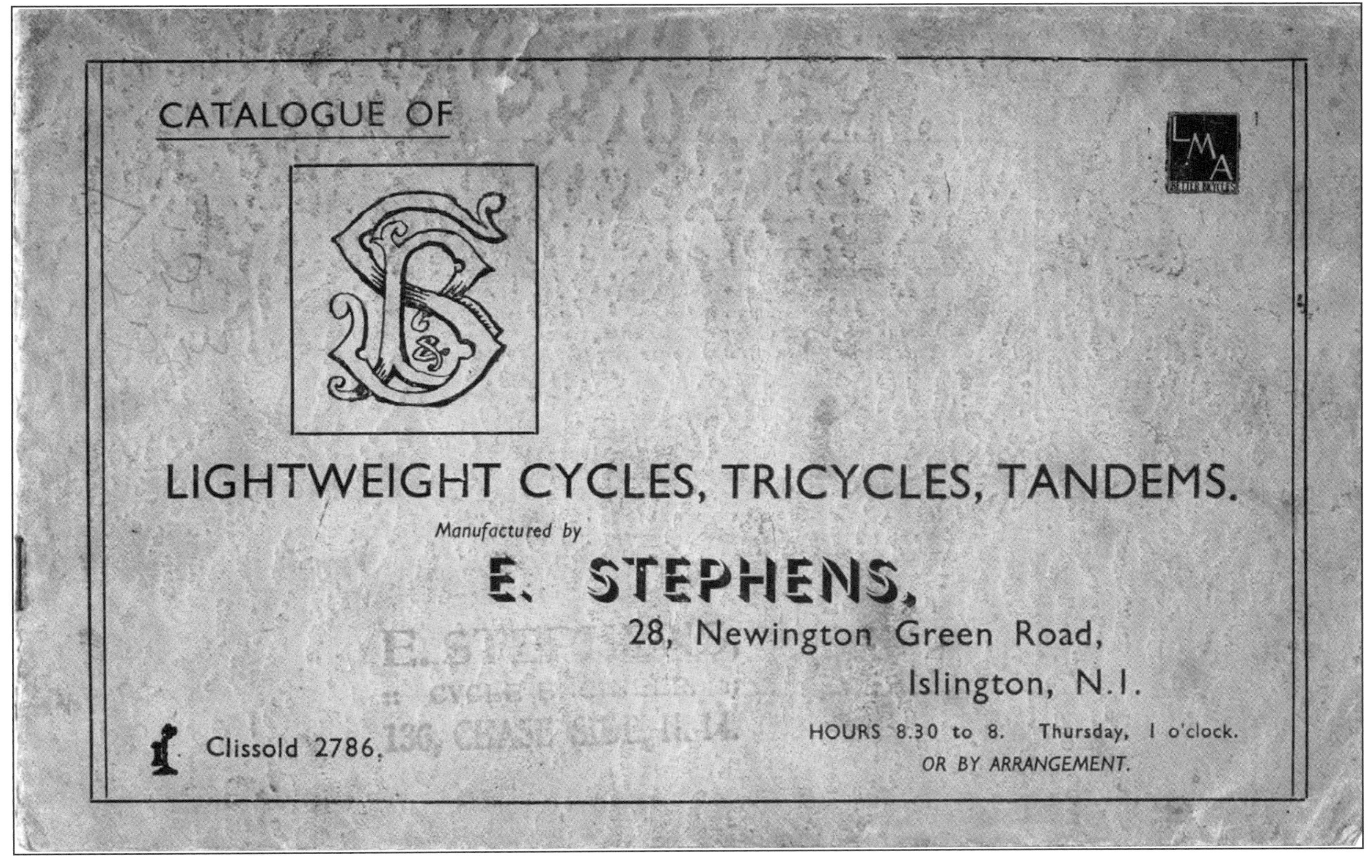
CATALOGUE OF
LMA
LIGHTWEIGHT CYCLES, TRICYCLES, TANDEMS.
Manufactured by
E. STEPHENS,
28, Newington Green Road,
Islington, N.1.
Clissold 2786.
HOURS 8.30 to 8. Thursday, 1 o'clock.
OR BY ARRANGEMENT.

INTRODUCTION.

In presenting to you my latest Catalogue of B. & S. Cycles, Tricycles and Tandems, I am confident that no more honest value for money can be offered or given. Each machine bearing my transfers is an individual job. I do not build low grade or cheap cycles, for those built under mass-production principles cannot give the same service (including after sales service), comfort or lasting reliability as a machine built by an expert who specializes in quality first, and understands a cyclist's requirements from a personal experience.

In this enlarged edition I have shown those models that I found to be in most demand, but there is no limit to the variations of frame design, or equipment that can be made into a " Stephens " Bicycle. Each machine is built to suit the rider's individual requirements, and I am always pleased to forward per return an estimate to cover your particular needs.

When purchasing a " Stephens " Cycle you are assured at all times of personal attention.

Chromium Plating is standard at no extra charge.

A VERY POPULAR MODEL OF PROVED VALUE WITH A LONG RECORD OF SERVICE.

B. & S. CLUB MODEL C.1

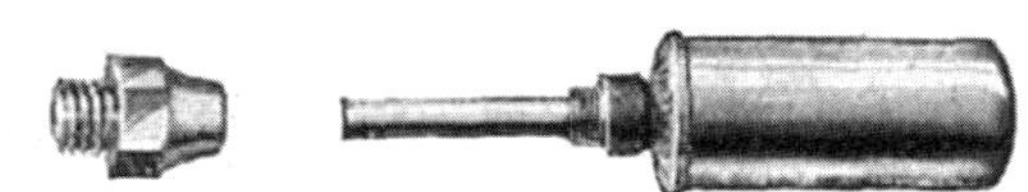

Tecalemit lubrication throughout.

SPECIFICATION.

Frame.—Height to order (stock size 20½in.), 41½in. wheel-base, 10¾in. bracket height, 26lbs. approximate weight. Reynolds "A" quality tubes throughout. Selected lugs and interiors, Williams' best quality 3-arm chain-wheel and cranks. E. STEPHENS' forward opening rear ends, or any other type to order. Brazed guard eyes, pump hooks, chain rest and fork lamp bracket boss. Linered oil retaining bracket. All lugs cut out.

Forks.—D to O narrow crown. E. STEPHENS' reinforced principle. Machined tips.

Wheels.—26in. x 1¼in. or 1⅜in. Lightweight hubs, locked cones, double gear. Dunlop, Endrick or Constrictor steel rims, black or plated. Double butted spokes.

Tyres.—Dunlop, Palmer or John Bull speed or to order.

Chain.—Coventry or "Renold's."

Saddle.—Brooks' Champion range or Terry's.

Bars.—To order, fixed, adjustable clip or extension, black or plated.

Guards.—Bluemel's No-weight with extension, or separate. Special spring clip fixing.

Brake.—Pelissier bolt fixing, front or rear, or Resilion.

Equipment.—Bluemel's ⅞in. pump, Lucas "Challis" bell, Tecalemit oilgun, Bluemel's rear reflector and Safeti Flap.

Finish.—Frame and fork sandblasted, hand polished, enamelled one coat rustproof, three coats of best stove enamel. Crown and ends plated.

Price.—£7 7s. cash.

CHATER-LEA IS A BY-WORD FOR RELIABLE LIGHTWEIGHT FITTINGS.

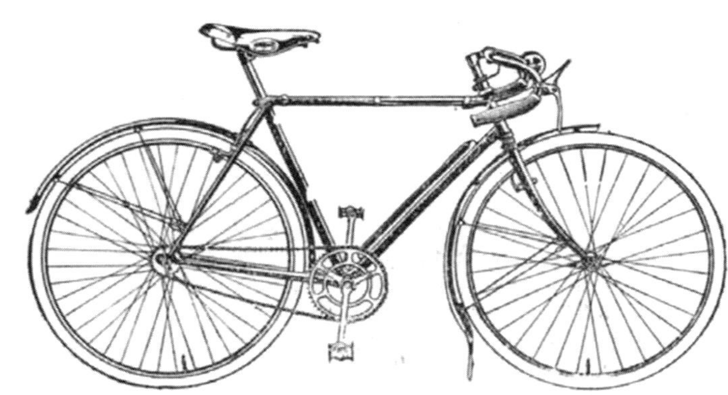

B. & S. CLUB MODEL C.2

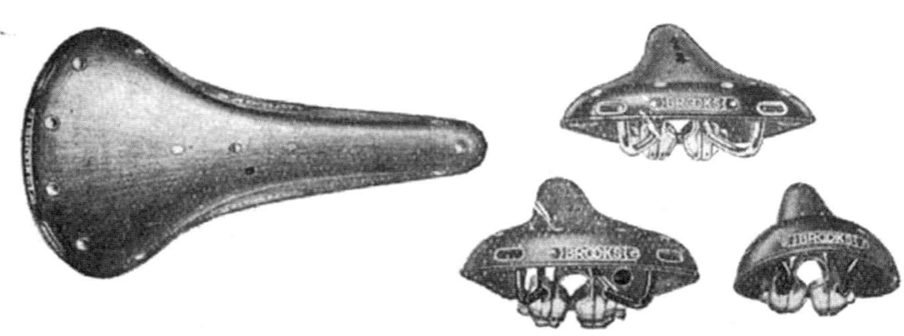

SPECIFICATION.

Frame.—Height to order (stock size 20½in.), 41½in. wheel-base, 10¾in. bracket height, 26½lbs. approximate weight, Reynolds' " A " quality tubes throughout. Chater-Lea lugs and interiors. Chater-Lea 3-pin chain wheel and cranks. E. STEPHENS' forward opening rear ends, or any other type to order. Brazed guard eyes, pump hooks, chain rest, and fork lamp bracket boss. Linered oil retaining bracket. All lugs cut out.

Forks.—⅞in. round, or D to O narrow crown. E. STEPHENS' reinforced principle machined tips.

Wheels.—26in. x 1¼in. or 1⅜in. Chater-Lea hubs, disc adjusting, Dunlop, Endrick or Constrictor steel rims. Black or plated. Double butted spokes.

Tyres.—Dunlop, Palmer or John Bull roadster, or to order.

Chain.—Coventry " Elite."

Saddle.—Brooks' B18, B10, or Champion range, or Terry's.

Bars.—To order, fixed, adjustable clip, or extension, black or plated.

Guards.—Bluemel's No-weight with extension or separate, special spring clip fixing.

Brake.—Pelissier bolt fixing, front and rear, or Resilion.

Equipment.—Bluemel's ⅞in. pump. Lucas " Challis " bell, Tecalemit oilgun, Bluemel's rear reflector and Safeti Flap.

Finish.—Frame and fork sandblasted, hand polished, enamelled one coat rustproof, three coats of best stove enamel. Crown and ends plated.

Price.—£9 9s. cash.

A CLUB CHAMPIONSHIP MODEL WITH THE FAMOUS B.S.A. FITTINGS.

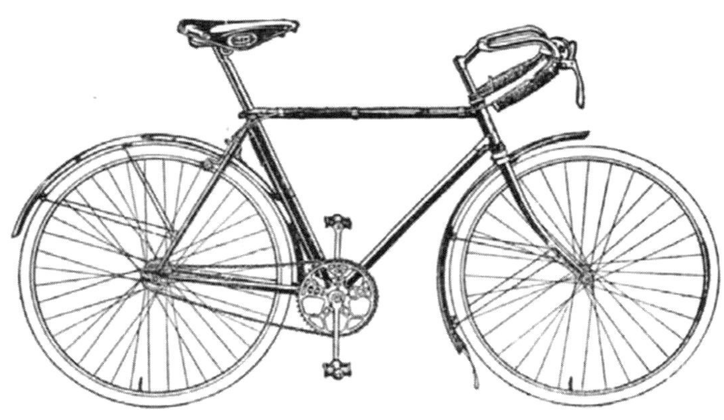

B. & S. CLUB MODEL, C.3.

SPECIFICATION.

Frame.—Height to order (stock size 20½in.), 41½in. wheel-base, 10¾in. bracket height, 26lbs. approximate weight. Reynold's "A" quality tubes throughout. Selected B.S.A. lugs and interiors. B.S.A. 5-screv chain wheel and cranks. E. STEPHENS' forward opening rear ends, or any other type to order. Brazed guard eyes, pump hooks, chain rest and fork lamp bracket boss. Linered oil retaining bracket. All lugs cut out.

Forks.—⅞in. round, or D to O narrow crown. E. STEPHENS' reinforced principle, machined tips.

Wheels.—26in. x 1¼in., or 1⅜in. B.S.A. hubs, locked cones, double gear. Dunlop, Endrick or Constrictor steel rims. Black or plated. Double butted spokes.

Tyres.—Dunlop, Palmer, or John Bull roadster, or Constrictor, or to order.

Chain.—Coventry "Elite."

Saddle.—Brooks' B18, B10, or Champion range, or Terry's.

Bars.—To order, fixed, adjustable clip or extension. Black or plated.

Guards.—Bluemel's No-weight with extension or separate special spring clip fixing.

Brake.—Pelissier bolt fixing, front or rear, or Resilion.

Equipment.—Bluemel's ⅞in. pump, Lucas "Challis" bell, Tecalemit oilgun, Bluemel's rear reflector and Safeti Flap.

Finish.—Frame and forks sandblasted and hand polished. Enamelled one coat rustproof, three coats of best stove enamel. Crown and ends plated.

Price £9 15s. cash.

A LIGHT, RIGID CYCLE, DESIGNED SPECIALLY FOR THE "FAIR" SEX.

B. & S. LADIES CLUB MODEL

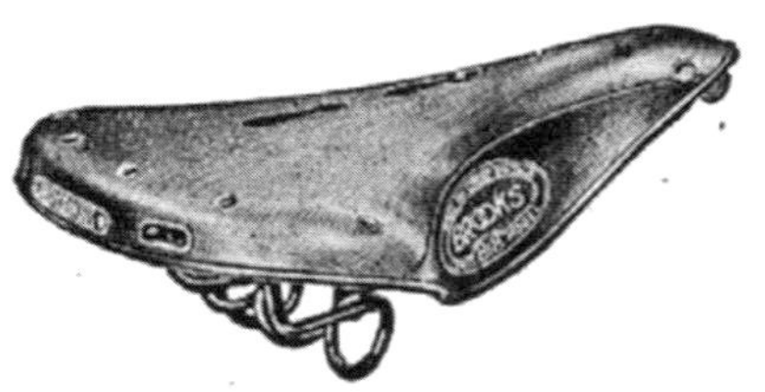

SPECIFICATION.

Frame.—Special design, height to order, (stock size **19in.**), 41½in. wheelbase, 10¼in. bracket height, **26lbs.** approximate weight. Reynold's "A" quality tubes throughout. E. STEPHENS' forward opening rear ends, or any other type to order. Brazed guard eyes, pump hooks, chain rest and fork, lamp bracket boss. Linered oil retaining bracket. All lugs cut out.

Forks.—D to O narrow crown. E. STEPHENS' reinforced principle. Machined tips.

Wheels.—26in. x 1¼in., or 1⅜in., double gear. Dunlop, Endrick or Constrictor steel rims, black or plated. Double butted spokes.

Tyres.—Dunlop, Palmer, or John Bull roadster, or Constrictor, or to order.

Chain.—Coventry "Elite."

Saddle.—Brooks' B18L, B10L, or Champion range, or Terry's.

Bars.—To order, fixed, adjustable clip or extension. Black or plated.

Guards.—Bluemel's No-weight with extension, or separate. Special spring clip fixing.

Brake.—Pelissier bolt fixing, front or rear, or Resilion.

Equipment.—Bluemel's ⅞in. pump, Lucas "Burbury" bell, Tecalemit oilgun, Bluemel's rear reflector and Safeti Flap.

Finish.—Frame and fork sandblasted and hand polished. Enamelled one coat rustproof, three coats of best stove enamel. Crown and Ends Plated.

Price.—L.4 : Brampton fittings, **£7 10s.** cash.
L.5 : Chater-Lea fittings, **£9 9s.** cash.
L.6 : B.S.A. fittings, **£10** cash.

A MACHINE THAT MEETS THE DEMAND OF THE ALL WEATHER RIDER.

B. & S. All Weather Model

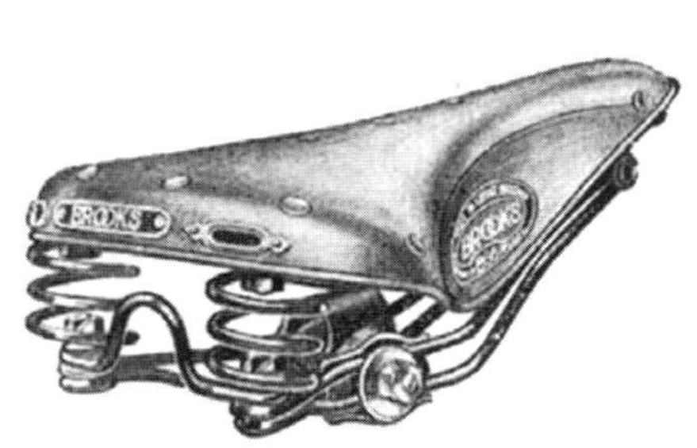

SPECIFICATION.

Frame.—Height to order (stock size 19in. or 20in.), 43in. wheel-base, 10¼in. bracket height, 28lbs. approximate weight. Reynold's "A" quality tubes throughout, E. STEPHENS' forward opening rear ends, or any other type to order. Brazed guard eyes, pump hooks, chain rest and fork lamp bracket boss. Linered oil retaining bracket. All lugs cut out.

Forks.—D to O blades or Reynold's "S.R." Machined tips, E. STEPHENS' reinforced principle.

Wheels.—26in. x 1¼in., or 1⅜in. locked cones. E. STEPHENS' narrow section. Dunlop, Endrick, or Constrictor steel rims. Double butted spokes. All black.

Tyres.—Dunlop, Palmer, or John Bull roadster, or Constrictor, or to order.

Chain.—Coventry "Elite."

Saddle.—Brooks' B10, B18, B66, or Champion range, or Terry's spring.

Bars.—14in., 15in., or 16in., flat. N.R. flat or North-road celluloid covered. Stem fixed or adjustable ; or to order.

Guards.—Bluemel's No-weight.

Brakes.—Pelissier bolt fixing, front and rear, or Resilion.

Equipment.—Bluemel's 15in. by ⅞in. pump, Lucas "Challis" bell, Tecalemit oil-gun, Bluemel's rear reflector and Safeti Flap.

Finish.—Frame and forks sandblasted, hand polished, enamelled one coat rustproof, four coats of best black stove enamel, all other parts stove black.

Price.—A.7 : Brampton fittings, **£8** cash.
A.8 : Chater-Lea fittings, **£9 15s.** cash.
A.9 : B.S.A. fittings, **£10** cash.
Built in oil-bath chain case £1 10s. extra.

IN designing and producing the "SPECIAL B. & S." Lightweight Models illustrated, I have endeavoured to present a machine that is the LAST WORD in cycle engineering. Each design aims at rigidity, liveliness and reduction of weight wherever possible, but the reduction of weight does not in the smallest degree sacrifice the safety of the rider. They are built under my personal supervision and are constructed of the finest materials procurable.

The frame is made of Reynolds' butted high manganese tubes in conjunction with lugs made for me by a reputable manufacturer.

The whole assembly embodies theory, practice, experience, best materials and workmanship, and I have every confidence in putting this machine before you.

Cash Price for Frame only.—£4 5s. Weight.—8¼lbs.

Instantly Detachable Mudguard Stays.

best materials and workmans
putting this machine before y

Cash Price for Frame

SPECIFICATION.

Frame.—E. STEPHENS' own design. Standard height 20½in., wheel-base 41in., bracket height 10¾in. Reynold's butted high manganese tubes, round, tapered chain and seat stays. Superfine cutaway and filed lugs (to safety limits). Brazed on pump pegs chain rest, and special guard eyes. Williams light C.1000 chain wheel and cranks. Finest quality bracket and head interiors, linered bracket shell. H.M. seat-pin. Tecalemit oilers in head and bracket.

Forks.—Reynold's ⅞in. round D to O, or S.R. taper-gauge blades with E. STEPHENS' adjustable fork lamp-bracket.

Finish.—Silver, gold, or red flambovant on nickel, with chrome ends, or to order. All parts Chrome Plated.

Wheels.—26in. or 27in. Constrictor-Bastide 13mm. (first choice), flat rims, built with 16 x 18 gauge finest quality plated spokes, on Constrictor light steel hubs, direct spoking on front and tangent on rear, bound and soldered, double cog.

Tyres.—Constrictor No. 50's, file or smooth band or Dunlop.

Pedals.—B.O.A. or Brampton solid centre.

Saddle.—Brooks' B.17, Mansfield Ormond, or to order.

Guards.—Bluemel's No-weight.

Chain.—Coventry Elite ½in. x ⅛in.

Brake.—Special front Pelissier, Tabucchi Duralumin, or Resilion.

Bars.—High manganese bend, brazed to stem and lugs as required, or adjustable.

Equipment.—Spearpoint extension, Bluemel's ⅝in. pump, Lucas bell, Tecalemit oil-gun.

Weight—18lbs.

Cash Price for Complete Machine.—£11 with Sprints.

e "SPECIAL B. & S." Lightweight
ndeavoured to present a machine
engineering. Each design aims
ion of weight wherever possible,
es not in the smallest degree
They are built under my personal
of the finest materials procurable.

eynolds' butted high manganese
made for me by a reputable

odies theory, practice, experience,
, and I have every confidence in
.

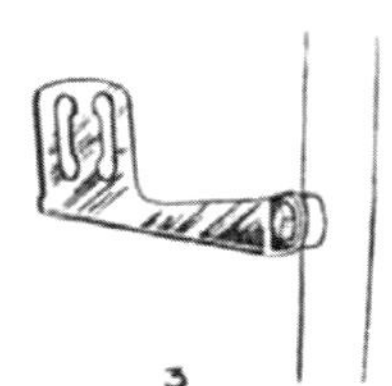

Adjustable and Detachable Lamp Bracket.

ıly.—£4 5s. Weight.—8¼lbs.

SPECIFICATION.

Frame.—E. STEPHENS' own design. Standard height 20½in., wheel-base 41in., bracket height 10¾in. Reynold's butted high manganese tubes, round, tapered chain and seat stays. Superfine cutaway and filed lugs (to safety limits). Brazed on pump pegs chain rest, and special guard eyes. Williams' light chain wheel and cranks. Finest quality bracket and head interiors, linered bracket shell. H.M. seat-pin. Tecalemit oilers in head and bracket.

Forks.—Reynolds' ⅞in. round D to O, or S.R. taper-gauge blades with E. STEPHENS' adjustable fork lamp-bracket.

Finish.—Silver, gold, or red flamboyant on dull nickel, with chrome ends, or to order.

Wheels.—26in. x 1¼in., or 1⅜in., built with 16 x 18 gauge finest quality plated spokes, on Constrictor light steel hubs, direct spoking on front and tangent on rear, bound and soldered, double cog.

Tyres.—Dunlop "Sprite."

Pedals.—B.O.A. or Brampton solid centre.

Saddle.—Brooks' B.17, Mansfield Ormond, or to order.

Guards.—Bluemel's No-weight.

Chain.—Coventry Elite ½in. x ⅛in.

Brake.—Special front Pelissier, Tabucchi Duralumin, or Resilion.

Bars.—High manganese bend, brazed to stem and lugs as required, or adjustable.

Equipment.—Spearpoint extension, Bluemel's ⅞in. pump, Lucas bell, Tecalemit oil-gun.

Weight.—22lbs.

Cash Price for Complete Machine.—£9 15s. with **Endricks.**
£10 with Dunlop High Pressure.

NOT A ROAD FRAME ADAPTED, BUT A FRAME DESIGNED SOLELY FOR ITS PURPOSE.

B. & S. Path Racing Model

SPECIFICATION.

Frame.—E. STEPHENS' design. Height to order (stock size 21in.), 42in. wheel-base, 11¼in. bracket height. Weight under 20lbs. (with duralumin parts, approximately 15lbs.), superfine cut out lugs, straight seat stays. Straight round 1in. chain stays, Reynolds' special "H.M." quality tubes. Rear opening rear fork ends with adjustors. All lugs cut out.

Forks.—1in. or ⅞in. round, or D to O narrow crown machine tips. Head-clip handle-bar fixing.

Wheels.—26in. or 27in. x 12mm. flat Constrictor-Bastide rims. Wide flanged hubs. Best butted spokes 16 x 18 gauge, tied and soldered at crossings.

Tyres.—Dunlop.

Chain.—Renold or "Elite," 1in. x ⅛in., or ½in. x ⅛in.

Saddle.—Brooks' Sprinter, or to order.

Bars.—Special path bend, brazed in lug, or to order.

Finish.—Frame and forks carefully filed, and hand polished. Enamelled transparent on dull nickel plating, dull copper or coloured enamel. Usual parts plated.

Price.—P.10 : Brampton fittings, **£8 15s.** cash.
P.11 : Chater-Lea fittings, **£10 4s.** cash.
P.12 : B.S.A. fittings, **£10 10s.** cash.

Important.—When ordering please state whether for cement or grass, or for both.

DESIGNED FOR A NOTED TRICYCLE EXPONENT, OF PROVED SPEED AND RIGIDITY WITH EASE OF STEERING.

B. & S. RACING TRICYCLE

SPECIFICATION.

Frame.—E. STEPHENS' own design, very rigid and fast. Height to order (stock size 21in.), 38in. wheelbase, 9¼in. bracket height, 28lbs. approximate weight, Reynolds' " A " quality tubes, one piece chain stays, brazed-on front guard eyes, pump hooks and fork lamp bracket boss, linered oil retaining bracket, Abingdon axle, 27in. or 30in. width.

Forks.—⅞in. round, or D to O narrow crown ; E. STEPHENS' reinforced principle, machined tips.

Wheels.—26in. or 27in. Constrictor-Bastide, 14mm. flat or round reinforced rims, butted spokes, tied and soldered at crossings.

Tyres.—Constrictor No. 3's, Dunlop or Merlin tubulars.

Chain.—Coventry " Elite."

Saddle.—Brooks' B.66 or Champion range, or Terry's Spring.

Bars.—To order, fixed, adjustable, or extension. Plated or black.

Guard.—Bluemel's front No-weight. Separate extension.

Brake.—Resilion.

Equipment.—Bluemel's ⅞in. pump, Tecalemit oil-gun, Lucas " Challis " bell, rear reflector.

Finish.—Frame and forks sandblasted, hand polished, enamelled one coat rust-proof, three coats of best stove enamel. All usual parts plated.

Price.—S.14 : Brampton fittings, **£18** cash.
S.15 : Chater-Lea fittings, **£19** cash.
S.16 : B.S.A. fittings, **£20** cash.

THE WELL KNOWN RECORD MODEL, HOLDER OF MANY CLUB RECORDS, OR THE NEW C.L. SHORT DRIVE.

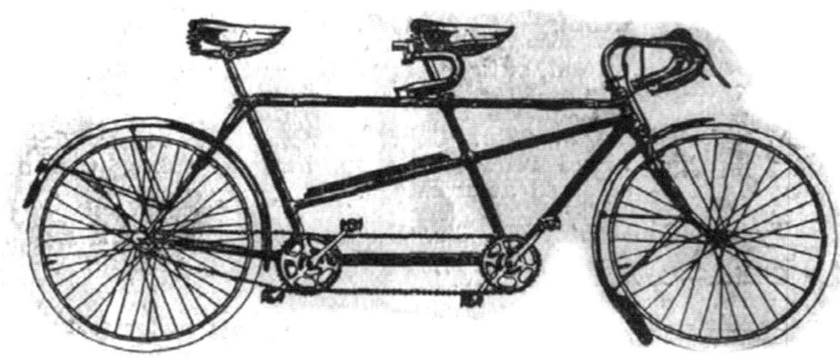

B. & S. TANDEM MODEL

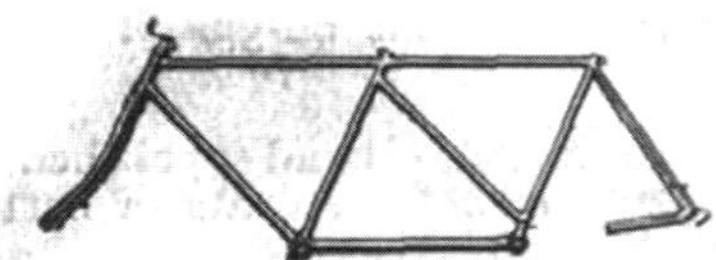

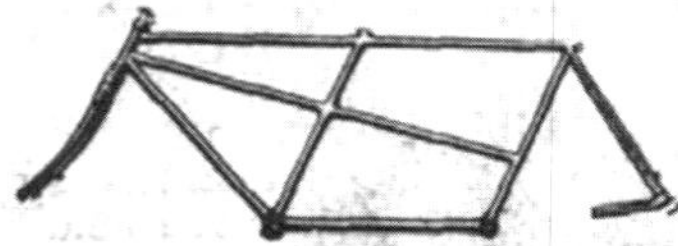

Alternate Types of Frames that can be Built.

SPECIFICATION.

Frame.—Special design. Height to order (stock size 20½in.), 64in. wheel base (62in. cross-over drive), 10¾in. bracket height, 46lbs. approximate weight, all on. Reynolds' "A" quality tubes throughout, round tapered chain and seat stays. E. STEPHENS' forward opening rear ends, or any other type to order. Brazed on guard eyes, pump hooks, chain rest and fork lamp bracket boss. All lugs cut out.

Forks.—Oval to round or D to O. E. STEPHENS' reinforced principle. Machined tips.

Wheels.—26in. x 1¼in., 1⅜in., or 1½in. Dunlop, or Endrick tandem rims. Black or plated. Special heavy butted spokes. Locked cones, double gear.

Tyres.—Dunlop, ~~Palmer, John Bull, Constrictor, or to~~ order.

Chains.—Coventry "Elite." ✓

Saddles.—Brooks' ~~B10, B18~~, ~~or Champion Range~~, ~~or Terry~~'s ~~spring~~. 13-14

Bars.—To order, both adjustable. Marsh brome. 18·20

Guards.—Bluemel's "No-weight" with extension or separate. ✓

Brakes.—Resilion's, front and rear. ✓

Equipment.—Bluemel's ⅞in. pump, "Telcalemit" oil-gun, Lucas "Challis" bell, Bluemel's rear reflector. ✓

Finish.—Frame and forks sandblasted, hand polished. Enamelled one coat rustproof, three coats of best stove enamel. All usual parts plated. Crown and ends plated. Green & ends Plated

Price.—T.17 : Brampton fittings, **£14** cash. ✓
~~T.18~~ : Chater-Lea ~~fittings~~, **£16 16s.** cash.
~~T.19~~ : "~~Special H.M.~~" model, **£17 17s.** cash.

Important.—Prices quoted are for fully equipped machines. Prices for stripped tandems will be forwarded on application.

DESIGNED FROM PRACTICAL EXPERIENCE OF TANDEM RIDING.

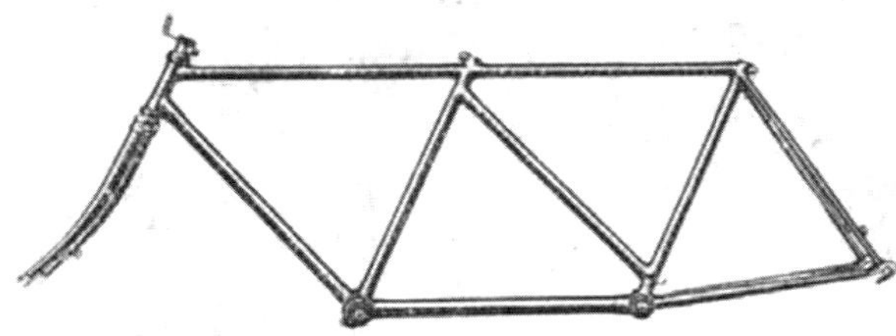

B. & S. TANDEM FRAMES

Alternate Types of Frames that can be Built.

SPECIFICATION.

E. STEPHENS' own special design, very rigid. **Reynolds' "A"** quality tubes throughout, finely **tapered** and cut-out lugs. Complete with all ball **races, lamp** brackets, seat pillars (L.T. straight or **curved), chain** wheel and cranks. E. STEPHENS' **forward opening** rear ends or any other type to **order. Front forks** oval to round, narrow crown, **reinforced principle**, machined tips. · **Brazed-on mudguard eyes, pump hooks**, chain rest, and **fork lamp bracket boss**. Linered oil bath **bracket. Tecalemit nipples** for oiling, 62in. and **65in.** wheel-base, **10¾in.** bracket height, **18½** lbs. approximate weight, **20½in.** stock size, or to order.

Finish.—Frame and forks sandblasted and hand polished, enamelled one coat rustproof, three coats best stove enamel. Crown of forks and ends chrome plated.

Built of BRAMPTON Fittings	£8 0 0	**Cash**
,, **CHATER LEA**	£10 0 0	,,
,, ,, ,, **Special "H.M."**	£11 10 0	,,
"H.M." Tubes Extra	15 0	,,

BUILT UP ON SOUND PRINCIPLES FROM A PRACTICAL EXPERIENCE.

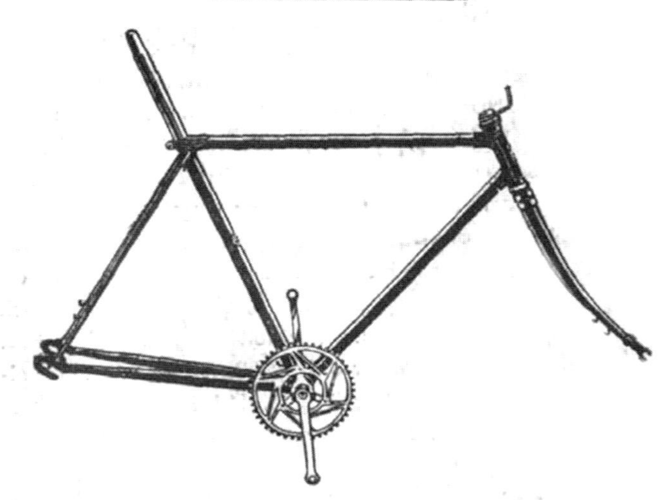

B. & S. FRAMES

FRONT FORKS

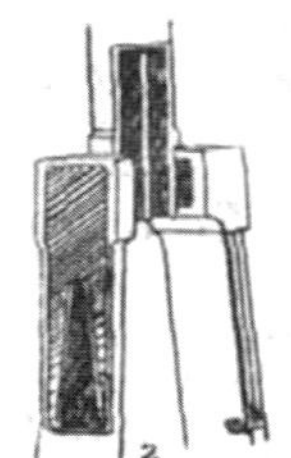

SHOWING STRENGTHENING LINERS.

SPECIFICATION.

E. STEPHENS' own special design, very rigid. Reynolds' "A" quality tubes throughout, finely tapered and cut-out lugs. Complete will all ball races, lamp bracket, seat pillar (L straight or curved), chain wheel and cranks. E. STEPHENS' forward opening rear ends or any other type to order. Front forks ⅞in. round, or D to O narrow crown, reinforced principle, machined tips. Brazed-on mudguards eyes, pump hooks, chain rest, and fork lamp bracket boss. Linered oil bath bracket. Telcalemit nipples for oiling. 41½in. wheel-base, 10¾in. bracket height, 9½lbs. approximate weight, 20½in. stock size, or to order.

Finish.—Frame and forks sandblasted and hand polished, enamelled one coat rustproof, three coats best stove enamel. Crown of forks and ends chrome plated.

Built of BRAMPTON Fittings	£3	0	0	Cash
,, CHATER LEA Fittings	£4	0	0	,,
,, B.S.A. Fittings	£4	5	0	,,
"SPECIAL" Model	£4	5	0	,,
Taper Tube Extra		5	0	,,
"H.M." Tubes		10	0	,,

EXTRAS.

However much I should like to, it is not possible, even in this new enlarged catalogue, to quote separate prices for every model incorporating the numerous additions and variations to every specification. Exact prices of any model in which the following items may be required can be arrived at by reference to the specification of the model concerned and the undermentioned extra charges, or I shall be pleased to quote by return:—

Sturmey-Archer T.F.	20/-
Sturmey-Archer K. 3-speed gear	20/–
Sturmey-Archer K.S. 3-speed gear	26/–
Sturmey-Archer K.B. 3-speed Brake Hub	26/–
EXTRA: Brakes charged at list price ruling.	
Hub Brake in lieu of Rim Brake, each	2/6
Cyclo Gear 2-speed	23/–
Cyclo Gear 3-speed	27/–
Cyclo Gear 3-speed Tank model	35/–
Trivelox	27/-

PLATING.

Front Forks, Chromium	6/-
Front Forks, Chromium (Tandem)	7/6

ENAMELLING.

Colours, Cycle or Frame	2/6
Colours, Tandem	4/6
Flamboyant, any Colour, Cycle or Frame	8/–
Flamboyant, any Colour. Tandem	18/–
Brazing Bars and Stem, "Special" Light	4/–

Types of handle bars, stems and seat pillars that can be supplied fitted to B. & S. cycles:—

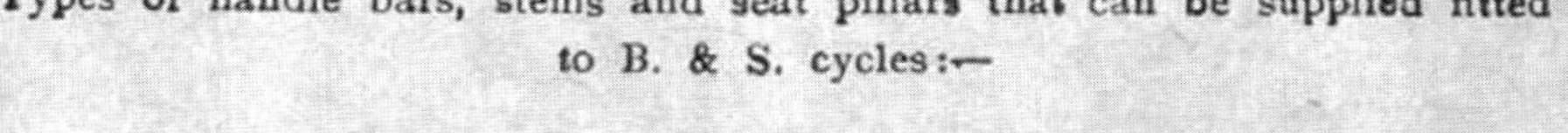

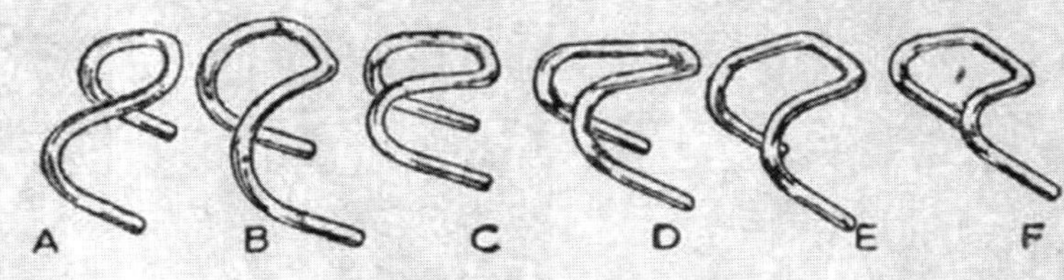

FLAT AND SHALLOW DROP TYPES.

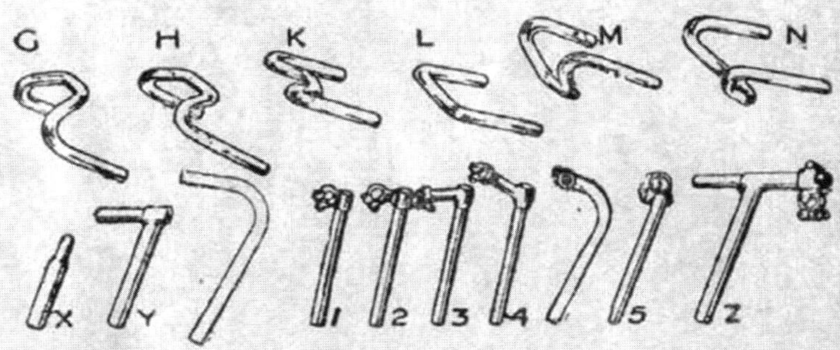

Conditions of Sale and Guarantee.

Every Cycle Frame, Complete Cycle, Tricycle, or Tandem which is sold by me carries the following express agreements which take the place of and exclude all conditions, warranties and liabilities whatsoever which exist either by Common Law, Statute or otherwise. Any statement, description, condition, or representation contained in any catalogue, advertisement, leaflet, or other publication shall not be construed as enlarging, varying, or over-riding these.

1.—I give no guarantee as to performance, quality, or fitness for any particular purpose. Should any defect be alleged in material or workmanship within two years after purchase from me I undertake on the immediate return of the part which is alleged to be defective to my Works, carriage paid, within such period to examine the same, and should any fault be found by me on examination to be solely due to defective material or workmanship I will repair the defective part or supply a new part in the place thereof, free of charge. I do not undertake to bear the cost of any work involved in re-instating a repaired or inserting a new part.

2.—This guarantee as to material or workmanship does not extend to (1) a second-hand Pedal Bicycle, or (2) to a Pedal Bicycle which has been used for "Hiring-out" purposes, or (3) a Pedal Bicycle from which my transfer or manufacturing numbers have been removed, or (4) which has carried a greater weight than it is designed to bear. And this guarantee does not extend to defects caused by racing, wear and tear, dirt, neglect, misuse, or accident.

3.—My responsibility is limited to the terms of this guarantee, and I will not be answerable for any contingent or resulting liability or loss arising through any defect or for any claim for labour, material, or other expenditure incurred in remedying any defect.

4.—When claiming under this guarantee the claimant must furnish me with the number of the machine which will be found stamped on the head lug of the frame and the fork crown, and the date of purchase.

5.—This guarantee shall apply to parts repaired or replaced under clause 1, and such guarantee shall run concurrently with, and shall terminate on the same date as the guarantee under clause 1, all the aforesaid implied conditions, liabilities, and warranties being excluded.

6.—When returning machines for repairs all accessories should be removed. This guarantee shall not apply to any parts of a Pedal Bicycle which are not manufactured by me, and all conditions, warranties and liabilities whatsoever implied, either by Common Law, Statute or otherwise relating to such parts are hereby excluded, but I will assist the purchaser by any guarantee given to him by the manufacturer of such parts as shall not have been made by me.

Cash Terms: 20% of total cost with order, balance when machine is ready.

H.P. Terms: Deposit as stated when ordered.

A Two Years' Signed Guarantee is given with every "Stephens" Frame or Cycle.

All machines sent carriage paid.

I reserve the right to revise without notice the specifications and/or prices as set out in this Catalogue.

VIKING CYCLES

Viking's origins started with a brave decision made by Alfred Victor Davies in 1908 to get into the cycle trade.

When he set up his repair shop Vic Davies was working as a clerk for the London Midland Railway. The railway company would not permit an employee to work elsewhere. He was faced with the choice of staying with the company and accepting low wages, or seek to earn a living from providing for the now well-established sport of cycling. He had the vision to see that cycling was going to be a growth area and that there was a good market to be served. He left the railway company to work full-time in his own cycle repair shop at Heath Town. Motorcycles were also serviced and repaired, but, as his cycle trade grew, bicycles became the sole focus of the business.

At first the new enterprise struggled, but later with his son Reg also in the business, things began to improve. Reg was bright and although money in the Davies household was tight, he won a scholarship to the Grammar School, where he did well in many subjects. Unfortunately, there was not enough money for Reg to go to university, but that misfortune was the Viking company's gain.

For many years, the firm made and sold well-constructed roadsters at its shop premises in Broad Street, where it had moved to in 1928. Broad Street was soon outgrown and, in 1934, the firm moved to Midland Chambers, 34 Princess Street. In 1935, a building in nearby Princess Alley was acquired, leaving the Princess Street address as offices and showroom. Frames were now being made on a regular basis. Things were beginning to move and by 1939 the firm is said to have been making up to 800 cycles a year. Also in 1939, Viking Cycles Limited was formed and the shop then traded as Victor Davies Cycles.

During World War II, the firm was well engaged making munitions for the war effort and nothing of exceptional note emerged until the years immediately following the war.

Vic Davies had retired in the late 1930s just before the war started and from then on Reg was the man in full command. Reg had been a useful club rider and knew how to put together reliable designs. High standards were set, and quality was the watchword. Open hearth brazing was the method for frame manufacture and again Viking paid particular attention to detail, using both TI and Reynolds tubes as appropriate. Good brazing by skilled craftsmen was the order of the day. Wheels were built using bought-in parts – rims, spokes and hubs. Finish was seen as very important and frames were always given several coats of good primer and well rubbed down before the finishing coats were applied. Save for BSA, Raleigh, Royal Enfield and Rudge, few British firms enjoyed much in the way of an export trade, but in the immediate post-war years, Viking succeeded in exporting a fair quantity of its cycles.

With Percy Stallard's formation of the British League of Racing Cyclists (BLRC), and the organisation of many mass start road races, the demand for lightweight club cycles boomed. A local Wolverhampton clubman, Bob Thom, was making a big name for himself, getting good places and winning many key events. Before the War he had been a keen amateur and from 1921 onwards he had been winning some notable race events.

Bob Thom joined the firm in 1948 and throughout his time with it, he was very closely involved with the lightweights' design, development and component selection. Bob's first work at Viking was with frame building and for a time he was in charge of the department. In 1953 he became a Sales Representative and finally, from 1954 onwards, he was Sales Manager and Team Manager. Under Managing Director Reg Davies, Works Manager Les Bremmer and Head of Frame Building Jack Robinson, production soared. In the course of the 1940s Viking was edging towards production of 2,000 cycles per year, most of them sports models.

In 1948, Reg Davies played a master stroke. The Viking road race team was formed. Much of Viking's success in the market place of the 1950s and 1960s was due to the Team's high profile successes and the skill of its manager.

The top riders in those days were: Dave Bedwell, Geoff Clarke, Ted Jones, Ken Jowett, George Lander, Les Scales, Ken Russell, Alec Taylor and Bob Thom. For the Viking Team's cycles there were arrangements with Airlite hubs; Cyclo gears; GB brakes, bars, etc; Gardiol tubular tyres; Perry chains and a few others. The first Viking team included Bill Allan, Harold Johnson, Bob Thom, Len West and Ben Whitmore. The team won the BLRC Championships in 1948, 1949 and 1951. Viking's 1951 team was: Ted Jones, Fred Nicholls, Bob Thom and Johnny Welch.

Ian Steel, previously a member of the Glasgow United Cycling Club, soon joined the teamand became its star rider and leader. He won the 1951 Tour of Britain and the 1952 Warsaw – Berlin – Prague Race. He worked for Viking on frame inspection and later as a sales representative. Other senior Viking staff, well-known personalities in the cycling world of their day, were: Les Holland, Roger Kowalski and Don Wilson.

In essence, the Viking Road Race Team was a semi-professional group of riders. They were all well experienced, well led and managed, but they were not full-time salaried professional riders. They subsisted on a mix of support via supply of cycles and kit, and Viking employment in other roles.

VIKING CYCLES

So, not unlike Jaguar Cars in their Le Mans years, Viking had the race-bred commercial success that it well deserved. The different cycles Viking sold all used quality components and materials, carefully built and well finished.

Bob Thom was the chief inspiration of Viking's several lightweight designs. When he first became involved, the Viking's frame builders did not quite know what to make of his ideas and insistence on the importance of frame angles, weight factors and how to get the best results. At the time Bob owned and rode a Hobbs of Barbican Blue Riband. One day he took it to the frame department and said, 'that's what a lightweight bicycle needs to be like'. The message was well received and Viking began to produce some remarkable quality lightweights at affordable prices.

A 1952 Viking advertisement elatedly said 'over 110 firsts and 80 team wins!' The top Viking was the 1952 Tour of Britain bicycle. Viking also produced the Trackmaster, Severn Valley, Mileater, Clubmaster, Hosteller models and several others.

The pattern for frame numbers is unknown but, from known machines, the frame numbers appeared to be placed on the left-hand rear drop out until about the end of 1960 and are thought to be sequential up to then.

However, the special machines had their own alpha prefix: S for Ian Steel and H for Hosteller. Numbers after 1960 were placed under the bottom bracket. Known frame numbers are:

Model	Number	Date
SS	082F	early to mid-50s
Mileater	AF489	1954
Tour of Britain	519	??
Unknown	3 688	early-50s
Ian Steel	S 4871	1958
Ian Steel	S 10475	1960
Grandtour	138457	1961/62
Hosteller	H 13972	1959
Severn Valley	118648	??
Severn Valley	135623	??
Severn Valley	488604	??
Severn Valley	1828281	1967
Trophy/Conquest	142433	early-60s
Hosteller	198413	mid-60s

The Viking successes were not maintained as the riders began to age, and other firms' fully professional teams did well. Reg Davies' strategy of investing profits in the firm's expansion caused strain because there was little in reserve to counter the downturn being experienced across the whole trade. In effect the bank was getting worried. At its peak Viking had employed some 80 people, but by mid-April 1967, it was down to about 25. Raleigh was approached about a take-over, but they decided to go with the acquisition of Carlton instead. In December 1967, Viking Cycles Limited went into liquidation.

John Gleave and Tom Jeffery

Catalogue and price list, on loan from John Gleave, are from 1951.The catalogue is printed in two colours, black and blue. It may be difficult to see the racing results as they are white text out of the pale blue background

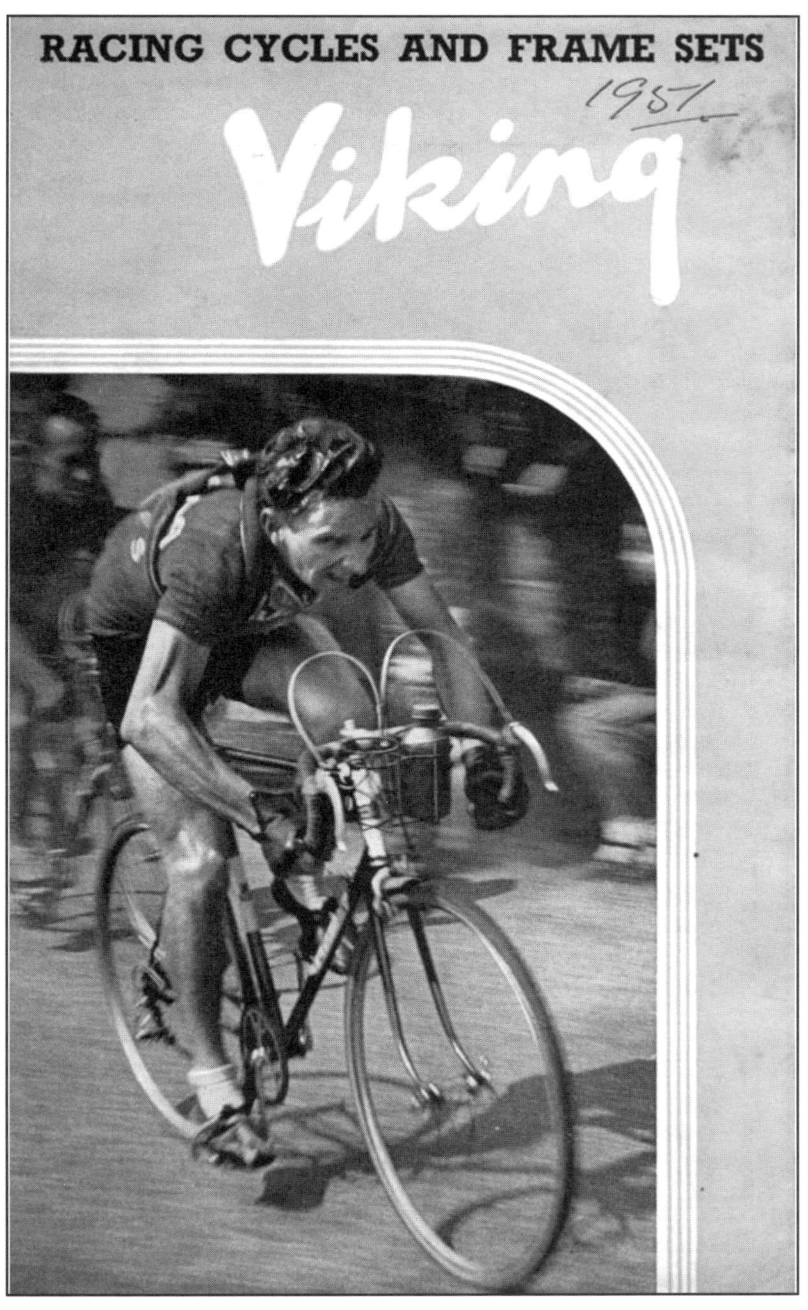

FOR THE HARD RIDING CLUBMAN

The "CLUBMASTER"

FRAME & FORK : Viking " MASTER " Series " SS," as specification on back page.
WHEELS & TYRES : Dunlop 27″ High Pressure on GNUTTI (or similar) Lightweight Hubs ; built with 15/17 gauge Double Butted Spokes.
BARS: Strata or Reynolds' Alloy to choice, on Steel or Alloy Extension.
BRAKES: G.B. (or equal) Alloy.
SADDLE: Brooks' B.17 Narrow or Standard.
CHAINWHEEL SET: Williams C.34, or similar.
CHAIN: ½″ x ⅛″ Perry or Coventry.
PEDALS: Webb, Brampton B.8, or similar.
MUDGUARDS: Alloy or Bluemels' Celluloid.
GEARS : Cyclo " BENELUX " or Simplex, or other Derailleur 3- or 4-speeds, to choice.
EQUIPMENT : Capacious Touring Bag, Tools, and 18″ Inflator.

Guarantee that all reasonable precautions are taken in the manufacture of our cycles to ensure excellence of materials and workmanship and that we will repair or replace FREE OF CHARGE any part of such machines as may be found by us to be faulty or defective, AT ANY TIME WHILST THE MACHINE REMAINS THE PROPERTY OF THE FIRST RETAIL PURCHASER, subject to the following conditions:

(1) The part which is claimed to be defective must be returned to us, carriage paid, with a covering letter stating the name and address of the sender, date of purchase, and the number stamped on the frame of the machine.
(2) Our responsibility is limited to the repair or replacement of the defective part, and we shall not be answerable for any contingent or resulting liability or loss arising through any defect or for any claim for labour, material, or other expenditure incurred in remedying any defect.
(3) We give no guarantee as to performance, quality or fitness for any particular purpose, and shall not be responsible for defects caused by racing, accident, wear and tear, misuse or neglect, nor for any machine which has been used for hiring-out purposes or from which our trade marks or manufacturing numbers have been removed.
(4) We bear no responsibility whatsoever for any part which is not manufactured by us ; but we will give the purchaser every possible assistance to obtain the benefit of the guarantee given by the manufacturer of such part.
(5) This guarantee takes the place of and excludes all conditions, warranties and liabilities whatsoever which exist either by Common Law, Statute, or otherwise ; and we shall not be held responsible for any statement, written or verbal, which may be construed as enlarging, varying or over-riding the above conditions.

Introducing the new... *Viking* 'SEVERN VALLEY'

- The ultimate expression of racing cycle perfection.
- Designed and used by Britain's Leading Team of Racing Cyclists.
- Protected and adorned by the finest coloured finishes in the cycle trade.

FRAME & FORK: Viking "SEVERN VALLEY," as specification on back page.

WHEELS & TYRES: DUNLOP Alloy Tubular 27" on GNUTTI (or similar) Quick Release Racing Hubs; built with 15/17 gauge Double Butted Spokes.

BARS: [illegible]" Alloy Maes (or to choice) on Alloy or Steel Extension.

BRAKES: G.B. (or equal) Alloy.

SADDLE: Brooks' B.17 Narrow or Standard.

CHAINWHEEL SET: Williams' C.1200 or Continental 3-pin.

PEDALS & TOECLIPS: Racing Rattrap to choice, Steel or Alloy.

GEAR: Cyclo "BENELUX" or Simplex 4-speed, or to choice. Double Chain Wheel (as illustrated) at EXTRA charge.

EQUIPMENT: 18" Inflator, "Carlton" Tyre-savers.

FOR BOARD, CEMENT, CINDER, AND GRASS TRACKS

The "TRACKMASTER"

FRAME & FORK: Viking "MASTER" Series "SS/T," as specification on back page.

WHEELS & TYRES: Dunlop Alloy Tubular 27" on GNUTTI (or similar) Racing Hubs; built with 15/17 gauge Double Butted Spokes.

BARS: Strata "Madison" (or to choice) on Steel Extension.

CHAINWHEEL SET: B.S.A. or Continental 5-pin, 1" pitch.

CHAIN: Renold Twin-Roller, 1" pitch. **GEARS:** Fixed.

PEDALS & TOECLIPS: Racing Rattrap to choice, Steel or Alloy.

SADDLE: Brooks' B.17 Narrow or Sprint.

SOLE MANUFACTURERS

VIKING CYCLES LTD.

WORKS No. 1	Registered Office:	WORKS No. 2
(Rough Stores and Frame Building)	PRINCESS LANE	(Finished Stores, Assembly and Packing)
PRINCESS LANE	PRINCESS STREET	1, ST. PETER'S SQ.
WOLVERHAMPTON	WOLVERHAMPTON ENGLAND	WOLVERHAMPTON

Telegrams: VIKING, WOLVERHAMPTON. Telephone: WOLVERHAMPTON 20475

VIKING

"MASTER" SERIES "SS"

1950 SPECIFICATION

"SEVERN VALLEY" FRAME SET

FRAME SIZES: 22½"-24". TOP TUBE: 22½"c/c. WHEELBASE: 41½". FRAME SIZES: 20"-22". TOP TUBE: 21½"c/c. WHEELBASE: 40½". ANGLES: 72° Head and Seat. WHEEL SIZE: Designed for 27", but will fit 26". BRACKET: 10½". FORK: 2½" Rake. FORKENDS: Stallard Standard or Osgear. BRAZINGS: 18" Pump Pegs on Bottom Tube. Brake and Gear Cable Eyes. Fork Lamp Brackets at EXTRA charge (NOT fitted unless specified). FINISH: Pre-treated by "Jenolite" process, providing a rust-proof base for a superb range of plain or metallic colours with modern decorations. Chromium Plating (Front Fork, Rear Ends, Head Lugs, etc.) at EXTRA charge. Flamboyant Finishes at EXTRA charge. HEAD & BRACKET BEARINGS: Highest Grade Continental. SEAT PILLAR: Alloy. Chainwheel Sets at EXTRA charge (NOT fitted unless specified).

MODEL "S S" FRAME SET

FRAME SIZES: 22½"-24". TOP TUBE: 23"c/c. WHEELBASE: 41½" FRAME SIZES: 20"-22". TOP TUBE: 22"c/c. WHEELBASE: 40½" ANGLES: 73° Head, 71° Seat. WHEEL SIZE: Designed for 27", but will fit 26". BRACKET: 10¾". FORK: 2½" Rake. FORKENDS: Stallard Standard or Osgear. BRAZINGS: 18" Pump Pegs on Bottom Tube; Brake & Gear Cable Eyes. Fork Lamp Brackets at EXTRA charge (NOT fitted unless specified.) FINISH: Pre-treated by "Jenolite" process, providing a rust-proof base for a superb range of plain or metallic colours; Lined, Lugs edged, and Olympic Bands; Front Fork 3/4 CHROMIUM PLATED as standard. Flamboyant finishes EXTRA; Chromium Plated Rear Ends EXTRA. HEAD BEARINGS: Lytaloy or Best Continental. SEAT PILLAR: Best Alloy. BRACKET BEARINGS: Bayliss Wiley, with Drilled Axle. Chainweel Sets at EXTRA charge (NOT fitted unless specified).

MODEL "SS/T" FRAME SET

FRAME SIZES: 22½"-24". TOP TUBE: 23"c/c. WHEELBASE: 40½" FRAME SIZES: 20"-22". TOP TUBE: 22"c/c. WHEELBASE: 39½" ANGLES: 74° Head, 73° Seat. WHEEL SIZE: 27". FORKENDS: Track Type. BRACKET: 11¼". FORK: 1½" Rake. BRAZINGS: To order at EXTRA charge. FINISH: Pre-treated by "Jenolite" process, providing a rust-proof base for a superb range of plain or metallic colours; Lined, Lugs edged, and Olympic Bands; Front Forks 3/4 CHROMUIM PLATED as standard. Flamboyant finishes EXTRA; Chromium Plated Rear Ends EXTRA. HEAD BEARINGS: Lytaloy or best Continental. SEAT PILLAR: Best Alloy. BRACKET BEARINGS: Bayliss Wiley, with Drilled Axle. Chainwheel Sets at EXTRA charge (NOT fitted unless specified).

IMPORTANT: The revised standard "SS" dimensions are the result of comprehensive and rigorous road and bench tests, and are scientifically balanced to give best results under all conditions. They can therefore only be varied at EXTRA charge, and without guarantee that the non-standard design will retain the liveliness and responsiveness for which VIKING Racing Cycles have become famous.

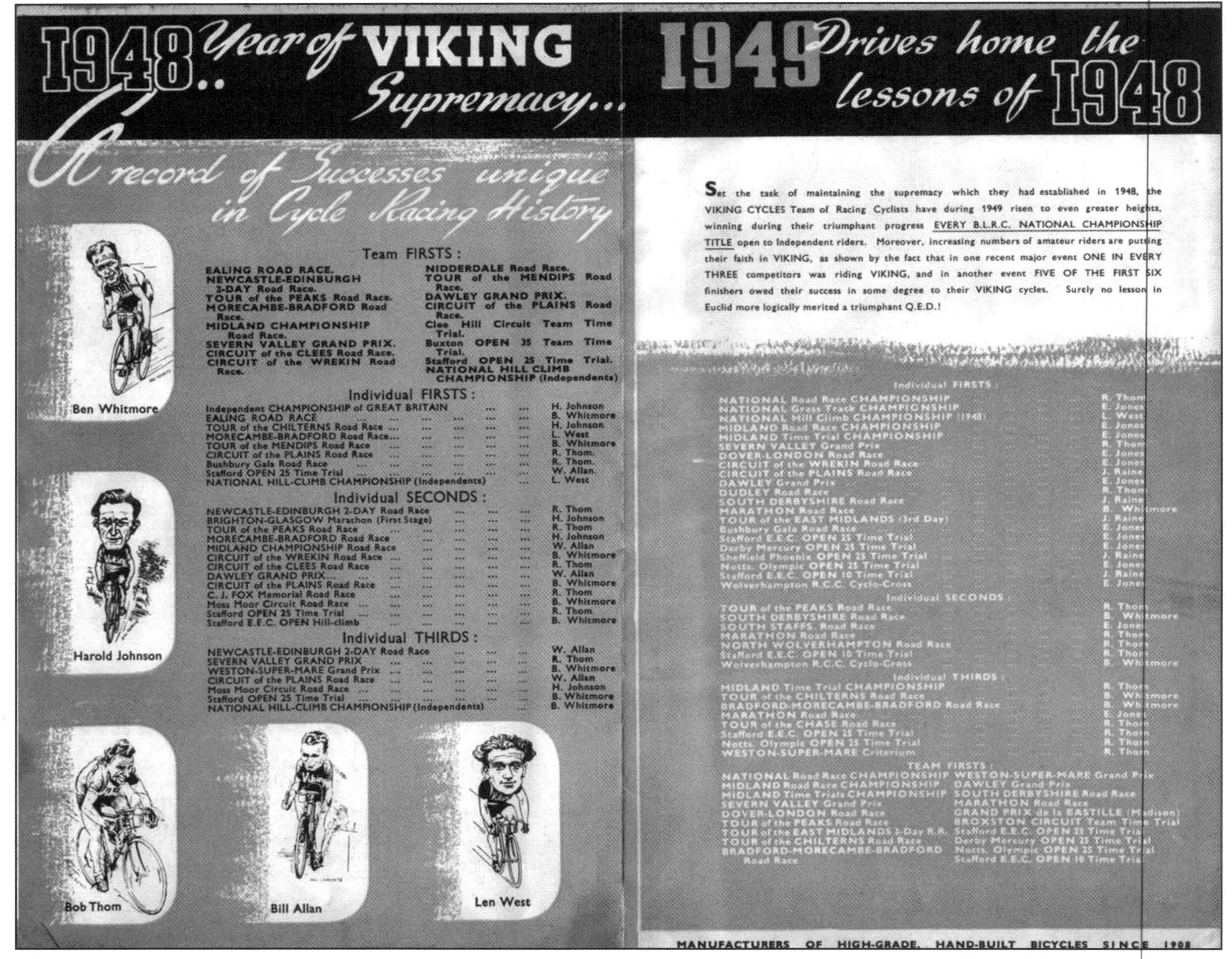

1948.. Year of VIKING Supremacy...

A record of Successes unique in Cycle Racing History

Team FIRSTS :

EALING ROAD RACE.
NEWCASTLE-EDINBURGH 2-DAY Road Race.
TOUR of the PEAKS Road Race.
MORECAMBE-BRADFORD Road Race.
MIDLAND CHAMPIONSHIP Road Race.
SEVERN VALLEY GRAND PRIX.
CIRCUIT of the CLEES Road Race.
CIRCUIT of the WREKIN Road Race.
NIDDERDALE Road Race.
TOUR of the MENDIPS Road Race.
DAWLEY GRAND PRIX.
CIRCUIT of the PLAINS Road Race.
Clee Hill Circuit Team Time Trial.
Buxton OPEN 35 Team Time Trial.
Stafford OPEN 25 Time Trial.
NATIONAL HILL CLIMB CHAMPIONSHIP (Independents)

Individual FIRSTS :

Independent CHAMPIONSHIP of GREAT BRITAIN	H. Johnson
EALING ROAD RACE	B. Whitmore
TOUR of the CHILTERNS Road Race	H. Johnson
MORECAMBE-BRADFORD Road Race...	L. West
TOUR of the MENDIPS Road Race	B. Whitmore
CIRCUIT of the PLAINS Road Race	R. Thom.
Bushbury Gala Road Race	R. Thom.
Stafford OPEN 25 Time Trial	W. Allan.
NATIONAL HILL-CLIMB CHAMPIONSHIP (Independents) ...	L. West

Individual SECONDS :

NEWCASTLE-EDINBURGH 2-DAY Road Race	R. Thom
BRIGHTON-GLASGOW Marathon (First Stage)	H. Johnson
TOUR of the PEAKS Road Race	R. Thom
MORECAMBE-BRADFORD Road Race	H. Johnson
MIDLAND CHAMPIONSHIP Road Race	W. Allan
CIRCUIT of the WREKIN Road Race	B. Whitmore
CIRCUIT of the CLEES Road Race	R. Thom
DAWLEY GRAND PRIX...	W. Allan
CIRCUIT of the PLAINS Road Race	B. Whitmore
C. J. FOX Memorial Road Race	R. Thom
Moss Moor Circuit Road Race	B. Whitmore
Stafford OPEN 25 Time Trial	R. Thom
Stafford E.E.C. OPEN Hill-climb	B. Whitmore

Individual THIRDS :

NEWCASTLE-EDINBURGH 2-DAY Road Race	W. Allan
SEVERN VALLEY GRAND PRIX	R. Thom
WESTON-SUPER-MARE Grand Prix	B. Whitmore
CIRCUIT of the PLAINS Road Race	W. Allan
Moss Moor Circuit Road Race	H. Johnson
Stafford OPEN 25 Time Trial	B. Whitmore
NATIONAL HILL-CLIMB CHAMPIONSHIP (Independents) ...	B. Whitmore

Ben Whitmore

Harold Johnson

Bob Thom

Bill Allan

Len West

1949 Drives home the lessons of 1948

Set the task of maintaining the supremacy which they had established in 1948, the VIKING CYCLES Team of Racing Cyclists have during 1949 risen to even greater heights, winning during their triumphant progress EVERY B.L.R.C. NATIONAL CHAMPIONSHIP TITLE open to Independent riders. Moreover, increasing numbers of amateur riders are putting their faith in VIKING, as shown by the fact that in one recent major event ONE IN EVERY THREE competitors was riding VIKING, and in another event FIVE OF THE FIRST SIX finishers owed their success in some degree to their VIKING cycles. Surely no lesson in Euclid more logically merited a triumphant Q.E.D.!

Individual FIRSTS :

NATIONAL Road Race CHAMPIONSHIP	R. Thom
NATIONAL Grass Track CHAMPIONSHIP	E. Jones
NATIONAL Hill Climb CHAMPIONSHIP (1948)	L. West
MIDLAND Road Race CHAMPIONSHIP	E. Jones
MIDLAND Time Trial CHAMPIONSHIP	E. Jones
SEVERN VALLEY Grand Prix	R. Thom
DOVER-LONDON Road Race	E. Jones
CIRCUIT of the WREKIN Road Race	E. Jones
CIRCUIT of the PLAINS Road Race	J. Raine
DAWLEY Grand Prix	E. Jones
DUDLEY Road Race	R. Thom
SOUTH DERBYSHIRE Road Race	J. Raine
MARATHON Road Race	B. Whitmore
TOUR of the EAST MIDLANDS (3rd Day)	J. Raine
Bushbury Gala Road Race	E. Jones
Stafford E.E.C. OPEN 25 Time Trial	E. Jones
Derby Mercury OPEN 25 Time Trial	E. Jones
Sheffield Phoenix OPEN 25 Time Trial	J. Raine
Notts. Olympic OPEN 25 Time Trial	E. Jones
Stafford E.E.C. OPEN 10 Time Trial	J. Raine
Wolverhampton R.C.C. Cyclo-Cross	E. Jones

Individual SECONDS :

TOUR of the PEAKS Road Race	R. Thom
SOUTH DERBYSHIRE Road Race	B. Whitmore
SOUTH STAFFS. Road Race	E. Jones
MARATHON Road Race	R. Thom
NORTH WOLVERHAMPTON Road Race	R. Thom
Stafford E.E.C. OPEN 10 Time Trial	R. Thom
Wolverhampton R.C.C. Cyclo-Cross	B. Whitmore

Individual THIRDS :

MIDLAND Time Trial CHAMPIONSHIP	R. Thom
TOUR of the CHILTERNS Road Race	B. Whitmore
BRADFORD-MORECAMBE-BRADFORD Road Race	B. Whitmore
MARATHON Road Race	E. Jones
TOUR of the CHASE Road Race	R. Thom
Stafford E.E.C. OPEN 25 Time Trial	R. Thom
Notts. Olympic OPEN 25 Time Trial	R. Thom
WESTON-SUPER-MARE Criterium	R. Thom

TEAM FIRSTS :

NATIONAL Road Race CHAMPIONSHIP
MIDLAND Road Race CHAMPIONSHIP
MIDLAND Time Trials CHAMPIONSHIP
SEVERN VALLEY Grand Prix
DOVER-LONDON Road Race
TOUR of the PEAKS Road Race
TOUR of the EAST MIDLANDS 3-Day R.R.
TOUR of the CHILTERNS Road Race
BRADFORD-MORECAMBE-BRADFORD Road Race
WESTON-SUPER-MARE Grand Prix
DAWLEY Grand Prix
SOUTH DERBYSHIRE Road Race
MARATHON Road Race
GRAND PRIX de la BASTILLE (Madison)
BROXSTON CIRCUIT Team Time Trial
Stafford E.E.C. OPEN 25 Time Trial
Derby Mercury OPEN 25 Time Trial
Notts. Olympic OPEN 25 Time Trial
Stafford E.E.C. OPEN 10 Time Trial

MANUFACTURERS OF HIGH-GRADE, HAND-BUILT BICYCLES SINCE 1908

VIKING CYCLES LTD.,
Midland Chambers.
Princess Street.
WOLVERHAMPTON.

LIST R.M. RETAIL PRICES.
Racing Frames
& Cycles.
January 1951.

	Retail Price (EXCLUDING TAX)	PURCHASE TAX	RETAIL PRICE (TAX INCLUDED)
FRAME SETS:			
Model "SS" / " "SSL" / " "SS/T"	£13. 5s. 0d.	NIL	£13. 5s. 0d.
"SEVERN VALLEY"	£14. 14s. 0d.	NIL	£14. 14s. 0d.
EXTRAS:			
Flamboyant colours.	7s. 0d.	-	7s. 0d.
Fork Lamp-bracket.	2s. 9d.	-	2s. 9d.
RACING CYCLES.			
"SEVERN VALLEY" Road Model.	£41. 15s. 2d.	£9. 14s. 10d.	£51. 10s. 0d.
"RACEMASTER" (as above but with 'SS' Frame)	£40. 2s. 8d.	£9. 7s. 4d.	£49. 10s. 0d.
"TRACKMASTER"	£33. 0s. 10d.	£7. 14s. 2d.	£40. 15s. 0d.
"CLUBMASTER" (excluding touring-bag)	£27. 9s. 4d.	£6. 8s. 2d.	£33. 17s. 6d.
FLAMBOYANT COLOURS.	7s. 0d.	1s. 8d.	8s. 8d.

ALL PREVIOUS LISTS CANCELLED - PRICES SUBJECT TO ALTERATION WITHOUT NOTICE.